Advance Praise for Timothy Gallagher's
The Discernment of Spirits

"In Gallagher's faith-filled presentation of the rules for discernment, the bare and laconic quality of Ignatius's language disappears. In its place there emerges the life-giving character of the rules which enable individuals to have a deeper understanding of their spiritual experience and to respond more wisely to it."
> —Gill K. Goulding, I.B.V.M., Assistant Professor of Systematic Theology and Spirituality, Regis College, Jesuit Graduate School of Theology, University of Toronto

"I recommend *Discernment of Spirits*. It is a thorough, solid contribution to the literature on discernment of spirits. The author shows a profound understanding of Ignatius's rules for discernment and uses good examples to illustrate them."
> —William A. Barry, S.J.

Renewed interest in Ignatian spirituality and mysticism—especially his focus on the discernment of spirits—awakened around the time of the Second Vatican Council. One can find detailed and ponderous studies on these rules—of great aid to scholars but not to the average person. One also finds popular, superficial studies that do justice neither to Ignatius, nor to his rules, nor to those reading such studies. Father Timothy Gallagher's pellucid prose, meticulous reading of the rules, skillful exposition of the material, helpful illustrative quotations, and apposite use of examples has gone a long way to remedy this situation. His book presents the "First Week" rules for the discernment of spirit in a relatively complete way, yet simply enough in terms of style and content so that Christians with little background in this area will be able to absorb the material. . . . By providing a sound understanding of Ignatian principles and applying them in a skillful way to daily life, Father Gallagher meets the pressing needs of retreat directors, retreatants, students of spiritual theology, and others interested in deepening their spiritual lives. I know of no comparable volume that proves so helpful.
> —Harvey D. Egan, S.J., Professor of Systematic and Mystical Theology, Boston College (from the book's foreword)

The Discernment of Spirits

An Ignatian Guide for Everyday Living

Timothy M. Gallagher, O.M.V.

A Crossroad Book
Crossroad Publishing Company
New York

The Crossroad Publishing Company

Permissions continued on p. ix.

This book is set in 10/12 Sabon.
The display type is Tiepolo Book.

Printed in the United States of America

Library of Congress Cataloging-in-Publication Data

Gallagher, Timothy M.
     The discernment of spirits : an Ignatian guide for everyday living /
Timothy M. Gallagher.
          p. cm.
     Includes bibliographical references and index.
     ISBN 0-8245-2291-5 (alk. paper)
     1. Spiritual life—Catholic Church. 2. Ignatius, of Loyola, Saint,
1491-1556. I. Title.
BX2350.G35 2005
248.4'82—dc22

Contents

Acknowledgments

〜

I am deeply grateful to the many people whose assistance and support have made this book possible. I express my thanks to Fr. William Brown, O.M.V., provincial, for the encouragement that led me to undertake this project and for providing the concrete circumstances that allowed me to write. I am also profoundly grateful to David Beauregard, O.M.V., for his ongoing assistance throughout the writing of this book, to Harvey Egan, S.J., for his reading of the manuscript and for writing the foreword to this book, and to Claire-Marie Hart for her reading, her generous assistance in the writing itself, and for her help in the final preparation of the manuscript.

My heartfelt thanks go also to those whose accompanied me in the writing process through their reading, their comments on the manuscript, and their personal support: Rose Blake, Claire Callahan, S.N.D., Susan Dumas, James Gallagher, Gill Goulding, I.B.V.M., Elizabeth Koessler, Ed O'Flaherty, S.J., Gertrude Mahoney, S.N.D., Germana Santos, F.S.P., Ernest Sherstone, O.M.V., and Mary Rose Sullivan.

I express my sincere gratitude also to Bernadette Reis, F.S.P., for her highly competent help with technical issues regarding publication, and to Carol McGinness for her invaluable aid with computer skills and in preparing the manuscript for publication.

Finally, I am deeply grateful to the many persons from whose teaching, writing, and experience I have learned about Ignatian discernment of spirits over the past thirty years. In particular, I am indebted to Miguel Angel Fiorito, S.J., Daniel Gil, S.J., and Jules Toner, S.J., without whose profound systematic study of the Ignatian rules for discernment this book would not have been possible.

Thanks also are expressed to the following publishers for permission to reprint copyrighted material.

Excerpts from *Angela of Foligno: Complete Works*, translated with an introduction by Paul Lachance, O.F.M., from The Classics of Western Spirituality. Copyright © 1993 by Paul Lachance, O.F.M., Paulist Press, Inc., New York/Mahwah, N.J. Used with permission of Paulist Press. www.paulistpress.com.

Excerpt from *The Autobiography of St. Ignatius Loyola*, by John C. Olin, ed. Copyright © 1974 by John C. Olin and Joseph F. O'Callaghan. Reprinted by permission of HarperCollins Publishers Inc.

Excerpts from *A Commentary on Saint Ignatius' Rules for the Discernment of Spirits: A Guide to the Principles and Practice,* by Jules Toner, S.J. Used with permission. © The Institute of Jesuit Sources, St. Louis, Mo. All rights reserved.

Excerpt from *Confessions,* by Saint Augustine. Translated with an introduction by R. S. Pine-Coffin (Penguin Classics, 1961). Copyright © R. S. Pine-Coffin, 1961. Reprinted by permission of Penguin Group (UK).

Excerpts from "Consciousness Examen," in *Review for Religious,* by Fr. G. Aschenbrenner. Jesuit Center for Spiritual Growth, 1972. Used with permission of Fr. G. Aschenbrenner.

Excerpts from *Discernimiento según San Ignacio: Exposición y Comentario Practico de las Dos Series de Reglas de Discernimiento de Espíritus Contenidas en el Libro de los Ejercicios Espirituales de San Ignacio de Loyola (EE 313–336),* by Daniel Gil, S.J. Used with permission of the Secretariatus ad Promotionem Spiritualitatis Ignatianae.

Excerpts from *Discernimiento y Lucha Espíritual: Comentario de las Reglas de Discernir de la Primera Semana del Libro de los Ejercicios Espirituales de San Ignacio de Loyola,* by Miguel Angel Fiorito, S.J. Used with the permission of the Jesuit Province of Argentina.

Excerpts from *Emily Dickinson: Selected Poems & Letters of Emily Dickinson,* R. Linscott, ed. Used with permission granted from the estate of Robert N. Linscott.

Excerpts from Grail Psalms used with permission. Copyright © 1976 by Ladies of the Grail, administered by GIA Publications, Inc. All rights reserved.

Excerpts from *The Jesuits: Their Spiritual Doctrine and Practice: A Historical Study,* 1986. Used with permission. © The Institute of Jesuit Sources, St. Louis, Mo. All rights reserved.

Excerpts from *Julian of Norwich: Showings,* translated from the critical text with an introduction by Edmund College, O.S.A., and James Walsh, S.J., from The Classics of Western Spirituality. Copyright © 1978 by Paulist Press, Inc., New York/Mahwah, N.J. Used with permission of Paulist Press. www.paulistpress.com.

Excerpt from *Letters of St. Ignatius of Loyola,* by William J. Young, S.J. Loyola Press, 1959. Reprinted with permission of Loyola Press. To order copies of this book, call 1-800-621-1008 or visit www.loyolabooks.org.

Excerpt from *Mrs. Seton,* by Joseph I. Dirvin. Copyright © 1962 by Farrar, Straus & Cudahy Inc. Copyright renewed © 1990 by Farrar, Straus & Cudahy Inc. Reprinted by permission of Farrar, Straus & Giroux, LLC.

Excerpts from the New American Bible with Revised New Testament and Psalms. Copyright © 1991, 1986, 1970 Confraternity of Christian Doctrine, Washington, D.C., and used by permission. All rights reserved. No part of the New American Bible may be reprinted without permission in writing from the copyright holder.

Excerpts from *A New Introduction to the Spiritual Exercises of St. Ignatius,* by J. Dister, ed. Used with permission of Liturgical Press, Collegeville, Minn.

Excepts from *St. Francis of Assisi, Writings and Early Biographies: English Omnibus of the Sources for the Life of St. Francis,* ed. Marion Habig. Franciscan Press, 1973. Used with permission of Franciscan Press, Quincy University, 1800 College Ave. Quincy, Ill.

Excerpts from *The Seven Storey Mountain* by Thomas Merton. Copyright © 1948 by Harcourt, Inc. and renewed 1976 by the Trustees of the Merton Legacy Trust, reprinted by permission of the publisher. Copyrighted © 1948 by Harcourt Brace and Company, renewed reprinted by permission of Curtis Brown, Ltd. Copyright by Sheldon Press UK, reprinted permission by publisher SPCK, 36 Causton St., London SW1P 4ST.

Excerpts from *Spirit of Light or Darkness: A Casebook for Studying Discernment of Spirits,* by Jules Toner, S.J., 1995. Used with permission. © The Institute of Jesuit Sources, St. Louis, Mo. All rights reserved.

From *Story of a Soul,* translated by John Clarke, O.C.D. Copyright © 1975, 1976, 1996 by Washington Province of Discalced Carmelites, ICS Publications, 213 Lincoln Road N.E., Washington, DC 20002-1199 U.S.A. www.icspublications.org. Used with permission.

Excerpt from *Weeds among the Wheat: Discernment: Where Prayer & Action Meet,* by Thomas H. Green, S.J. © by Ave Maria Press, P.O. Box 428, Notre Dame, Indiana 46556. Used with permission of the publisher. www.avemariapress.com.

Foreword

╭─╮

Ignatius of Loyola. Even today, his name rarely evokes neutrality or indifference. Ever since he appeared on the Christian scene, many have considered him either their champion or their foe. Even within the church that canonized him, some find it difficult to mention his name, and they regard him with suspicion. Nonetheless, he commands awe and respect—if only grudgingly at times—from most who know anything at all about his extraordinary accomplishments.

The name "Ignatius of Loyola" calls forth a variety of images: founder of the controversial Society of Jesus, whose members are sometimes called the "pope's commandos"; father of the advance guard of the Counter-Reformation, which allegedly taught that the end justifies the means; the first "Black Pope," who claimed to owe obedience to no man on earth save the pope and who taught his followers blind obedience to the pontiff. The very name "Jesuit" is for many synonymous with casuistry, craftiness, and intrigue. Was it not the image of Ignatius of Loyola that stood behind Dostoevsky's portrait of the infamous Grand Inquisitor in the *Brothers Karamazov* and Camus' unsavory Jesuit in *The Plague*?

Contemporary commentators—closer to the mark—often depict Ignatius as a courtier, a gentleman, and a soldier. After a profound religious conversion, he became a wandering pilgrim for the sake of Christ and attained heroic sanctity. For apostolic purposes, "to help souls," he decided to study to become a priest. He gathered a group of companions in Christ, founded a renowned religious family, established colleges, universities, and charitable institutions, and always kept his hand in pastoral activity. He oversaw a vast missionary network and undertook sensitive diplomatic appointments. Moreover, he authored the highly influential *Spiritual Exercises,* the Jesuit *Constitutions,* and thousands of letters that demonstrate his far-reaching sociopolitical involvement. To be with the trinitarian Christ to serve the church may well summarize the goal of this complex saint.

His Spiritual Exercises has changed the history of spirituality from the sixteenth century to the present day. Too many still view this classic as a step-by-step recipe book that teaches an asceticism of the will, a technically attained voluntarism, and a pragmatic spirituality centered almost exclusively on practical resolutions. In fact, some contend that these Exercises teach only highly discursive, image-bound, and somewhat mechanical methods of prayer, suitable only for beginners, and an actual barrier to deeper, more mystical levels of prayer.

That the first serious attacks on the Exercises were directed at their purported overemphasis on the mystical dimension of prayer refutes in no small way the skewed caricature. Recent studies have shown that these Exercises contain no less than twenty different methods of prayer and that the underlying dynamic of each day of the Exercises is the gradual deepening and simplification of prayer. In the early years of the Society of Jesus, many who made these Exercises later joined contemplative orders. The first crisis in the nascent Jesuit order arose because of a demand from many Jesuits for longer hours of prayer—a request Ignatius opposed with all his strength. If one uses the spirituality and mysticism of Ignatius himself as the hermeneutical key to the Exercises, their mystical dimension is self-evident.

In short, the Ignatian Exercises can lead persons at almost any level of spiritual development into ever-deeper realms of the spiritual life—even into the mystical life. His richly incarnational, iconistic spirituality and mysticism find God in all things and all things in God. They never separate love of God, neighbor, and world. This is a spirituality and mysticism of joy in the world, an Easter spirituality that loves the earth because the trinitarian God creates, redeems, loves, and transforms it. Ignatius's trinitarian and christocentric spirituality and mysticism founded a community of love for effective apostolic service—service that includes both social and political dimensions.

If one reads Ignatius's *Autobiography,* one discovers that his first insights into the discernment of spirits occurred almost simultaneously with his religious conversion. His foundational enlightenment experience on the banks of the Cardoner River in Manresa, Spain, transformed him into a new man with a new understanding of matters of faith and of learning. During a vision in a small chapel at La Storta, near Rome, he experienced the Eternal Father placing him with his cross-bearing Son. The Father spoke interiorly to Ignatius's heart: "I shall be favorable to you [plural] at Rome," and "I want you, my Son, to take this man as your servant." Then Christ said to Ignatius: "I want you [singular] to serve us [Father and Son]." The graces at La Storta confirmed Ignatius's trinitarian, Christ-centered service and ecclesial mysticism. The autobiography also attests to other dramatic mystical experiences, including his developing mystical ability to discern spirits.

The other important text, his *Spiritual Diary,* is perhaps the most remarkable document on trinitarian and christocentric mysticism ever written. It offers an astonishing record of Ignatius's mystical intimacy with each person of the Trinity, the Divine Essence, the God-Man, and Mary. Mystical tears, trinitarian visions and illuminations, various kinds of locutions, profound mystical consolations, mystical touches, experiences of reverential love, mystical repose, and melodic inner voices permeate this short document. These experiences enabled him to discern the variety of spirits that stirred him to discover God's particular will for him.

Ignatius's apostolic successes and those of the Jesuits from his time to the present seem to have overshadowed the importance of his mysticism—a mysticism he never sought for its own sake but mainly for its ability to teach and to confirm God's will. That Ignatius usually closed his nearly seven thousand letters with the words "May Christ our Lord help us all with His bountiful grace, so that we may know His holy will and perfectly fulfill it" attests to this. These same apostolic successes have also obscured the centrality of the discernment of spirits in Ignatius's spirituality and mysticism. The proper understanding of his rules for the discernment of spirits requires an understanding of his life as the seeking and carrying out of God's will.

I once called Ignatius the "mystic of moods and thoughts." This oversimplifies a saint who took into consideration almost everything that influences Christian life and Christian decisions: the Holy Spirit, good angels, demons, what flows from the human spirit's rational and volitional structure, what comes from one's imagination, one's memory, one's emotions, one's sinful and disordered nature, what one eats and drinks, light and darkness, and even the seasons of the year.

The discernment of spirits is hardly an anomaly in the Judeo-Christian tradition. The biblical texts show clearly that God guides the upright person. Adam and Eve learned the hard way that one can be deceived by great promises. Jeremiah was well aware of the tangles of the human heart. God instructed the Jews on ways to discern the authentic prophets from false ones.

The early Christian community knew, too, that it had to discern and test the various influences that affected it. St. Paul understood that only through the Spirit could the community differentiate authentic from false prophetic utterances and charismatic phenomena. Even leaders had to pass the test of the Spirit, for they could sometimes be "false and deceitful workers." The "works of the flesh" were clearly from the evil spirit; the fruits of the Spirit spoke for themselves. Against love, joy, peace, patience, kindness, self-control, and goodness "there is no law."

The early Christians were thus exhorted to follow the Spirit, to live in the Spirit, and to be guided by the Spirit. The Spirit would pray in them, enabling them to say "Abba, Father" and "Jesus is Lord." The Spirit empowered them to discern God's mysterious and hidden wisdom: Christ himself, the norm of all discernment, the very "consolation of Israel."

Early in the Christian tradition, Origen taught that thoughts may come from God, the angels, the devils, or our very own selves. Many of the church fathers after him counseled paying strict attention to the thoughts that arise from the heart and to the thoughts that enter the heart, carefully studying their footprint. In time, the discernment of spirits involved the meticulous study of all factors that influence Christian life, especially that of decision and choice. Affective states of consolation and desolation, reasoning processes, thoughts, imaginings, phantasms, dreams, visions, locutions, and the like were to be subjected to the question: Do these come from God, the angels, the devils, or only ourselves? One of the most quoted apocryphal sayings attributed to Jesus, "become shrewd money-changers," focused on the ability to discern pure gold from base metals, that is, the ability to discern spirits.

Ignatius's emphasis on discreet love may well be the hallmark of his spirituality and mysticism. He is the paradigm of that "shrewd money changer" so admired in the Christian tradition. No matter how intense Ignatius's religious experiences were, he always subjected them to discretion, critical reflection, and the content of Christian faith.

Karl Rahner, the famous German theologian and admirer of St. Ignatius, contended that his relatively brief rules for the discernment of spirits provided a practical and formal systematic method for discovering God's will for an individual. He also maintained that these rules were the first and the only detailed attempt at such a systematic method in the history of Christian spirituality. Some first generation Jesuits—experts in the Christian spiritual heritage—said of Ignatius's rules for the discernment of spirits that they contain "a great deal that is new and heretofore unheard of."

These rules represent the formal codification of insights and responses that aroused and found justification in Ignatius's own spiritual life and pastoral experience. Although definitely within the tradition of the discernment of spirits, Ignatius was strangely innocent of it. He learned what he did mainly from his own spiritual experience, as attested to in his *Autobiography* and *Spiritual Diary*. His schematization, the concise codification, and the internal structure of his rules contribute to the heritage of Christian spirituality in a way in which no author before or after him has done. They are *sui generis*.

Karl Rahner maintained that there is not only a history of Christian dogma but also one of Christian holiness. The saints incarnate ways of being an authentic Christian in their own historical period, and Rahner also viewed Ignatius this way. But Rahner also found in Ignatius someone who explicated and codified the supernatural logic of the saints. He considered Ignatius to be as important for the church as Aristotle is for the field of philosophy. Through Aristotle logic became the first science of philosophy; through Ignatius, the logic of existential decision, the discernment of spirits, became the science of the saints.

Rahner, however, spoke of Ignatius as more a master of brevity than one of clarity. The terse simplicity and sometimes imprecise wording of his rules for the discernment of spirits can be misleading. Only through an appropriation of the Ignatian spirit which desires to know Christ more deeply, to love him more ardently, and to follow him more faithfully—as well as a meticulous reading of the texts—does one begin to fathom the spiritual profundity of the rules drawn up by this mystical titan.

Renewed interest in Ignatian spirituality and mysticism—especially his focus on the discernment of spirits—awakened around the time of the Second Vatican Council. One can find detailed and ponderous studies on these rules—of great aid to scholars but not to the average person. One also finds popular, superficial studies that do justice neither to Ignatius, nor to his rules, nor to those reading such studies.

Father Timothy Gallagher's pellucid prose, meticulous reading of the rules, skillful exposition of the material, helpful illustrative quotations, and apposite use of examples have gone a long way to remedy this situation. His book presents the "First Week" rules for the discernment of spirit in a relatively complete way, yet simply enough in terms of style and content so that Christians with little background in this area will be able to absorb the material.

Of course, no definitive book on these rules exists. Father Gallagher, however, fulfills solidly what Ignatius desired: that is, for Christians of good will—whatever their background—to attain the ability to understand "to some extent, the different movements produced in the soul and . . . recognizing those that are good to admit them, and those that are bad, to reject them." By providing a sound understanding of Ignatian principles and applying them in a skillful way to daily life, Father Gallagher meets the pressing needs of retreat directors, retreatants, students of spiritual theology, and others interested in deepening their spiritual lives. I know of no comparable volume that proves so helpful.

Harvey D. Egan, S.J.
Professor of Systematic and Mystical Theology
Boston College

Introduction

⤳

At the Heart of the Spiritual Life

In Leo Tolstoy's *Anna Karenina*, Levin, a main character in the story, has just encountered God in an experience of deep joy.[1] The witness of an upright man who lives for God has opened for Levin the way to spiritual clarity. Tears express the profound happiness of his heart in the Lord. His faith has grown strong and new spiritual life opens before him. Levin hopes that the spiritual richness he has received will strengthen and deepen his relationship with his family. He is disheartened to find, however, that he continues to struggle as he interacts with various people of his household. When, finally, he is alone for a moment, Levin reflects on his recent spiritual experience:

> He was glad of a chance to be alone to recover from the influence of ordinary actual life, which had already depressed his happy mood. He thought that he had already had time to lose his temper with Ivan, to show coolness to his brother, and to talk flippantly with Katavasov.
>
> "Can it have been only a momentary mood, and will it pass and leave no trace?" he thought. But the same instant, going back to his mood, he felt with delight that something new and important had happened to him. Real life had only for a time overcast the spiritual peace he had found, but it was still untouched within him.[2]

Joy in God—then the depressing of that joy. A happy mood—then interactions that discourage and raise doubts about authentic spiritual progress. Anxiety that what seemed to be strong faith may have been only a passing mood—then again delight. Spiritual peace—then an overshadowing of that peace. Finally, untouched peace in God. . . . In this description of Levin's thoughts and emotions, Tolstoy illustrates something fundamental in every life of faith: the alternations of joy and fear, peace and anxiety, hope and discouragement that the human heart experiences as it journeys toward God.

1

These alternations matter. The joy of experiencing God's closeness instills new energy into the effort to love and serve. The darkness of discouragement and fear chills that quest and may overwhelm it completely. All faithful persons in all walks of life experience some form of these inner spiritual fluctuations: times of energy and desire for the things of God, and other times when that energy and attraction wane. Are we helpless in the face of such contrasting movements of the heart? Is there a way for us to understand this complex spiritual experience? Can we learn how to respond wisely to these changes in our hearts? If any teaching can answer these questions, clearly we will benefit immensely by learning that teaching. Such wisdom is, literally, at the heart of the spiritual life.

Ignatius of Loyola

All who have preceded us in the journey of faith have experienced such movements of the heart, and they, like us, have made choices in response to these movements, accepting or rejecting them. From the experience of the first human beings described in the Book of Genesis and throughout both the Old and New Testaments, we encounter persons who must distinguish between attractions that are of God and those that are not. Through the centuries, figures of holiness have offered assistance to dedicated people in understanding and responding to these stirrings of the heart: Origen, Anthony of Egypt, Augustine, John Cassian, Bernard of Clairvaux, and Catherine of Siena, to name a few.[3]

Among them, however, one emerges in a distinct way: Ignatius of Loyola (1491–1556), the spiritual guide whose teaching on discernment will be the focus of this book. As we will see, in a way all his own, Ignatius found practical language to explain these contrasting movements of the heart and taught effective ways of responding to them.

Ignatius's own interior life was characterized by rich affectivity and a remarkable spiritual self-awareness. References to this keen spiritual awareness abound in the writings of those who knew him personally and are classic in the Ignatian tradition. Jerónimo Nadal, one of those closest to Ignatius, affirms that Ignatius's special grace was "to see and contemplate in all things, actions, and conversations the presence of God and the love of spiritual things, to remain a contemplative even in the midst of action."[4] Many other witnesses express similar thoughts.[5]

In his life and writings, and through the words of witnesses, Ignatius appears as a person deeply attuned to the spiritual movements of his heart, sensitive to these stirrings and careful to distinguish in them what is and what is not of God. For Ignatius, this spiritual awareness was critically important, and he was vigilant to maintain it throughout the hours of the day; it was at the heart of his entire spiritual life and writings. Such awareness of the contrasting spiritual movements of the heart, coupled with an effort to understand and respond wisely to them, is known as the *discernment of spirits*, the subject of this book.

Discernment, in the sense intended here, signifies the process of distinguishing one thing or idea from another. To *discern* (from the Latin *discernere*—to separate things according to their qualities, to distinguish between one thing and another) is to identify one spiritual reality as different from another.[6] The phrase *of spirits* describes *what* is to be discerned, that is, *which spiritual realities* are to be distinguished, one from the other. The word *spirits*, as Ignatius uses it in this context, indicates those affective stirrings in the heart—joy, sadness, hope, fear, peace, anxiety, and similar feelings—with their related thoughts, that influence our life of faith and our progress toward God.

At this point, therefore, we may say that, for Ignatius, discernment of spirits describes the process by which we seek to distinguish between different kinds of spiritual stirrings in our hearts, identifying those that are of God and those that are not, in order to accept the former and to reject the latter.[7] This book is concerned with explaining, illustrating, and applying "discernment of spirits" to the ordinary, daily spiritual experience of dedicated people.

Our basic text in Ignatius's writings will be the rules for the discernment of spirits that he includes in his Spiritual Exercises.[8] These rules are the clearest and most concrete teaching on discernment of spirits contained in our spiritual tradition. As Green writes regarding the practice of discernment of spirits:

> The classic source is the Rules for the Discernment of Spirits in the Spiritual Exercises of St. Ignatius Loyola. Even today these rules, written 450 years ago, are the church's canonical *locus* on discernment. What St. Augustine has done for the problem of evil, or St. Teresa of Avila and St. John of the Cross for the phenomenology of prayer, St. Ignatius, by the grace of God, has done for the art of discernment.[9]

A Personal Word

Twenty years ago my work in retreats and spiritual direction first drew my attention to discernment of spirits in a particular way. I began to discuss these rules in retreats and, later, in seminars on discernment. The enthusiastic response to this teaching I regularly encountered convinced me that, in these rules, Ignatius had touched something fundamental in the experience of all who sincerely seek the Lord. I realized that Ignatius here provides an unparalleled resource for overcoming what is generally the

major obstacle faithful persons encounter in their efforts to grow spiritually: discouragement, fear, loss of hope, and other troubling movements of
the heart.

I was struck to see how often, at the end of a retreat or seminar, such
persons would say that Ignatius had supplied them with an invaluable set
of spiritual tools for overcoming discouragement and fear. They sensed that
Ignatius had assisted them in the struggles of the moment and had
equipped them with the spiritual means to conquer similar trials in the
future. With this learning came new hope.

Over the years I developed the method of presenting these rules that I
am following in this book. This method is based on two convictions. The
first is that the most effective way to convey the full teaching of these rules
is to examine attentively what Ignatius actually says in them: to explore the
rules, phrase by phrase, at times word by word, just as he wrote them.[10]
This is all the more necessary since Ignatius's style is, as de Guibert says,
hard, complicated, and difficult.[11] In fact, I have found that on first receiving the text of the rules, at times people feel disappointed. When first read,
the rules may appear to say little, or little that the person does not already
know. Only when a person examines them phrase by phrase, attentively
exploring their dense wording, does their full and vital richness emerge.

The second conviction is that, since these rules are born of experience,
they are best explained by constant reference to experience. Ignatius wrote
these rules as a digest of spiritual experience—his own and that of many
others he assisted. For this reason I have chosen to present these rules less
through abstract considerations than in the light of examples drawn from
spiritual experience. Each rule will be discussed through examples taken
from the lives of various people, some well known in our spiritual tradition, others less so. Our commentary on these examples will reveal the
meaning of the rule itself.

In this way, the rules come alive. I have often observed how Ignatius's
rules are, in a sense, transformed when they are related to spiritual experience. This approach situates the rules in their original and proper setting,
and something electric occurs. The bare and laconic quality of the language
disappears, and dedicated persons realize, with a sense of marvel, how profoundly Ignatius understands and describes their own spiritual experience
and how skilled he is in assisting them to respond wisely to it. It is my hope
that the examination of the rules in this book will foster a similar realiza-
tion in those who read it.

The Purpose of This Book

My aim, then, is to offer an experience-based presentation of Ignatius's
rules for discernment of spirits in order to facilitate their ongoing applica-

tion in the spiritual life. In accord with the nature of the rules themselves, I have kept this practical purpose constantly in mind. This is a book about living the spiritual life.[12]

In his Spiritual Exercises, Ignatius provides two sets of rules for discernment.[13] In this book I will discuss the first set, composed of fourteen rules. My intention is to comment also on the second set of rules in a separate volume. Ignatius himself, in fact, indicates that the second set of rules should not be discussed simultaneously with the first, and that to do so is unhelpful to persons engaged in applying the first set of rules (*SpirEx*, 9). As we will see, the growth involved in assimilating the first set of rules is already great. By focusing our reflections in this book on the first set of rules, the material remains manageable and will be more easily understood and applied in our lives.[14]

Ignatius composed these rules for those who guide others in the Spiritual Exercises, a time of prayer and of seeking the will of God. He presumes that these guides will know the rules well and will explain them to the retreatants in accordance with the retreatants' spiritual needs (*SpirEx*, 8). In this pedagogy, Ignatius desires that with the help of their guides the retreatants will increasingly develop a personal ability to apply these rules to their own experience, an ability that they will retain when the days of retreat have concluded.[15]

These rules for discernment, therefore, do not apply only to the formal time of retreat but also to the ongoing spiritual experience of all who seek the Lord. Once they have been learned and, with the continuing assistance of a competent spiritual guide, dedicated persons will find these rules irreplaceable in understanding and responding to the daily spiritual stirrings of their hearts.

This book is intended for all who desire deeper understanding of Ignatius's rules for discernment in order to apply them in their spiritual lives. It is written for those giving and for those receiving spiritual guidance, and may serve them as a resource in transmitting and receiving Ignatius's teaching on discernment. It envisages those striving to live these rules both in the context of the Spiritual Exercises and in daily life. This book may serve as a systematic introduction to the fourteen rules or be used, according to need, as a reminder of individual rules. As the choice of examples throughout will demonstrate, the teaching contained in this book applies to persons of every walk of life and vocation. The same examples also indicate that this book is concerned not with remote spiritual phenomena but with the ordinary spiritual experience of all faithful persons.

Excellent literature on the rules for discernment already exists. A gap, however, remains in that literature, a gap that explains in part why the rules for discernment continue to be too little known and too seldom utilized. Some of the writing is extensive, thorough, and conceptually rich but, by that very fact, inaccessible except to specialists. Other writing helpfully simplifies and renders the rules more accessible to many readers, but cannot, in a few pages, describe them fully. The presentation of the rules in this book seeks to combine both accessibility and essential completeness. Each rule is the subject of a separate chapter and is discussed in depth. By examining what Ignatius actually writes in each rule, without attempting to explore further issues and complexities, we respect Ignatius's own pedagogical choices and permit an intelligible and substantial discussion of each rule without undue length or difficulty of exposition.[16] The explanation of the rules through use of examples lightens the reading, sets the teaching in its original experiential context, and clarifies the rules themselves.

In the fourteen rules, as will be evident, Ignatius first instructs us regarding the nature of discernment and then, when we have grasped this, offers practical guidelines for living according to the discernment we have come to understand. Most readers will find that from the third chapter forward this book will apply directly to their personal experience and will offer practical guidelines for spiritual action. The first two chapters, in keeping with Ignatius's sound pedagogical sense, supply the necessary foundation for a fruitful understanding of those that follow.

The basic message of Ignatius's fourteen rules for discernment is liberation from captivity to discouragement and deception in the spiritual life. One of my happiest experiences in working with these rules has been to witness consistently how they awaken new hope in those with whom they are shared. Dedicated persons, at times long subject to the spiritual discouragement mentioned above, find in Ignatius's rules a teaching that begins to set them free. The words that Jesus proclaimed in the synagogue of Nazareth as a summation of his entire redemptive mission also express the central theme of this book: "The Spirit of the Lord is upon me, / because he has anointed me / to bring glad tidings to the poor. / He has sent me to proclaim *liberty to captives* . . . / to *let the oppressed go free*" (Luke 4:18; *emphasis added*). This is a book about setting captives free. Each rule, as we will see it in the following chapters, will guide us one step further toward that freedom.

The Text of the Rules[1]

Rules for becoming aware and understanding to some extent the different movements which are caused in the soul, the good, to receive them, and the bad to reject them. And these rules are more proper for the first week.

First Rule. The first rule: in persons who are going from mortal sin to mortal sin, the enemy is ordinarily accustomed to propose apparent pleasures to them, leading them to imagine sensual delights and pleasures in order to hold them more and make them grow in their vices and sins. In these persons the good spirit uses a contrary method, stinging and biting their consciences through their rational power of moral judgment.

⟿

Second Rule. The second: in persons who are going on intensely purifying their sins and rising from good to better in the service of God our Lord, the method is contrary to that in the first rule. For then it is proper to the evil spirit to bite, sadden, and place obstacles, disquieting with false reasons, so that the person may not go forward. And it is proper to the good spirit to give courage and strength, consolations, tears, inspirations, and quiet, easing and taking away all obstacles, so that the person may go forward in doing good.

⟿

Third Rule. The third is of spiritual consolation. I call it consolation when some interior movement is caused in the soul, through which the soul comes to be inflamed with love of its Creator and Lord, and, consequently when it can love no created thing on the face of the earth in itself, but only in the Creator of them all. Likewise when it sheds tears that move to love of its Lord, whether out of sorrow for one's sins, or for the passion of Christ our Lord, or because of other things directly ordered to his service and praise. Finally, I call consolation every increase of hope, faith, and charity, and all interior joy that calls and attracts to heavenly things and to the salvation of one's soul, quieting it and giving it peace in its Creator and Lord.

⟲

Fourth Rule. The fourth is of spiritual desolation. I call desolation all the contrary of the third rule, such as darkness of soul, disturbance in it, movement to low and earthly things, disquiet from various agitations and temptations, moving to lack of confidence, without hope, without love, finding oneself totally slothful, tepid, sad and, as if separated from one's Creator and Lord. For just as consolation is contrary to desolation, in the same way the thoughts that come from consolation are contrary to the thoughts that come from desolation.

⟲

Fifth Rule. The fifth: in time of desolation never make a change, but be firm and constant in the proposals and determination in which one was the day preceding such desolation, or in the determination in which one was in the preceding consolation. Because, as in consolation the good spirit guides and counsels us more, so in desolation the bad spirit, with whose counsels we cannot find the way to a right decision.

⟲

Sixth Rule. The sixth: although in desolation we should not change our first proposals, it is very advantageous to change ourselves intensely against the desolation itself, as by insisting more upon prayer, meditation, upon much examination, and upon extending ourselves in some suitable way of doing penance.

⟲

Seventh Rule. The seventh: let one who is in desolation consider how the Lord has left him in trial in his natural powers, so that he may resist the various agitations and temptations of the enemy; since he can resist with the divine help, which always remains with him, though he does not clearly feel it; for the Lord has taken away from him his great fervor, abundant love, and intense grace, leaving him, however, sufficient grace for eternal salvation.

⟲

Eighth Rule. The eighth: let one who is in desolation work to be in patience, which is contrary to the vexations which come to him, and let him think that he will soon be consoled, diligently using the means against such desolation, as is said in the sixth rule.

⤺

Ninth Rule. The ninth: there are three principal causes for which we find ourselves desolate. The first is because we are tepid, slothful, or negligent in our spiritual exercises, and so through our faults spiritual consolation withdraws from us. The second, to try us and see how much we are and how much we extend ourselves in his service and praise without so much payment of consolations and increased graces. The third, to give us true recognition and understanding so that we may interiorly feel that it is not ours to attain or maintain increased devotion, intense love, tears or any other spiritual consolation, but that all is the gift and grace of God our Lord, and so that we may not build a nest in something belonging to another, raising our mind in some pride or vainglory, attributing to ourselves the devotion or the other parts of the spiritual consolation.

⤺

Tenth Rule. The tenth: let the one who is in consolation think how he will conduct himself in the desolation which will come after, taking new strength for that time.

⤺

Eleventh Rule. The eleventh: let one who is consoled seek to humble himself and lower himself as much as he can, thinking of how little he is capable in the time of desolation without such grace or consolation. On the contrary, let one who is in desolation think that he can do much with God's sufficient grace to resist all his enemies, taking strength in his Creator and Lord.

⤺

Twelfth Rule. The twelfth: the enemy acts like a woman in being weak when faced with strength and strong when faced with weakness. For, as it is proper to a woman, when she is fighting with some man, to lose heart and to flee when the man confronts her firmly, and, on the contrary, if the man begins to flee, losing heart, the anger, vengeance and ferocity of the woman grow greatly and know no bounds, in the same way, it is proper to the enemy to weaken and lose heart, fleeing and ceasing his temptations when the person who is exercising himself in spiritual things confronts the temptations of the enemy firmly, doing what is diametrically opposed to them; and, on the contrary, if the person who is exercising himself begins to be afraid and lose heart in suffering the temptations, there is no beast so fierce on the face of the earth as the enemy of human nature in following out his damnable intention with such growing malice.

⤳

Thirteenth Rule. The thirteenth: likewise he conducts himself as a false lover in wishing to remain secret and not be revealed. For a dissolute man who, speaking with evil intention, makes dishonorable advances to a daughter of a good father or to a wife of a good husband, wishes his words and persuasions to be secret, and the contrary displeases him very much, when the daughter reveals to her father or the wife to her husband his false words and depraved intention, because he easily perceives that he will not be able to succeed with the undertaking begun. In the same way, when the enemy of human nature brings his wiles and persuasions to the just soul, he wishes and desires that they be received and kept in secret; but when one reveals them to one's good confessor or to another spiritual person, who knows his deceits and malicious designs, it weighs on him very much, because he perceives that he will not be able to succeed with the malicious undertaking he has begun, since his manifest deceits have been revealed.

⤳

Fourteenth Rule. The fourteenth: likewise he conducts himself as a leader, intent upon conquering and robbing what he desires. For, just as a captain and leader of an army in the field, pitching his camp and exploring the fortifications and defenses of a stronghold, attacks it at the weakest point, in the same way the enemy of human nature, roving about, looks in turn at all our theological, cardinal, and moral virtues; and where he finds us weakest and most in need for our eternal salvation, there he attacks us and attempts to take us.

∽

What Is Discernment of Spirits?

∽

If we could lift the veil and if we watched with vigilant attention, God would endlessly reveal himself to us and we should see and rejoice in his active presence in all that befalls us. At every event we should exclaim: "It is the Lord!"
—Jean Pierre de Caussade

"Until One Time His Eyes Were Opened a Little"

We will begin our reflections by exploring the account of Ignatius's conversion on his convalescent bed in Loyola as he described it years later to one of his companions, Luis Gonçalves da Câmara.[1] This experience is the watershed moment in Ignatius's life. Prior to that moment, his life was directed principally to achieving renown through feats of arms and chivalry. After this experience, Ignatius dedicated himself to the service of the eternal king and began that quest for holiness which would so bless generations to come.

We will read this narrative attentively, focusing especially on the patterns of *thought* and *affectivity* contained within it, and all that these reveal about Ignatius's spiritual experience at this crucial moment in his spiritual pilgrimage. It is the moment from which everything else flows in his teaching on discernment of spirits.

Wounded during his courageous but ill-fated attempt to battle the French troops in Pamplona, Ignatius has returned to his native Loyola. He undergoes a first and then a second operation on his leg. His health is good in every way, except that he cannot stand and is confined to his bed as the slow process of healing occurs. To pass the time, he asks for reading materials. Since his more accustomed reading, centering on feats of arms and chivalry, is not to be found in the house, he is given more devout books: a life of Christ and a book of the lives of the saints. Lacking another choice, he begins, somewhat reluctantly, to read these books as the long days pass.

11

But gradually his interest is awakened. The following is his description of what takes place as he reads. The emphasis on *thoughts* and *thinking* is evident in his account:

> As he read them over many times, he became rather fond of what he found written there. Putting his reading aside, he sometimes stopped to *think* about the things he had read and at other times about the things of the world that he used to *think* about before. Of the many vain things that presented themselves to him, one took such a hold on his heart that he was absorbed in *thinking* about it for two or three or four hours without realizing it: he imagined what he would do in the service of a certain lady, the means he would take so he could go to the country where she lived, the verses, the words he would say to her, the deeds of arms he would do in her service. He became so conceited with this that he did not consider how impossible it would be because the lady was not of the lower nobility nor a countess nor a duchess, but her station was higher than any of these.[2]

The framework of Ignatius's experience here is his extended and intense *thought* about the things of the world, and one of these in particular. Within these lengthy periods of thought other faculties in Ignatius are active as well. Affectivity comes into play: the worldly oriented project takes a strong "hold on his heart." His imagination, too, is extensively involved as Ignatius considers this worldly project. We may further note the element of unnoticed unreality in all this thinking. Ignatius simply says that he becomes so immersed in thinking about the project that he fails to perceive its radical impossibility. Something already does not ring true in the unfolding of this interior experience.

A second project, born of the sacred reading that also occupies Ignatius's thoughts, alternates with the worldly project. Now Ignatius begins to consider imitating, with great energy, the holy life of the saints. Once again the focus on thinking is present:

> Nevertheless, Our Lord assisted him, causing other *thoughts* that arose from the things he read to follow these. While reading the life of Our Lord and of the saints, he stopped to *think*, *reasoning* within himself: "What if I should do what St. Francis did, what St. Dominic did?" So he *pondered* over many things that he found to be good, always proposing to himself what was difficult and serious, and as he proposed them, they seemed to him easy to accomplish. But his every *thought* was to say to himself, "St. Dominic did this, therefore, I have to do it. St. Francis did this, therefore, I have to do it." These *thoughts* also lasted a good while, but when other matters intervened, the worldly *thoughts* mentioned above returned, and he also spent much time on them. (23–24)[3]

The sacred project, the choice to live like the saints, also becomes a focus of concentrated and protracted thought. The accent on thought is abundantly evident in the repeated references to "thoughts," "thinking," "reasoning," "pondering," and related words.

As he continues to describe his interior experience, Ignatius explicitly emphasizes his concerted application of thought to these two contrasting projects, one sacred, the other worldly:

> This succession of such diverse *thoughts* lasted for a long time and he always dwelt at length on the *thought* before him, either of the worldly deeds he wished to achieve or of the deeds of God that came to his imagination, until he tired of it and put it aside and turned to other matters. (24)

Now, however, a shift occurs. Thus far, although Ignatius has mentioned affective and imaginative elements in his experience, the primary accent has been on thought, divided between the two contrasting projects. At this point, while *thought* will remain important, *affectivity* will come to the fore and the stage is set for the powerful moment of grace that will change everything in Ignatius's life:

> Yet there was this difference. When he was thinking about the things of the world, he took much *delight* in them, but afterwards, when he was tired and put them aside, he found that he was *dry* and *discontented*. But when he thought of going to Jerusalem, barefoot and eating nothing but herbs and undergoing all the other rigors that he saw the saints had endured, not only was he *consoled* when he had these thoughts, but even after putting them aside, he remained *content* and *happy*. (24)

The framework of the two contrasting periods of thought remains, but now Ignatius begins to focus primarily on the affective experience that accompanies his thinking. The use of affective words makes this clear: "delight," "dry," "discontented," "consoled," "content," "happy."

On the level of thought there is a certain equality to the two projects: both the sacred and the worldly project are capable of intensely engaging his thought for hours at a time. Periods of thought centered on one or the other alternate. The only difference seems to be in the object of the thought, whether sacred or worldly. As regards the reflective experience itself there appears to be an essential similarity: both continue at length, both are engaging.

But things are very different on the affective level. Here there is a fundamental inequality which Ignatius describes according to a chronological pattern in the unfolding of his experience: during and after. It is true that *during* the periods of thought centered on either project there is no significant affective difference; both times of thought are accompanied by welcome, happy affectivity, a kind of delight. *After*, however, when the period of thought has finished, the same is no longer true. When Ignatius ceases reflecting on the worldly project he finds himself "dry and discontented." Yet after he has considered the project of imitating the saints, the delight remains. He continues enduringly to be "content and happy."

And then, the moment of grace occurs:

> He did not wonder, however, at this; nor did he stop to ponder the difference until one time *his eyes were opened a little*, and he began to marvel at the difference and to reflect upon it, realizing from experience that some thoughts left him sad and others happy. Little by little he came to recognize the difference between the spirits that agitated him, one from the demon, the other from God. (24)

It would be difficult to overstate the spiritual power of this brief phrase: "his eyes were opened a little." At this moment Ignatius steps into a whole new spiritual arena. A contrasting affective experience, linked to two contrasting projects of life, has been taking place in Ignatius's heart, but *he has not been aware of it*. Now the experience continues to occur, but his spiritual eyes have been opened a little, enough so that he is now *aware* of these differing patterns within his heart. In this moment, when Ignatius first notices the contrasting affective spiritual experience in his heart, his teaching on discernment of spirits is born. This teaching arises directly from his personal experience and, in the first place, from this time of grace on his convalescent bed. That is why we begin our exploration of his discernment of spirits here; this is the privileged point of entry for all that follows.

Ignatius, however, is not content with awareness alone, significant as this is. In the attentive manner characteristic of his entire spirituality, he begins now to "ponder" the difference of which he has become aware, and to "to reflect on it." This reflection leads him to "realize from experience" and "little by little to come to recognize" the meaning of the diverging patterns of affective spiritual experience of which he has become aware. He now finds himself increasingly able to *understand* "the difference between the spirits that agitated him," whether from the bad spirit or from God.

Ignatius has become aware that certain patterns of affectivity customarily accompany the different kinds of thinking he has been doing. The contrasting affectivity that he notes after the thoughts are completed (i.e., that the sacred project leaves him enduringly happy while the worldly project leaves him ultimately sad) becomes the object of focused reflection. And he concludes that if thoughts of one project (the worldly) cause a delight that consistently turns into sadness, then this project does not have the "feel" of God's action but rather of the bad spirit. And if thoughts of the other (sacred) project cause a delight that consistently lasts, then this project does have the "feel" of God's workings in his heart.

The sequel belongs to history. Ignatius faithfully *takes action* in accord with this insight. His new awareness and understanding lead him to *accept* the sacred project as of God and to *reject* the worldly one as of the bad spirit. With remarkable generosity he sets out on his new life according to the God-inspired project. He travels to Manresa; he begins (not without some initial imprudence) to imitate the saints; he undertakes the pilgrimage to Jerusalem; and his life finds its new direction.

This, then, is the spiritual process that Ignatius experiences during his convalescence in Loyola, a process articulated according to the three steps described: *becoming aware*, *understanding*, and *taking action* (accepting, rejecting). The powerful impact of this moment for good in his own life and in the life of the church even to the present day confirms that we have touched here upon something of crucial importance in Ignatius's life and in the spiritual life generally. What if Ignatius's eyes had not been "opened a little"? What if he had not reflected on his new awareness? Had not acted accordingly? Had followed the worldly project that so drew him? And what of our own lives if our spiritual eyes are not so opened in daily living? What will occur if they are?

Ignatius's initial experience alone of discernment of spirits renders immediately clear the great value of spiritually identifying the movements of our hearts. It also reveals to us the inestimable benefit we will find in a practical and usable teaching about discernment of spirits. If our spiritual tradition can offer us an instruction capable of permitting us also to live our daily lives with discernment, then that tradition is offering us an invaluable treasure. The fourteen guidelines for discernment that we will consider in the rest of this book provide just such a teaching.

We have analyzed Ignatius's convalescent experience here because it is the living context of and the best introduction to the title of his rules, the subject of this chapter. In the highly summarized wording of his title Ignatius codifies the experience in Loyola that we have just described. Seen in the light of this life-changing event, the sober language of the text assumes its full richness.

The Title of the Rules

Ignatius prefaces his teaching on discernment of spirits with a densely packed introductory statement:

> Rules for *becoming aware* and *understanding* to some extent the different movements which are caused in the soul, the good, to *receive* them, and the bad to *reject* them. And these rules are more proper for the first week.[4]

This brief text announces many key elements of discernment and merits our careful attention. It is structured according to the threefold paradigm already evidenced in our consideration of Ignatius's convalescent experience and which will govern his teaching on discernment of spirits in general. Our commentary will follow the language of this text.

The first word of the title indicates the literary genre Ignatius employs. He describes his teaching on discernment as a series of *rules*. Ignatius is not composing a developed spiritual treatise such as those written, for example, by Francis de Sales, John of the Cross, or others. Rather, he is composing short, essential statements with a twofold purpose. They are directed, first, toward *instructing* us concerning the elements involved in discernment of spirits and, second, toward giving us practical *norms* regarding the corresponding action to be taken with respect to the instruction we have received.[5] They are concise guidelines related to specific spiritual realities in discernment, containing directives concerning how to handle them. They are practical rather than speculative. In this sense, Ignatius calls his text a set of rules.

In writing these rules, as is clear from their context in the Exercises, Ignatius presumes they will be discussed with one knowledgeable in their content.[6] They are to be explained by such a person to those who find themselves in the spiritual situation the rules describe and who will, consequently, benefit from this teaching in learning how to respond appropriately to this specific spiritual experience. With the help of both the wisdom of these rules and of one who can impart this instruction opportunely, the persons so aided are increasingly enabled to make spiritual sense out of their experience, and so to live ever more attuned to the Lord's will. This is the goal of all discernment.

Ignatius notes that his fourteen rules will assist "to some extent" in the discernment of spirits. The wording tells us that while these rules will assist in the art of discerning, they do not attempt to say everything that can be said about discernment of spirits. Various interpretations of this phrase are possible: it may well be that Ignatius has in mind here the further content of the second set of rules for discernment of spirits. It is enough for our purposes now to be aware that these fourteen rules, with all their richness, do not exhaust Ignatius's thinking on discernment of spirits.

The humility of this "to some extent" can be deceptive. These rules contain the most practically usable instruction in the entire Christian tradition regarding discernment of spirits. In an unparalleled way and precisely because Ignatius has chosen the genre of *rules*, these fourteen directives constitute a uniquely valuable instrument toward making spiritual sense of the movements of our hearts.

A Threefold Paradigm

In his title Ignatius next outlines the three key steps in discernment of spirits. These mirror exactly the experience of Ignatius on his convalescent bed in Loyola when he first becomes alive to discernment. We can identify these steps though the verbs Ignatius employs in the title: become aware, understand, accept-reject. The following paradigm is thus established:

BE AWARE
UNDERSTAND
TAKE ACTION (ACCEPT/REJECT)

BE AWARE: this is the effort to *notice* what is happening in our inner spiritual experience, what is spiritually stirring in our hearts and thoughts; UNDERSTAND: the *reflection* on the stirrings we have now noticed that allows us to recognize what in them is of God and what is not; TAKE ACTION, that is, to *accept* and live according to what we have recognized as of God, and to *reject* and remove from our lives what we have recognized as not of God. These three steps are presumed in everything Ignatius will say subsequently about discernment, and it is important that we be deeply familiar with them. We need, then, to take a closer look at each of them.

"Be Aware"

In Ignatius's own experience this is the moment when his "eyes were opened a little." This moment expresses a crucial transition from one spiritual situation to another. In the first situation stirrings of thought and affectivity are occurring and impacting the direction of a person's spiritual journey, but the person does not perceive this, is not aware that this is happening. In the second situation these inner stirrings are taking place, but the person perceives this, now is aware that this is occurring. These are the persons whose spiritual eyes are now "opened a little" and who have *noticed* their interior spiritual experience. Without this transition no discernment of spirits is possible; "becoming aware" is the gateway to all discernment.

And we cannot take this awareness for granted. How aware are we of our own interior spiritual experience? How habitually are we aware of it? How often during the day do we advert to it? Do we ever consciously stop to become aware of what is stirring spiritually within? This is a major question in the spiritual life, and it cannot be emphasized too much. It is the issue that Ignatius highlights at the outset of his rules for discernment.

Augustine, as he reviews in his *Confessions* the moment when his own eyes were "opened a little," writes his classic words:

You were within, and I was without. . . . You called, you shouted, and you broke through my deafness. You flashed, you shone, and you dispelled my blindness.[7]

Looking back over his experience, Augustine realizes that God was active within him, in his heart, in his interior world, and that he, Augustine, was without, looking outward, fixed on the world beyond himself, unaware of God's activity within him.

Augustine utilizes two energy-filled images to describe the action of God within him. God "calls," even "shouts" within him; God "flashes" and "shines" within him. God's voice cries out with great strength in his interior spiritual hearing; God's light floods with brilliance his interior spiritual sight. And yet, until the moment of grace arrives, Augustine does not hear, does not see, *is not aware* of God's action within him: "you were within, and I was without."

All too often the culture that surrounds us lives "without," unaware of a divine activity "within." And we ourselves, more often than we would want, find our awareness focused "without," less aware than we would like of what is happening "within." This, again, is the first and most basic Ignatian teaching on discernment: *be aware*, seek to be sufficiently "within" so that what is stirring spiritually in our hearts becomes present to our consciousness.

The Courage to Be Spiritually Aware

Consideration of such awareness leads us to a question fundamental to all discernment of spirits and to the spiritual life in general: why is it that we find spiritual awareness so difficult? Why do we not perceive more of the ongoing spiritual stirrings of our hearts? Why, so often, do we incline more spontaneously toward living "without" than "within," such that, unless we make an explicit effort to be aware of what is "within," we will not gain this awareness? And why does this effort itself cost us as it does? Why do we find it so difficult to sustain day after day? Since interior spiritual awareness is the indispensable point of entrance into all else in discernment, this issue merits our close attention, if we would pursue a life of effective discernment of spirits. The attempt to answer this question will also offer us a deeper appreciation of what is involved in achieving such spiritual awareness.

Any adequate approach to this question must consider the many dimensions of the human person who seeks this awareness. A first consideration is the simple need for instruction in the area of discernment. What the fifth-century writer John Cassian affirms concerning the struggles all encounter in the spiritual life applies in a particular way to the spiritual stirrings of the heart and awareness of them:

> Although the causes of these passions, once they have been set forth by the teachings of the elders, are immediately recognized by all, nonetheless, before they are revealed, though we are all harmed by them and they are present in everyone, no one knows of them.[8]

The same may be said of this interior spiritual world of affective movements and the thoughts that occasion them or spring from them. These
exist in us all. All of us are affected by them. Yet without a helpful instruction regarding them we tend to have only a generic and vague sense of their
existence in us. Because we do not know clearly what we are to look for
"within," we find it all the more difficult to "be aware." This is the need
that Ignatius meets with unique practical clarity in his rules for discernment
of spirits.

A further reason is suggested by the Thomistic teaching regarding the
difference between what gives delight on the level of the senses and what
gives delight on the level of the intellect. Goods of the senses are more visible, more tangible, and more readily apparent to us than those of the mind
and of the spiritual order. Consequently we are easily drawn "without,"
toward what our senses can grasp, while greater effort is required to attend
to the less perceptible world "within."[9]

Jules Toner, in discussing spiritual awareness, points to additional factors involved in the resistance to being "within": the effects of human sinfulness, deceptions of the bad spirit, difficulty in disciplining our power of
attention which "tends to wander aimlessly, responding to any present
stimulus." And,

> Even when we do get attention focused on our inner motions of mind
> and heart, these motions themselves are so manifold and mobile, so
> complexly interrelated in a swift flux, that a distinct perception of
> any particular motion within the flow is difficult to achieve except in
> the case of unusually intense or prolonged motions.[10]

Who of us cannot recognize the truth of this in daily living? It is no easy
task to untangle and identify the innumerable threads in the tapestry of our
daily affective and reflective life. Multiplicity of movements, rapidity, and
varying degrees of consciousness all render the task more complicated.
"Being aware" cannot be taken for granted.

Much is also said of the impact of contemporary culture in diminishing
interior awareness. Thoreau's world that "lives too fast," lives even faster
today. Electronic means of filling the quiet spaces continue to multiply:
portable televisions, cell phones, the Internet, and the like. A secularized
worldview questions faith and the reality itself of an interior spiritual life.
Accordingly, the value of noticing different spiritual voices in our hearts is
simply unrecognized.

While these contemporary factors undeniably increase the difficulty of
reaching interior awareness, they themselves are nonetheless expressions
and consequences of a deeper resistance to living "within," a resistance that
lies at the heart of the entire struggle itself. Blaise Pascal powerfully explores
this deepest resistance in his striking description of *diversion,* wherein we
find his classic affirmation: "I have often said that the sole cause of man's

unhappiness is that he does not know how to stay quietly in his room."[11] Diversion, as Pascal explains it, is essentially a flight from our own limitedness. Since to live consciously "within" is necessarily to encounter our human limitations, it is simpler, though ultimately unsatisfying, to live "without," to *divert* our awareness toward what is external. Contemporary technology simply offers new means of exercising this age-old tactic of diversion. In our time we have become, indeed, "virtuosi of diversion."[12]

It must be admitted that living "within" does mean facing an imposing array of human limitations. We are ontologically limited as contingent, finite beings. The biblical theology expressed in Genesis 3 indicates that we carry a historically inflicted wound affecting the wholeness of our humanity. In addition, the hurt that can accumulate psychologically over the years of our individual life history may be very difficult to face. Though we know of God's mercy, moral weakness remains uncomfortable, and something comparable can be said of our spiritual struggles in general. None of this is easy to face, even in settings where we are sure of understanding and acceptance.

When to this deep resistance we add the other factors mentioned above: our need for instruction in spiritual awareness, the intangibility of interior movements and their complexity and rapid flux, we can understand clearly the strength in the pull to divert our awareness outward, and why diversion readily appeals to us all. Only when we learn experientially the truth that there is a "light that shines in the darkness" (John 1:5), and that to be "within" is above all to encounter the personal presence, the love and healing of our Savior, does this resistance begin to diminish.

The sustained courage to face this challenge makes discernment of spirits possible, and Ignatius invites us to be conscious of this from the beginning, from the title itself of the rules. This is the first and most basic choice that faces the one who, like Ignatius, would live able to discern the movements of the heart. And, as his experience reveals, the choice to live "within" changes everything in the spiritual life and opens up a new journey with the Lord.

A Specifically Spiritual Awareness

A key question remains. Our inner life is richly complex, and there are many levels of stirrings in our interior world. It is necessary, then, to specify more exactly within this complexity the precise type of interior movements of which Ignatius would have us be aware. A grasp of the specific object of discernment is key to a discernment that would be truly discernment *of spirits*.

When Ignatius speaks of the daily meeting of the director with the retreatant in the *Spiritual Exercises*, he writes that the one giving the retreat "should not desire to ask or to know the personal thoughts or the sins of the one making the Exercises, but rather should be faithfully informed regarding the various agitations and thoughts that the different spirits bring the person."[13] An approach to our question is suggested here. Daniel Gil writes:

> The seventeenth annotation distinguishes clearly the thoughts that belong to our psychological awareness ("personal thoughts") from those corresponding to our moral awareness ("sins") and from those pertaining to our spiritual awareness ("the various agitations and thoughts which the different spirits bring the person").

He continues: "It is these agitations and thoughts which, in the title of the rules, are called good or bad. They are clearly distinguished from what may be the sin or the self-engendered thoughts of the retreatant."[14]

Examination of these three closely interrelated but distinguishable kinds of interior awareness will enable us to situate more exactly the spiritual awareness that is the focus of Ignatian discernment of spirits. The following schema represents these three forms of awareness:

KINDS OF INTERIOR AWARENESS

PSYCHOLOGICAL
MORAL
SPIRITUAL

Each of us responds to the surrounding world in a great variety of affective ways. If we are attentive, we become increasingly able to notice these affective responses in the different situations of our lives. In so doing we gain deeper knowledge regarding our emotional patterns, our affective strengths and struggles. This first type of interior awareness is the *psychological awareness* that is professionally pursued in the counseling process and which we also gain through many channels in daily life: feedback from friends, our own effort to notice the affective states we experience in the events of the day, reflection on our interactions with others, and similar means.

Thus we may discover that in certain situations we habitually become angry or fearful, feel more or less secure, find ourselves uplifted or discouraged, and tend to act accordingly. This greater awareness regarding our individual psychological patterns and their causes leads to greater clarity and freedom in making emotionally healthy choices, with increased energy for the tasks of life. Such psychological awareness is obviously an extremely valuable resource for living. This, however, is not the specific awareness that Ignatius proposes in his rules for discernment of spirits.

A second kind of interior awareness involves a being "within" that permits us to grasp the moral quality of our lives. How faithful or unfaithful to the gospel of Jesus Christ are our actions, our words, our choices, and our relationships with others? Are we living according to the Sermon on the Mount, the New Commandment, to Paul's description of the qualities of love? This is the *moral awareness* we seek at the beginning of each Eucharist, when we approach the sacrament of reconciliation, or any time we confront our lives with the Word of God. It is born of a love for Christ that desires to live in union with his own life and teaching. This moral awareness, too, is of great value in the spiritual life: without it, a key piece would be missing in any genuine desire to love the Lord and live as his follower. But neither is this the awareness that Ignatius intends in his guidelines for discernment.

Discernment of spirits focuses rather on a third kind of interior awareness, a specifically *spiritual awareness*. Whereas the concepts of both psychological and moral awareness are relatively familiar to us, the same may not necessarily be true of spiritual awareness. Our task at this point in our reflections, in keeping with the introductory title we are examining, is simply to outline this spiritual awareness in general terms. We will explore further and repeatedly exemplify this awareness in our discussion of the rules that follow. Our examination of Ignatius's convalescent experience in Loyola, however, offers a first approach to spiritual awareness and an initial way of comparing it to the psychological and moral awareness already described.

In reflecting on the two projects that present themselves to him Ignatius experiences two different sets of interior movements. The thoughts relative to one project leave him "dry and discontented"; those corresponding to the other leave him "contented and happy." While his experience of discontent or happiness is indeed an affective psychological experience, it is apparent in his narrative that this awareness is not limited to the psychological level alone. Ignatius is aware that these repeating affective patterns are directly related to his Christian life and contain a message regarding the direction in which the Lord is leading him in life. There is an essentially *religious* dimension to this awareness; it presupposes Christian faith and a Christian understanding of God at work in the various factors which influence human interior life.[15] Ignatius becomes aware of these movements not simply as indicative of his psychological condition but as signifying which of these projects will lead him toward or away from God's will.

Ignatius's experience, then, teaches him that certain movements among the many that stir in our hearts have special significance for our life of faith and our pursuit of God's will. These are the focus of spiritual awareness, the kind of interior awareness that takes note of these spiritually significant affective movements with their related thoughts, as these impact our life of faith and our pursuit of God's will. For the person who has faith in Jesus Christ, it is clear that this spiritual awareness is more than psychological awareness alone.

It is also clear that both the dryness and the happiness Ignatius experiences are *spontaneous* affective movements. Ignatius simply finds them within his heart and, indeed, for a time, though they are affecting him, he is not even aware of them. Obviously, then, these are pre-moral movements; since they are spontaneous, no dimension of moral responsibility can apply to them. The time for decisions with moral significance regarding these movements may indeed arrive later, but, at this point, the moral plane has not yet been reached. Ignatius's awareness of these contrasting states of the heart, then, is not a moral awareness. It is, however, an awareness with immense importance for the whole of his spiritual life as what follows in his narrative powerfully demonstrates. We find here, therefore, not a moral nor a simply psychological awareness but a specifically *spiritual* awareness, of the greatest value for the life of faith.

Although we have distinguished these three kinds of interior awareness for the sake of the necessary precision in discernment, it is also important to note the close interconnection of each with the others. All three are found in the one human person. The developed or undeveloped quality of each will strengthen or slow the growth of the others. An expanding psychological self-awareness increases the space for spiritual awareness as well, and all efforts toward deepening our psychological awareness are of great value toward discernment. In addition, spiritual awareness presumes a solid moral awareness regarding our Christian life. Such moral awareness creates a firm base for spiritual awareness, fosters the integration of our entire life in the process of discernment, and assists in avoiding blind spots that, if undetected, could diminish the clarity of spiritual awareness. It may also be said, conversely, that effective spiritual awareness will assist the human person in making psychologically healthy choices and wise moral decisions.

"Understand"

The first step, then, in discernment is to move from a consciousness projected "without" to a consciousness sufficiently directed "within" that we *notice* what is stirring spiritually in our hearts and thoughts. Being "within," however, is not an end in itself. Though it is key, spiritual awareness of itself is not yet discernment of spirits. Such awareness is indispensable because this awareness alone creates the possibility of the second equally essential step in discernment. Everything in spiritual awareness is directed toward this next step, the moment in which we move from noticing to *understanding* the spiritual meaning of the interior movements we have noticed.

As soon as Ignatius becomes aware of the discontent and happiness that correspond to the thoughts of the contrasting projects, he moves immediately into this next step:

He began to marvel at the difference and to *reflect* upon it, *realizing* from experience that some thoughts left him sad and others happy.

Little by little he came to *recognize* the difference between the spirits
that agitated him, one from the demon, the other from God. (24)

The accent on cognitive activity is clear. Now that his spiritual eyes have
been "opened a little," Ignatius begins to reflect on the difference between
the two contrasting affective patterns he has noted. As he ponders, "little
by little" he perceives the meaning of this contrast: it arises from the two
opposing spirits at work in him. Gradually he comes to understand that
one of these is of God; the other is not. This is the interpretative step in discernment, and it too, like spiritual awareness, is an invaluable spiritual aid.
A clear perception of the origin and direction of the spiritual stirrings of
our hearts provides us with the necessary light to follow accurately the
guidance of the Spirit.

This second reflective step seeks the answer to questions such as these:
Are these stirrings indeed *spiritual* experience, that is, do they affect my life
of faith, hope, and love and my following of God's will? If they do, then
discernment of spirits is indeed necessary. In this case, do they bear the
signs of God (as, for example, the happiness in Ignatius accompanying the
holy project) or not (the sadness that accompanies the worldly project)?
When, through reflection, I have found sufficiently clear answers to these
questions and can name the spiritual experience as of God or not of God,
I have accomplished the second step of discernment of spirits; I *understand*
this spiritual experience.

"Take Action (Accept/Reject)"

The second, interpretative step is again not an end in itself but is in turn
directed to a third step. For Ignatius, even awareness and understanding
together are not yet discernment of spirits; both are aimed toward *action*.
Only when the person has become aware, has correctly interpreted and
then taken the appropriate action with respect to these spiritual movements, has true discernment of spirits taken place.

In his title Ignatius employs two verbs to express the spiritual action he
wishes to describe: "accept" and "reject." Here, too, Ignatius's own experience explains his words. Once Ignatius has understood from his consistent pattern of final discontent that the worldly project is not of God, he
rejects it. From this moment, in fact, Ignatius completely sets aside the
worldly project and will never consider it again. Having recognized God's
plan for him, however, through the experience of continuing joy associated
with the thoughts of the holy project, Ignatius *accepts* this project and
actively pursues it. He travels to Manresa and there begins a life in imita-
tion of the saints. He makes his pilgrimage to Jerusalem according to this
project, and his following of the Lord's plan has begun.

Everything in discernment of spirits is directed toward action: toward firmly accepting what is of God and equally firmly rejecting what is not. Through spiritual awareness and spiritual interpretation, accurate and decisive spiritual action is made possible. As the example of Ignatius himself indicates, the life of discernment calls for a person willing to act. Insightful understanding of spiritual realities alone is not enough; the discerning person must be ready to act in accordance with what has been understood.

This, then, is the fundamental paradigm that governs discernment of spirits: be aware; understand; take action. In his title Ignatius simply enunciates these three steps. The fourteen rules that follow will tell us in detail and with a wealth of practical insight how to put these steps into practice. We will return repeatedly to these three steps as we continue our reflections on discernment.

The Movements of the Heart

We have now examined the basic structure of discernment of spirits as outlined in the title. Before moving to the rules themselves there are further elements in the title to be noted at least briefly. These elements, too, are simply named in the title; they will return in our discussion as we explore the rules.

In discernment of spirits, Ignatius tells us, everything centers on "the different *movements*" that a person experiences interiorly. As we have already indicated, Ignatius has very specific movements in mind. His discernment focuses on the happy and heavy movements of our hearts and their related thoughts, as these tend of themselves to affect *our Christian life* of faith, hope, and love. In discernment of spirits Ignatius does not ask that we become aware of, understand, and act in regard to *all* the movements of our hearts (as valuable as this may be from other points of view), but rather with respect to those which may impact our adherence to the will of God, as strengthening or weakening this adherence.

Ignatius speaks of these movements as "good" or "bad." He asks that we become aware of and understand these different movements, "the *good* to receive them, and the *bad* to reject them." Clearly, from what we have said above, Ignatius is not speaking of moral goodness and badness here. These movements are good or bad inasmuch as they lead us toward or away from God's will, in keeping with Ignatius's primary objective in the *Spiritual Exercises* (*SpirEx*, 1). If the spontaneous feeling of joy we experience in conjunction with certain thoughts indicates in fact the direction God wishes us to pursue, then this movement is spiritually good. If a different spontaneous affectivity and its accompanying thoughts would lead us away from God's will, then this movement is spiritually bad. The movements that lead us toward God's will, toward a stronger life of faith, hope, and love, are *good* movements. Those that lead us away from God's will and weaken our life of faith, hope, and love are *bad* movements.

In the final words of his title, Ignatius tells us that these rules "are more proper *for the first week*." He is explicitly advising us that these fourteen rules do not contain everything he teaches about discernment of spirits; they pertain rather to one specific set of spiritual circumstances. It will suffice here to observe that Ignatius situates these rules in the context of the "first week" because "the purgative life" (*SpirEx*, 10) is the setting in which the kind of discernment these fourteen rules envisage is "more" likely to occur. As he will quickly indicate (rule 2), these fourteen rules essentially apply to the person who is generously striving to overcome sin and who is simultaneously growing in the service of the Lord, that is, to any dedicated and progressing Christian. If any person lives the Christian life seriously, then that person can expect to undergo the kind of spiritual experience these rules foresee. And that person will find in these rules an invaluable aid for the journey.

This means, consequently, that these fourteen rules will most likely apply to anyone reading this book. To learn about them will not be a speculative exercise alone; their teaching will speak to our own experience. It is now our task to explore that teaching.

1

⁓

When a Person Moves Away from God (Rule 1)

⁓

Halts by me that footfall:
Is my gloom, after all,
Shade of His hand,
outstretched caressingly?
—Francis Thompson

An Experience of Spiritual Liberation

Following the pattern of the previous chapter, we will once again approach Ignatius's text from the perspective of a concrete spiritual experience. As noted, because Ignatius's rules themselves arise from and describe spiritual experience, this methodology places the rules in their natural setting and more effectively permits us to uncover the full richness of the spare language Ignatius employs. In this chapter we will discuss the first of these rules. Since, however, the first and second rules are intimately related and must be understood together, we will explore one spiritual experience that incorporates both, returning to this experience in the following chapter when we examine the second rule.

Perhaps the best-known conversion experience in our spiritual tradition is that of Augustine, famously described in his *Confessions*. This is the grace-filled moment in the garden, under the fig tree, when Augustine's long search for spiritual renewal is finally fulfilled. Through his tears he hears the chanting of the child beyond the garden wall: "Take and read, take and read." He opens the Scriptures, and finds the words of St. Paul: "The night is far gone, the day is at hand. Let us, then, cast off the works of darkness and put on the armor of light . . ." (Rom 13:12ff.). In that instant Augustine's life is remade, and he commences a spiritual journey that will lead to great holiness.[1]

Our focus here will be the complex set of interior movements in Augus-

27

tine's heart that *immediately precedes* this moment of conversion. We will
see these first in their broader context and then specifically in their actual
unfolding.

In a very real sense, this story originates in Augustine's adolescent years
when he adopts an increasingly self-indulgent lifestyle. As he rather soberly
writes: "In my youth I burned to fill myself with evil things. . . . I dared to
run wild in different and dark ways of passion."[2] This process begins in the
idleness of his fifteenth year in Tagaste, when his studies were interrupted
for lack of economic means, and is solidified when he resumes these studies
in the larger city of Carthage. All this is tellingly captured in the energy-
packed words: "I burned. . . ." A powerful movement toward unrestrained
self-indulgence stirs in Augustine's young heart and largely shapes the
course of his life for years to come.

But this movement, though dominant, is increasingly challenged by
another. His life of "fruitless seedings of grief" and "restless weariness"[3]
weighs more and more on Augustine, and he yearns for a profound spiritual change in his life. Years pass as the tension between these two movements mounts, and still he remains unable to act.

As all this is stirring in Augustine, a day comes when he sits in conversation with Ponticianus, an official in the emperor's court, and Alypius, his
intimate friend.[4] Ponticianus, unaware of the impact his narrative will have
on Augustine, shares an anecdote of the day. Two acquaintances of his,
minor officials in imperial Rome, had been out walking, had entered the
house of some devout Christians and found there a copy of the *Life of St.
Anthony* by St. Athanasius. One of these officials had begun to read the
Life and learned of how the young Anthony had decisively and joyfully put
into practice the words of Jesus to the rich young man: "If you would be
perfect, go and sell what you have, give it to the poor . . . and come, follow me." He read of Anthony's holy life of total dedication to the Lord.
Deeply struck by this account, the official and his companion decided
immediately to do the same. They, too, gave up their former prospects in
life and dedicated themselves to following the Lord as had Anthony.

Ponticianus recounts this event and then takes his leave, without sus-
pecting the effect of his words on Augustine. The story of the two officials
awakens a profound anguish in Augustine as he compares their immediate
and vigorous response to God with his own protracted helplessness and
wavering. The inner distress Augustine feels is markedly evident as he
describes this moment:

> This was the nature of my sickness. I was in torment, reproaching
> myself more bitterly than ever as I twisted and turned in my chain. I
> hoped that my chain might be broken once and for all, because it was
> only a small thing that held me now. . . . And you, O Lord, never
> ceased to watch over my secret heart. In your stern mercy you lashed
> me with the twin scourge of fear and shame in case I should give way

once more and the worn and slender remnant of my chain should not be broken but gain new strength and bind me all the faster. In my heart I kept saying "Let it be now, let it be now!," and merely by saying this I was on the point of making the resolution. I was on the point of making it, but I did not succeed.[5]

The vocabulary is filled with tension. Augustine is in "torment"; he "reproaches" himself "more bitterly than ever"; he "twists and turns in his chain." Yet he is aware that *God is at work* in his affliction of heart and expresses this in his striking phrase "your stern mercy." His account continues:

I stood on the brink of resolution. . . . I tried again and came a little nearer to my goal, and then a little nearer still, so that I could almost reach out and grasp it. But I did not reach it. (175)

Clearly there has been a shift of direction in Augustine at this point. If we compare the direction he pursued earlier, that is, the quest for self-indulgence without regard for God, with the "goal" toward which he now "comes a little nearer," that is, a turning *toward God*, the change is evident. The two goals are radically opposed. He has pursued the self-indulgent goal for many years. Now, though in a fragile and hesitant way, he is moving in a contrary direction, toward God. Caught between these two goals, he lives a moment of intense spiritual struggle brought now to a high point of tension through the narrative of Ponticianus.

A subtle yet powerful movement of the heart restrains him from progressing toward his new goal:

I was held back by mere trifles, the most paltry inanities, all my old attachments. They plucked at my garment of flesh and whispered, "Are you going to dismiss us? From this moment we shall never be with you again, forever and ever. From this moment you will never be allowed to do this thing or that, for evermore. . . ." These voices . . . no longer barred my way, blatantly contradictory, but their mutterings seemed to reach me from behind, as though they were stealthily plucking at my back, trying to make me turn my head when I wanted to go forward. Yet in my state of indecision, they kept me from tearing myself away, from shaking myself free of them and leaping across the barrier to the other side, where you were calling me. (175–76)

The directional language is again worthy of note: "I was held *back*"; "their mutterings seemed to reach me *from behind*"; "they were stealthily plucking *at my back*"; "when I wanted to go *forward*." "Forward" and "back." Forward *toward God*, and backward *away from God*, back into the former life of self-indulgent separation from God. And the whisperings that pluck at his heart, the images of irretrievably lost opportunities of self-indulgence, do effectively hold him "back" from moving "forward." Still, though more attenuated now, the tense, conflicted tone remains.

But now something new enters this swirl of contrasting movements in Augustine's heart. A fresh movement, filled with peace and hope, meets the inner torment. His wording changes and becomes warm and heartening:

> But by now . . . I had turned my eyes elsewhere, and while I stood trembling at the barrier, on the other side I could see the chaste beauty of Continence in all her serene, unsullied joy, as she modestly beckoned me to cross over and to hesitate no more. She stretched out loving hands to welcome and embrace me, holding up a host of good examples to my sight. With her were countless boys and girls, great numbers of the young and people of all ages. . . . And in their midst was Continence herself, not barren but a fruitful mother of children, of joys born of you, O Lord, her Spouse. She smiled at me to give me courage, as though she were saying, "Can you not do what these men and women do? Do you think they find the strength to do it in themselves and not in the Lord their God? . . . Why do you try to stand in your own strength and fail? Cast yourself upon God and have no fear. He will not shrink away and let you fall. Cast yourself upon him without fear, for he will welcome you and cure you of your ills." (176)

Once more the directional vocabulary is evident, centered now on the forward movement toward God: "by now . . . I had turned my eyes elsewhere"; "on the other side"; "she modestly beckoned me to cross over."

And now, too, the twisting and turning, the sternness, the scourge of fear and shame, have faded and are replaced by a movement of serenity and joy. Augustine senses loving hands outstretched to welcome him, a smile that gives him courage. He perceives that he is not helplessly alone in his struggle to move toward God. New hope stirs within as he is led to consider the example of others who have struggled and have found strength in God to renew their lives spiritually. A warm invitation to trust rises in his heart: "Cast yourself upon God and have no fear . . . he will welcome you and cure you of your ills." As we read his words we sense something beautiful, something blessed at work in Augustine, gently and powerfully giving him hope, moving him "forward" toward God.

At this point Augustine can contain himself no longer and flings himself under the fig tree as his tears begin to fall. The decisive moment of grace is now at hand. He hears the voice of the child calling to "take and read," opens the Scriptures, finds the words of Paul to the Romans mentioned above . . . and his life is remade.

Augustine's account of the interior stirrings preceding his spiritual renewal is filled with drama; various movements of the heart, some assisting and some opposing movement *away from* God, others assisting or opposing movement *toward* God, succeed one another and conflict with each other. Clearly we are dealing here with *spiritual* movements impacting Augustine's journey away from or toward God; we are in the arena of discernment of spirits. Can we make spiritual sense out of these differing movements? Is there a way to discern the various threads in such spiritual experience so that a person may perceive how to respond effectively to them?

This is the type of experience Ignatius explains in his first two rules. As we explore them, we will find that these two rules clarify a foundational issue in all discernment of spirits: that the spirits we discern act in our hearts in contrasting ways depending upon the *fundamental direction* of our spiritual lives, away from or toward God.

Two Fundamental Directions of Life

We have already noted the directional language in Augustine's account of his experience. Two basic directions emerge. The first is a movement away from God and toward a self-indulgent life in which moral boundaries are ignored. This is the direction taken by the young Augustine. The second is born of the growing weariness of heart which this lifestyle engenders in his heart, and reverses the first. Augustine increasingly longs to repudiate this meaningless life of separation from God and to move instead toward God. Prior to his decisive conversion experience, though as yet inconclusively, he has begun to move in this second direction: "I tried again and came a little nearer to my goal, and then a little nearer still. . . ."

These two *fundamental directions* of the spiritual life, as evidenced in Augustine's experience, may be stated as follows: the *first* consists in movement *away from God* and *toward serious sin;* the *second,* the reverse of the first, consists in movement *toward God* and *away from serious sin,* indeed, away from every form of sin, serious or otherwise. In his first rule Ignatius describes the action of the two spirits, good and bad, in the person moving *away from God* and *toward serious sin,* as in the case of the young Augustine. In his second rule he describes the action of the two spirits in the person moving *toward God* and *away from serious sin,* as in the case of the later Augustine seeking spiritual renewal.

Ignatius thus highlights this all-important fact: to discern correctly which spirit is working in a person's heart (and so to know what we should accept or reject), we must first *identify* the *fundamental direction* of that person's spiritual life. This is the indispensable condition for correctly discerning which spirit is operative in the movement the person is experiencing. These two rules help us to identify and so equip us to respond rightly to a vast amount of potentially confusing spiritual experience. Our task now, in this chapter, is to examine the first of these two rules.

The Person Moving Away from God

Ignatius's first rule reads as follows:

First Rule. The first rule: in persons who are going from mortal sin to mortal sin, the enemy is ordinarily accustomed to propose apparent pleasures to them, leading them to imagine sensual delights and pleasures in order to hold them more and make them grow in their vices and sins. In these persons the good spirit uses a contrary method, stinging and biting their consciences through their rational power of moral judgment.

In this rule Ignatius is describing the action of the spirits in a precisely identified person: one who is going "from mortal sin to mortal sin."[6] The vocabulary focuses on a continuing direction of life, on "persons *who are going*," and on a direction of life moving *away from God* and *toward serious sin*. In rule 1 Ignatius clarifies how the spirits work in persons who find themselves in this harmful spiritual state.

Such, evidently, is not the case of the person engaged in the Ignatian Spiritual Exercises. It is equally unlikely to be true of any person seriously pursuing discernment of spirits. If Ignatius begins his rules speaking both of the person who, in the Pauline sense, lives utterly "according to the flesh" (rule 1) and of the person genuinely seeking God (rule 2), describing how the spirits work in both, it is because in this way a solid basis is established for the application of all the subsequent rules.[7] Rules 1 and 2 indicate that the first question always to be asked in discernment of spirits is this: is this person moving away from God and toward serious sin as a fundamental direction in life? Or is this person sincerely striving to overcome sin and grow closer to God as a fundamental direction in life? Only when we have answered this question can we accurately discern the spiritual movements the person is experiencing.

The "Enemy" of Our Spiritual Progress

In Augustine's account of his spiritual experience it is evident that some movements in his heart tend to pull him away from God. He shares the experience of every Christian that certain interior movements, if we are not aware of them, do not understand them, and do not reject them, will effectively distance us from God and his plan for our lives. Ignatius describes the source of such movements as the *enemy*: "in persons who are going from mortal sin to mortal sin, the *enemy* is ordinarily accustomed. . . ."

In these rules Ignatius most commonly speaks either of "the enemy" without further qualification or, more fully, of "the enemy of our human nature." Once he employs the plural: "all our enemies" (rule 11). Less frequently he speaks of "the evil spirit," the counterpart of "the good spirit." Ignatius, then, recognizes that when we seek to embrace God's love and follow God's will according to the full truth of our human nature, we will encounter something inimical to this seeking; we will be faced with an *enemy*. What exactly are we to understand by this "enemy" or "enemies" opposed to the human person who would move toward God?

Toner explains the meaning of the word "spirits" in discernment of spirits in the following way:

> There can be no doubt that, for Ignatius, this word referred to the Holy Spirit and to created spirits, both the good ones, those who are commonly called angels, and the evil ones, those who are commonly called Satan and demons. In using Ignatius's rules, we can and should give the term "evil spirits" a broader meaning which, besides Satan and demons, includes the tendencies in our own psyches which spring from egoism and disordered sensuality and also from other individual human persons or society insofar as these are an influence for evil in our lives.[8]

We may, therefore, consider the term "evil spirit" and its equivalent the "enemy" in a global way as indicating the several sources of those interior movements that would pull us away from God.

As Toner indicates, we may summarize these sources under various headings. In the first place, and in keeping with age-old Christian faith, Ignatius clearly understands the word "enemy" to designate the *personal angelic being* biblically named as the "adversary" (1 Pet 5:8), the "tempter" (Matt 4:3), and the "liar and the father of lies" (John 8:44). Ignatius expects that some of the God-opposed movements stirring within us will "come from without" (*SpirEx*, 32) and specifically from this source.

The word further signifies the *weakness of our humanity* as this tends to hold us back in various ways from moving toward God. Together with all the richness of what it means to be human, we are aware that some stirrings of our humanity, unless resisted, will distance us from God. In scriptural terms this is "the flesh" of which Paul says that it "has desires against the Spirit" (Gal 5:17). Such human fragility is also the "concupiscence" explored by classic Christian theology and the "seven capital sins," tendencies rooted within us focused on self and resistant to God. In various and overlapping ways, Christian reflection has always understood that one of the "enemies" we face in seeking God lies in our own redeemed but still fragile humanity.

This is the general human condition, the legacy we all share of a salvation history that includes both human falling and divine redemption. This general condition, however, takes further individual shape in our personal life history and in whatever wounds—hurt, fear, self-doubt, and similar burdens—we bear within as a result of that life history. The ancient spiritual dictum "Know thyself" is highly significant here.

Yet another source of such movements is *the world around us*, the society and culture in which we live and which affect us daily in significant ways. We are blessed to live in a world filled with goodness and wonder, the gift of the Creator to us all. Yet we are also aware that there is a "world" around us to which, as disciples of Jesus, we "do not belong" (John 17:14–16). Stirrings may be awakened in our hearts by contact with this "world" that, again, if not resisted, will lead us away from God.

The description of these various sources of God-opposed movements articulates our common experience: when we seek to move toward God, together with the saving power of grace, we experience other interior movements caused from within or without that tend to restrain our progress. The different causes of such movements, taken together, comprise the "enemy" of our spiritual progress. Henceforth we will use the term "enemy" in this global sense.

Simply in focusing our attention on the "enemy" Ignatius is rendering us a great service. To be unaware that we can expect resistance when we seek the Lord, or to be aware of this resistance only abstractly and very occasionally, if at all, in the actual living of our spiritual life, greatly increases the likelihood of encountering unexpected spiritual struggles. What is unexpected and finds us unprepared is difficult to overcome and can easily lead to discouragement. Certainly, God's love and grace at work in our lives is far more powerful than any resistance we may meet from the "enemy." Nonetheless, Ignatius tells us, there *is* an enemy and we can expect to encounter this enemy's hindering action. To know this and to understand how this enemy acts is of great assistance in progressing faithfully and perseveringly toward God. Ignatius intends that his rules for discernment assist us in precisely such spiritual understanding.

The Action of the Enemy: Strengthening the Pull Away from God

At this point Ignatius has placed before us two actors in the spiritual drama he is describing: the *person moving away from God* and choosing serious sin, and the *enemy*. In such persons, he writes, the enemy "is *ordinarily accustomed* to propose apparent pleasures . . . leading them *to imagine* sensual delights and pleasures in order to hold them more and make them grow in their vices and sins."

Here, as elsewhere in speaking of discernment (*SpirEx*, 10, 334), Ignatius refers to the *ordinary* ways in which the enemy is *accustomed* to act. Reflection on the spiritual experience he encounters reveals to him that the enemy, in certain kinds of people and in certain spiritual situations, *ordinarily* acts in certain ways. The codification in succinct and practical language of the enemy's customary patterns of action is one of the many efficacious aids Ignatius offers us in his rules. Once we have learned these patterns well, we will discern them more quickly and more accurately.

And, Ignatius tells us, in persons entrenched in serious sin the enemy ordinarily works on the *imagination*. He fills such persons' imagination with images of "sensual delights and pleasures" awakening, consequently, an attraction toward these "delights and pleasures" which confirms them all the more in their "vices and sins." This is the action of the enemy in the young Augustine: "In my youth I burned to get my fill of evil things." A great energy is stirred in Augustine, an energy that leads him away from God and toward "sensual delights and pleasures." If this working in the imagination is the ordinary tactic of the enemy in all ages, it would seem true to say that the stakes are higher in a "culture of the image" as is ours today.

The Good Spirit

Having examined the action of the enemy, Ignatius turns to the working of *the good spirit* in these same persons confirmed in ongoing serious sin. In such persons "the good spirit uses a contrary method." The term "good spirit," as was true of the term "enemy," is also to be understood in a comprehensive sense. The "good spirit" certainly indicates, above all, *God* in his direct action in the human heart. For Ignatius "good spirit" also signifies the *angels,* who, by God's design, serve as instruments of his love for his children.

The term expresses as well God's working in us through the gift of *grace* implanted in us at baptism: sanctifying grace, the theological, cardinal, and moral virtues, the gifts of the Holy Spirit, and individual charisms. "Good spirit" includes the manifold *influences for good* that surround us in the world and in the communion of the saints. Thus, for example, Ignatius's family members who give him spiritual books to read, and the books themselves, are instruments of the good spirit for him; so also Ponticianus and his account of the God-centered choice of the two officials is an instrument of the good spirit for Augustine. We may say, therefore, that all those persons and influences that move us toward the will of God are comprised in the term "good spirit." All of these are ultimately referable to God, their origin and their final goal. In our discussion of discernment we will use the expression "good spirit" in this inclusive sense.

The Action of the Good Spirit:
Weakening the Pull Away from God

Ignatius writes that the good spirit uses "a *contrary* method" with respect to the enemy in these persons. From the outset of his rules Ignatius emphasizes *the contrary nature* of the action of the two spirits. We will find this contrast emerging repeatedly in the rules that follow, and, indeed, this opposition will constitute a fundamental tool in the entire teaching on discernment these rules contain; if one spirit acts in one way, we can expect the other to act in exactly the contrary way. Assimilation of this principle will assist us greatly in applying these rules to our lives.

In persons moving away from God the good spirit works, "*stinging and biting* their *consciences* through their *rational power of moral judgment.*" The enemy places imagined delights before such persons, causing their way of life to appear desirable and thus confirming them in it. The good spirit, however, does precisely the opposite, "stinging and biting," arousing a sense of trouble in them and awakening them to their need for spiritual renewal and for God.

This action of the good spirit is dynamically exemplified in the Augustine still far from God:

I was in torment, reproaching myself more bitterly than ever as I twisted and turned in my chain. . . . And you, O Lord, never ceased to watch over my secret heart. In your stern mercy you lashed me with the twin scourge of fear and shame in case I should give way once more and the worn and slender remnant of my chain should not be broken but gain new strength and bind me all the faster. (175)

Augustine comprehends clearly that his inner distress is the action of God in him. God is at work in him with a "stern mercy," employing "the twin scourge of fear and shame" lest he be confirmed anew in the pattern of sin that has marked his life for so many years. The torment, the bitterness, the twisting and turning give rise in Augustine to that anguished longing for liberation which prepares the moment of new turning to God. The good spirit is powerfully operative in Augustine here.

If the enemy works in the *imagination* of these persons, the good spirit works in their *conscience*. And the good spirit works in their conscience through their *rational power of moral judgment,*[9] awakening in them a true understanding of their unhappy condition with an accompanying sense of inner trouble. Questions like these arise in the heart of such a person: Are you really happy living this way? Can you continue to live in such inner emptiness? Is not life meant to be more than this? Why do you hurt those who love and need you, living the way you do? In your deepest heart you yearn for a fulfillment that you cannot find living this way; why will you not seek it where it can be found? As it draws to its end, will you be happy to look back on the life you are leading now? Such stirrings are the action of the good spirit, arousing a "godly sorrow" that "produces a salutary repentance without regret" (2 Cor 7:10).

We speak, and truly, of our God as a God of peace. Yet our God is above all a God of love, a God who loves us too much to abandon us even when we turn from him in a habitual and confirmed way. In such cases it is the enemy who seeks to induce a sense of comfort and the good spirit who will not leave such a person in peace. Again the wisdom of Ignatius's rule is apparent: in order to discern accurately which spirit is at work in a person, we must identify the fundamental direction of that person's spiritual life.

Perhaps the richest literary representation of this working of the good spirit is found in Francis Thompson's lovely poem "The Hound of Heaven." The entire poem is a telling description of precisely this relentlessly troubling action of the good spirit, pursuing the human heart until that heart surrenders and is healed: "Is my gloom, after all, / Shade of His hand, / outstretched caressingly?" When people who have lived at length without God begin to see that their "gloom," their anguished sense of emptiness and failure in life, far from indicating that God has rejected them, is, rather, itself the surest sign that God has never ceased to love them and to call them to himself, something profoundly happy occurs within them. They begin to see that their "gloom" never was anything other than the "shade of His hand outstretched caressingly." To perceive this love at work in oneself or to assist another immersed in that "gloom" to perceive this love, is to discover a God who loves his children with unfailing fidelity.

This, then, is the way the two spirits work in a person moving away from God. In such a person the enemy awakens images of further delight and pleasure, in order to *conserve* the person's present spiritual situation. In direct contrast, the good spirit acts in the conscience of the person, stirring up a sense of distress in order to move the person to *change* the present spiritual situation, turning in a new way toward God. How will these two spirits act once the person *has* turned decisively toward God? Or, more broadly, how will they act in any person who is sincerely seeking God and his love? Ignatius addresses these questions in the following rule.

2

⌐

When a Person Moves toward God (Rule 2)

⌐

If I were to die tonight and were asked what moves me most in this world, I would perhaps reply: It is the way God passes through our hearts. Everything is swallowed up by love.
—Julien Green

"Rising from Good to Better"

Ignatius's second rule forms the counterpart to the first:

Second Rule. The second: in persons who are going on intensely purifying their sins and rising from good to better in the service of God our Lord, the method is contrary to that in the first rule. For then it is proper to the evil spirit to bite, sadden, and place obstacles, disquieting with false reasons, so that the person may not go forward. And it is proper to the good spirit to give courage and strength, consolations, tears, inspirations, and quiet, easing and taking away all obstacles, so that the person may go forward in doing good.

Ignatius begins rule 2 as he did rule 1, by specifying *which persons* he is considering in this rule. He describes two qualities of such persons: they are "intensely purifying their sins" and are "rising from good to better in the service of God our Lord." They are thus working simultaneously to eliminate something (sin) from their lives and to grow in something else (service of God). We have, then, a new fundamental direction in the spiritual life, the reverse of the previous; these persons are striving to move away from serious sin, and indeed all sin, and to move toward God.

Such persons have not overcome all sin but are seeking to diminish its presence in their lives and are doing so "intensely," that is, with constancy and generosity. They have already grown to a certain point in the service of God and are now applying themselves to "rise" in that service from

38

"good to better." As in rule 1, Ignatius again highlights a continuity in this fundamental direction; these persons also are "going on" in their spiritual movement, away from sin and toward God.

We have moved from the persons who "are going from mortal sin to mortal sin" (rule 1) to those who are "rising from good to better in the service of God our Lord" (rule 2). Here, in rule 2, Ignatius is manifestly speaking of his retreatants in the *Spiritual Exercises*. He is also describing those persons who are seeking to discern the spirits' action in their daily lives and so respond more fully to God's love and more faithfully follow his will. If this is so, then with rule 2 our discussion ceases to be even minimally abstract; from this point forward Ignatius will be describing the experience of all faithful persons.

The Action of the Enemy: Weakening the Movement toward God

Because the fundamental direction of the persons of rule 2 is directly contrary to that of the persons of rule 1, the action of the two spirits in rule 2 will be precisely the contrary of their action in rule 1: "in persons who are going on intensely purifying their sins and rising from good to better in the service of God our Lord, *the method is contrary* to that in the first rule." To the person moving *away* from God the enemy gave encouragement, and the good spirit trouble of heart (rule 1). To the person moving *toward* God the enemy now will give trouble of heart, and the good spirit encouragement (rule 2). In rule 2 Ignatius is essentially concerned with illustrating this action of the two spirits in the person moving toward God.

And first, the action of the enemy: "then *it is proper to the evil spirit* to bite, sadden, and place obstacles, disquieting with false reasons, so that the person may not go forward." Once more we find Ignatius speaking of the *customary patterns* of the enemy's action: "then it is proper to the evil spirit." What follows will outline the ordinary, habitual ways the enemy acts in those who are moving toward God. Again, the effort to learn these patterns well will render discernment all the more possible; we will become increasingly ready to be aware of, understand, and reject such action of the enemy.

Ignatius outlines several "discouraging" tactics of the enemy in the person moving toward God: "then it is proper to the evil spirit to *bite, sadden*, and *place obstacles, disquieting with false rea*sons." Each of these merits our attention. The goal of each tactic is the same: "so that the person may not go forward" toward God.

A "Biting" That Unsettles

In rule 1 Ignatius mentions a "biting" action of the good spirit in persons moving away from God. The good spirit works in such persons, "biting their consciences."[1] The word indicates an unsettling, troubling action of the good spirit in these persons. In rule 2 it is now the enemy who stirs up an unsettling "biting" movement in the hearts of those seeking God.[2] Such dedicated people will not easily succumb to sin, nor will the enemy begin by attempting to move them to sin. His tactic in such persons is rather a *biting*, gnawing action that triggers a sense of anxiety, diminishing their peace, and undermining their delight in God's service. And this approach is effective. If they—and we—are not aware of, do not understand, and do not reject this "biting" action, it will in fact diminish our energy in "rising from good to better." Further problems may ensue as well if we continue to yield to this troubling action of the enemy. To Sr. Teresa Rejadell, a woman of sincere love for God, Ignatius writes:

> The enemy is leading you into error . . . but not in any way to make you fall into a sin that would separate you from God our Lord. He tries rather to *upset* you and to *interfere with* your service of God and *your peace of mind*.[3]

It is vital, therefore, that we be aware of any such spiritual loss of heart and that we take appropriate steps to reject it.

Sadness

The enemy also enkindles a sense of *sadness* in those moving toward God. In rule 1 we saw that in persons moving away from God the good spirit stirs up a "godly sorrow" that, in Paul's words, "produces a salutary repentance" (2 Cor 7:10). The sadness of which Ignatius writes in rule 2 is very different. Nor is he speaking here of the natural, humanly healthy sorrow that accompanies certain moments in life: the loss of a loved one, a move away from beloved places, the termination of a fulfilling occupation, and so forth. Nor, finally, does he intend that purifying darkness in prayer which God sometimes gives to those close to him to increase their capacity for love. In rule 2 Ignatius highlights a different type of sadness: a sadness with respect to God, to prayer, to the love of others in God, that is, to everything involved in the pursuit of God's will. Such sadness diminishes the spiritual energy of the persons so afflicted, impeding their progress toward God. As Ignatius further tells Sr. Teresa Rejadell:

> We find ourselves sad without knowing why. We cannot pray with devotion, nor contemplate, nor even speak or hear of the things of God with any interior taste or relish.[4]

There is nothing salutary about this sadness. It, too, is a highly effective tactic and unless we are aware of, understand, and reject it, such sadness will undermine our spiritual vitality. We will lose heart and will gradually cease "to go forward" toward God, as the enemy intends. This type of dispiriting sadness, in fact, is one of the clearest signs of the enemy.

Obstacles

The enemy further, says Ignatius, "places obstacles" in the path of the person seeking God. A woman of deep faith, for example, senses God's love and feels a new strengthening of her desire to return that love. In the warmth of that love she plans new steps toward growth in serving the Lord and begins to put these into practice. She is "rising from good to better." Then another movement is triggered in her heart. She begins to see the difficulties involved, the problems she will encounter if she continues to seek this spiritual growth. She is led to consider her own weakness. Increasingly she feels that she is too weak to overcome the obstacles, that this spiritual newness, though attractive in itself, is not attainable for her. The enemy *places obstacles* in her path so that she may not go forward.

Ignatius continues in his letter to Sr. Theresa Rejadell:

The enemy as a rule follows this course. He places obstacles and impediments in the way of those who love and begin to serve God our Lord, and this is the first weapon he uses in his efforts to wound them. He asks, for instance: "How can you continue a life of such great penance, deprived of all satisfaction from friends, relatives, possessions? How can you lead so lonely a life, with no rest, when you can save your soul in other ways and without such dangers?" He tries to bring us to understand that we must lead a life that is longer than it will actually be, by reason of the trials he places before us and which no one ever underwent.[5]

A litany of questions: How can you? How can you? How can you? . . . Obstacles, impediments, suggestions of one reason after another why it will be too difficult . . . all leading the dedicated person to desist from going forward in "rising from good to better."

This is precisely the action of the enemy in the spiritually awakening Augustine, now seeking purification from sin and new closeness to God. He writes: "I was held back by mere trifles, the most paltry inanities, all my old attachments. They plucked at my garment of flesh and whispered, 'Are you going to dismiss us? . . .' From this moment you will never be allowed to do this thing or that, for evermore. . . ." These interior voices, says Augustine, "kept me from tearing myself away, from shaking myself free of them and leaping across the barrier to the other side, where you were calling me."[6]

These voices *place obstacles* in Augustine's path toward God. They dishearten him and effectively impede his progress toward God. The person seeking God will perceive anew the crucial need to discern: to be aware of, understand, and reject such movements, if we would indeed "go forward."

"False Reasons" That Disquiet

Finally, the enemy undermines the peace of such persons, "disquieting with false reasons" those seeking to grow in God's love. We have seen that the good spirit uses "the *rational power* of moral judgment" to sting the conscience of those far from God and so lead them back to God. In dealing with devout persons the enemy also employs reason. The enemy's "reasons," however, are *false reasons,* and their falsehood is further revealed by their affective consequence; they *disquiet* these committed persons, troubling their peace in God.

Lucia has just completed a time of retreat and is now traveling home. During her retreat she has felt close to a loving God. In the following account she relates to her retreat director what takes place in her heart as she travels:

> That experience I had as I was leaving after my retreat a month ago made quite an impression on me. It certainly took me by surprise! My mind was in such confusion that I couldn't comprehend what was happening to me. I didn't understand how I could feel so bad so fast after feeling so good for so long. On my way home I was second-guessing my entire retreat and felt that due to my failure it had been a complete waste of time. I figured that I must have some serious problem and that maybe I had been dishonest by not bringing it up during the retreat. And since I didn't even know what the "problem" was, I concluded that I was probably incapable of making a "good" retreat because I was incapable of being honest and open. The thought came to me that I should not waste your time and mine with these retreats. When I thought of calling you about it, I ran into still more obstacles. I felt that I really had no right to bother you—after all, my retreat was over. If things weren't resolved during the retreat, that was my own fault.[7]

The account is replete with "false reasons": "*I was second guessing* my entire retreat . . . *I figured* that I must have some serious problem . . . that maybe I had been dishonest by not bringing it up during the retreat." Within this movement even Lucia's inability to identify any such serious problem, far from reassuring her, becomes itself a further "reason" confirming her inability to make a good retreat: "And since I didn't even know what the 'problem' was, *I concluded* that I was probably incapable of making a 'good' retreat *because* I was incapable of being honest and open." Yet another "reason" indicates that Lucia should not speak of her present confusion to her retreat director: the retreat is over, and "if things weren't resolved during the retreat, that was my own fault." All of these "reasons" are manifestly disquieting: "I didn't understand how I could *feel so bad* so fast after feeling so good for so long." It is striking that within the time itself of this experience, all of these "reasons" seem plausible to this faith-filled woman.

At times a similar process occurs in the hearts of dedicated people as they seek the Lord. They review their spiritual situation and find one reason after another why they are deficient . . . and they are troubled. On such occasions they need to be very aware of what is taking place. When the three following elements are simultaneously present then we may be sure that the enemy is at work: persons "rising from good to better" in serving God; considerations ("reasons") regarding their spiritual situation which seem convincing to them; and, arising from these considerations as its cause, a disquiet that diminishes their affective strength in following the Lord. Such "false reasons" are not to be given credence but simply rejected.

Such are the hampering tactics of the enemy as Ignatius delineates them in rule 2. Once more, we are speaking of the "enemy" in the global sense described above: the "father of lies," our own weakness, external influences, or combinations of these various factors. The entry point of this action of the enemy may include emotional tendencies toward anxiety or sadness already present within us; misperceptions of events in our daily lives; difficult interactions with others in the day; burdensome situations in the work world or at home, and similar sources. It is vital to our spiritual journey that we be aware of how these factors impact us spiritually.

Thus far in his rules Ignatius has simply outlined the tactics of the enemy. In the title to the rules he has told us that we are to be aware of, understand and *reject* such tactics of the enemy. He has not yet advised us regarding *how* we are to reject these tactics. Ignatius will dedicate the greater part of his rules, rules 5 to 14, to addressing this crucial spiritual need.

The Action of the Good Spirit: Strengthening the Movement toward God

In those who are increasingly overcoming sin and growing in the service of God, the good spirit, too, is active. In such persons, "it is *proper* to the good spirit to give courage and strength, consolations, tears, inspirations, and quiet, easing and taking away all obstacles, so that the person *may go forward* in doing good." The action of the good spirit is precisely the opposite of the action of the enemy: if the enemy seeks to dishearten such persons, the good spirit seeks to encourage them. If the goal of the enemy's action is to hinder committed persons from going forward toward God, the working of the good spirit aims toward helping these persons to "go forward in doing good." This encouraging action is "proper" to the good spirit's operation in their hearts. Like the enemy, the good spirit, too, acts in customary, habitual ways in these persons. Again, by learning these patterns we become increasingly able to discern.

Ignatius sketches the good spirit's action succinctly: "it is proper to the good spirit to *give courage and strength, consolations, tears, inspirations, and quiet*, easing and taking away all obstacles." The enemy bites, saddens, places obstacles, and disquiets; the good spirit "gives." For Ignatius, *giving* is the sign of love: "love consists in a communication between the two parties, that is to say, in the lover's *giving and communicating to the beloved* what he has or out of what he has and is able to give" (*SpirEx*, 231).[8] The outpouring love of God is the first characteristic of the good spirit.

There is some overlapping in the qualities of the good spirit's action as Ignatius describes it here. We will discuss each of these characteristics briefly.

Courage and Strength

The good spirit gives "courage and strength."[9] A man has begun to pray with the Scriptures daily and finds that his new closeness to the Lord is deepening his love for his wife and children. Happy in this newness, he seeks to grow all the more in prayer and love for his family. Then difficulties arise, and he finds himself struggling to persevere in this effort; he becomes increasingly disheartened. In his discouragement he turns to prayer and recalls the words of Psalm 23: "The Lord is my shepherd, there is nothing I shall want." These words gently lift his heart, telling him that God's love and grace will always be enough for the task. With a quietly renewed strength he resolves to continue faithfully in his quest for a growing love of his family in the Lord. The good spirit, through the instrumentality of the Scriptures, has given him *courage and strength* to "go forward in doing good."

Consolations and Tears

The good spirit gives *consolations*. The entire third rule will be an illustration of the meaning Ignatius gives to this word: heartfelt experiences of God's love that energize and uplift the person, giving new ease in loving and serving the Lord. We will examine the word "consolation" at length in our next chapter. The *tears* that the good spirit inspires are healing, strengthening, blessed tears that physically express the consolation of the heart in God. Of these, too, Ignatius will speak in the third rule; we will return to them in our next chapter as well.

Inspirations

The *inspirations* that the good spirit gives to those progressing toward God assist such persons with the gift of *spiritual clarity*. A woman wishes to grow in prayer and, in conversation with her spiritual director, finds the way toward growth becoming clear to her. She knows that she has found her answer and is filled with new spiritual vitality. The words of a classic spiritual book slowly reveal to a faith-filled man the path that will bring him closer to the Lord. He silently expresses his gratitude to God for this new and energizing understanding. These are the moments when dedicated persons say with uplifted heart: "Now I see what I need to do; now I have found the way." The inspirations of the good spirit give clarity about *how* to "go forward in doing good."

A Strengthening "Quiet" of Heart

Finally, the good spirit gives such persons a peaceful and strengthening *quiet* of heart. We have seen that the enemy fosters *disquiet* in the hearts of committed persons through false reasons. The action of the good spirit quiets anxieties and instills peace in the Lord. A woman religious has found her sense of God's love and her own love for her religious calling growing over the years. She has many responsibilities in her apostolic mission, and, for some time, these have been a source of anxiety for her. Though her responsibilities have not diminished, this year in her prayer she experiences a growing sense of surety that the Lord is with her in the task. She has become less anxious and experiences a deepening peace that helps her find the Lord even in the midst of much activity. The good spirit is at work giving her a *quiet* heart in the Lord, assisting her to "go forward in doing good."

"Taking Away All Obstacles"

In all of this, says Ignatius, the good spirit is at work, "easing and taking away all obstacles," countering the enemy's tactic of "placing obstacles" in the way of one progressing toward God. A dedicated woman has begun to doubt that she will ever grow closer to the Lord in the way she desires. She has tried but finds herself failing again and again in the same habitual ways. Such growth seems impossible. Then one morning the smile of her child reveals afresh to her God's faithful love. Later in the day a moment of joy in prayer assures her once again of God's saving power at work in her. She senses now that the obstacles are not insurmountable and that "for God all things are possible" (Matt 19:26). New hope springs up within her that with God's grace she will overcome such obstacles and "go forward in doing good." She undertakes afresh her quest for spiritual growth. Such is the action of the good spirit, *easing and taking away all obstacles*. The word *all* is charged with hope; in the power of the good spirit's action in us, there is *no* obstacle that cannot be eased and overcome.

Here, as so often in these rules, Ignatius reveals his boundless confidence in the grace of God at work in the human heart.

This same "easing" action of the good spirit is revealed in the words of Augustine we have seen. In the voice of personified Continence, the good spirit stirs in Augustine's heart, "easing and taking away all obstacles" in his striving to move toward God: "On the other side I could see the chaste beauty of Continence in all her serene, unsullied joy, as she modestly beckoned me to cross over and to hesitate no more. She stretched out loving hands to welcome and embrace me, holding up a host of good examples to my sight. . . ." The good spirit shows Augustine how, fortified by the divine power, he can overcome what had appeared to be insuperable obstacles: "She smiled at me to give me courage, as though she were saying, 'Can you not do what these men and women do? Do you think they find the strength to do it in themselves and not in the Lord their God? . . . Why do you try to stand in your own strength and fail?" And then the loving and heartening invitation to action: "Cast yourself upon God and have no fear. He will not shrink away and let you fall. Cast yourself upon him without fear, for he will welcome you and cure you of your ills" (176).

A spiritual beauty that attracts, a loving invitation, a smile that gives courage, the reminder of God's faithful love, the assurance of a welcome that casts out fear: the good spirit is at work "easing and taking away" the obstacles which, within the movement of the enemy, had seemed so insurmountable. The questions of the enemy, the repeated "How can you . . ." with its intimation that the obstacles are too many and too grave to overcome, dulls the hope of going forward. The questions of the good spirit, on the contrary, give hope, revealing a power of divine love that removes all obstacles: "Can you not do what these men and women do? Do you think they find the strength to do it in themselves and not in the Lord their God? . . . Why do you try to stand in your own strength and fail? Cast yourself upon God and have no fear." This movement of the good spirit prepares Augustine's new and decisive step toward God. The obstacles have been taken away.

"Giving courage and strength, consolations, tears, inspirations, and quiet, easing and taking away all obstacles": such is the work of the good spirit in the person sincerely seeking God. The discerning person who is aware of, understands, and accepts this action will "go forward in doing good" securely and fruitfully.

In his first two rules Ignatius has established a foundation for discerning the action of the spirits at work in a person. If the person is *moving away* from God, the enemy encourages and the good spirit troubles. If the person is moving *toward* God, the enemy troubles and the good spirit encourages. From this point on, the rules presume the second type of person and discuss the *troubling* action of the enemy and the *encouraging* action of the good spirit in such persons. Ignatius will be speaking to all faithful persons about their own experience.

3

⤳

Spiritual Consolation (Rule 3)

⤳

Sometimes my heart would feel as though it were overflowing with joy, such lightness, freedom and consolation were in it. . . . Sometimes my eyes brimmed over with tears of thankfulness to God. . . .

—*The Way of a Pilgrim*

A Perceptible Experience of God's Love

In her journal entry for June 27, 1916, Raïssa Maritain, wife of the philosopher Jacques Maritain, author, and a woman of deep love of God, describes her experience of prayer on the morning of that day. She has been to Mass and now enters a time of personal prayer. The three hours from 9:00 AM to 12:00 PM are spent in nearly continuous "oraison," as she calls the prayer that so often absorbs her at this stage of her life. Initially her heart ranges freely. Then she attempts to pray the Litany of the Sacred Heart of Jesus and finds herself unable to move beyond the first three words, the simple appeal of the heart: "*Kyrie eleison*: Lord, have mercy." She writes:

> At the first invocation, *Kyrie eleison*, obliged to absorb myself, my mind arrested on the Person of the Father. Impossible to change the object. Sweetness, attraction, *eternal youth* of the heavenly Father. Suddenly, keen sense of his nearness, of his tenderness, of his incomprehensible love which impels him to demand our love, our thought. Greatly moved, I wept very sweet tears. . . . Joy of being able to call him Father with a great tenderness, to feel him so kind and so close to me.[1]

We sense immediately that we are on holy ground here and can only approach experiences like this with a great sense of reverence. In them the mystery of God's workings in the human heart is present. Ignatius names such experiences "spiritual consolation" and dedicates his third rule to describing this work of God's love in the human heart. The simple, unadorned language of this rule, like the preceding two, is born of and expresses a great richness of spiritual experience.

In his first four rules Ignatius sets out the groundwork for discernment; the *instructive* tone, therefore, that we have seen in the first two rules continues in the third and fourth. The first two rules are focused on the *fundamental direction* of a person's spiritual life and the impact of this direction on how the spirits operate. The third and fourth rules center on the *spiritual movements of the heart*, the spiritual stirrings that are the "material" of discernment. In this Ignatius further explicates a basic element of discernment already mentioned in his title; these are rules for becoming aware of, understanding, and accepting or rejecting "the *different movements* which are caused in the soul." These movements he names *spiritual consolation* (rule 3) and *spiritual desolation* (rule 4). Our concern in this chapter is with the first of these, spiritual consolation.

A Specifically Spiritual Consolation

In his third rule Ignatius writes:

Third Rule. The third is of spiritual consolation. I call it consolation when some interior movement is caused in the soul, through which the soul comes to be inflamed with love of its Creator and Lord, and consequently when it can love no created thing on the face of the earth in itself, but only in the Creator of them all. Likewise when it sheds tears that move to love of its Lord, whether out of sorrow for one's sins, or for the passion of Christ our Lord, or because of other things directly ordered to his service and praise. Finally, I call consolation every increase of hope, faith, and charity, and all interior joy that calls and attracts to heavenly things and to the salvation of one's soul, quieting it and giving it peace in its Creator and Lord.

The third and fourth rules alone begin with titles, a fact that invites us to observe these titles carefully. In the title for this rule Ignatius states: "The third is of spiritual consolation." Not simply "consolation," but consolation with a modifier: "*spiritual* consolation." The adjective "spiritual" indicates that in discernment of spirits Ignatius distinguishes between two different types of consolation: *spiritual* and *nonspiritual* consolation.[2] The distinction is crucial to discernment of spirits; indeed, accurate discernment of spirits is only possible when this distinction has been well assimilated. We need, consequently, to consider it carefully.

Ignatius employs the word *consolation* according to the common understanding of the word: something happy, uplifting, which instills joy and gives peace. The modifying word *spiritual* has already appeared in our description of *spiritual* awareness in chapter 1 and has the same meaning here. In discussing such spiritual awareness we noted that certain movements among the many that stir in our hearts have special significance for our life of faith and our pursuit of God's will. The kind of interior awareness, we said, that is attentive to these spiritually significant movements in the heart and to their related thoughts, as these impact our life of faith and our pursuit of God's will, is spiritual awareness. In an identical way, Ignatius here speaks of *spiritual* consolation: happy, uplifting movements of the heart (and so, "consolation") directly impacting our life of faith and our following of God's will (and so, "spiritual"). Some examples will serve to clarify the distinction between the two types of consolation, spiritual and nonspiritual.

The human person encounters many happy, uplifting experiences in life. These are the gift of a loving Creator, and we are the richer for them. Yet not all of these experiences are spiritual in the sense just delineated; not all have *direct and immediate reference* to our life of faith and our pursuit of God's will. Such experiences might include the elevation of heart we experience in contact with nature when we are moved and reenergized by its beauty and peace, or the stirrings we feel at the sound of beautiful music or at the sight of great works of art. Enjoyable company and warm conversation with family and friends will also impart a feeling of happiness. Healthy exercise may instill a sense of physical well-being and energy.[3] All of these experiences are good and willed for us by the Creator, but they are not spiritual consolations in the sense Ignatius intends here. They do not have *direct and immediate reference* to our life of faith and our pursuit of God's will. Of themselves, they are *nonspiritual* consolations. It is clear that the word *nonspiritual* has no negative implication. The term simply indicates that these consolations are found on a different level of our experience than the spiritual consolation Ignatius describes in his teaching on discernment.[4]

Though they are not strictly spiritual in themselves, nonspiritual consolations may readily serve as a *springboard* for specifically spiritual consolations. An example will further illustrate the difference, and the relationship that may exist between these two forms of consolation.

On June 7, 1897, in the final summer of her life, St. Thérèse of Lisieux visited with her older sister, Pauline, in the garden of their Carmelite monastery. Pauline recounts the incident that occurred that day:

Descending the steps leading into the garden, she saw a little white hen under a tree, protecting her little chicks under her wings; some were peeping out from under. Thérèse stopped, looking at them thoughtfully; after a while, I made a sign that we should go inside. I

noticed her eyes were filled with tears, and I said: "You're crying!"
She put her hand over her eyes and cried even more.

"I can't explain it just now; I'm too deeply touched."

That evening, in her cell, she told me the following, and there was
a heavenly expression on her face:

"I cried when I thought how God used this image in order to teach
us his tenderness toward us. All through my life, this is what he has
done for me! He has hidden me totally under his wings! Earlier in the
day, when I was leaving you, I was crying when going upstairs; I was
unable to control myself any longer, and I hastened to our cell. My
heart was overflowing with love and gratitude."[5]

Once more we are on holy ground. . . . Thérèse stands in the garden and
contemplates a charming scene from nature: a mother hen protecting her
helpless chicks in the safety of her wings. As Thérèse watches, a process of
thought and affectivity gradually develops. Initially she simply delights in
the scene itself. Then the prospect before her recalls Jesus' use of this very
image to describe his deep love for his people: "How many times I yearned
to gather your children together, as a hen gathers her young under her
wings" (Matt 23:37). The sight of the mother hen protecting her young
also evokes the words of the Psalm: "you have been my help; in the shadow
of your wings I rejoice" (Ps 63:7). As the scriptural understanding of this
scene unfolds in her thoughts, Thérèse's heart turns to God in joy and her
tears begin to fall: "I cried when I thought how God used this image in
order to teach us his tenderness toward us."

Then a further step takes place in this interior process. Thérèse has
already progressed from the sight before her in the garden to a *general*
teaching in Scripture; now she moves from this general teaching in Scripture to an awareness of how that teaching illuminates her *personal* life:
"All through my life, this is what he has done *for me*! He has hidden me
totally under his wings." At this point she is too affected even to speak and
tears well up, silently revealing the deep and joyful gratitude that fills her
heart before God.

This process begins with a gaze upon a pleasing scene from nature;
Thérèse finds delight in observing the mother hen protecting her chicks. We
may say that, at this point, Thérèse is experiencing a *nonspiritual*, natural
consolation. The moment elicits in Thérèse a gentle uplifting of heart, the
response of a humanly healthy heart to the beauty of nature that surrounds
us. It does not yet have direct and immediate reference to her life of faith
and pursuit of God's will.

Then the transition from what is *nonspiritually* consoling to what is
spiritually consoling occurs: "I cried when I thought how God used this
image in order to teach us his tenderness toward us." Now much more is
occurring than simple delight in a scene from nature. The scene from
nature has become the springboard for an awareness of a particular bibli-

cal expression of God's protecting love: the image of a God who shelters his people in the shadow of his wings. A scriptural message of a God who teaches us of his tenderness toward us all, followed by a powerful awareness of his protecting tenderness for her personally, now enter Thérèse's experience as she stands in the garden. Clearly the *level of faith* is now directly and immediately operative in the overflowing consolation her heart experiences. A nonspiritual consolation has become the springboard for a spiritual consolation.

We have paused to focus on the difference between spiritual and non-spiritual consolation since the ability to distinguish clearly between these two levels of consolation is critically important if we would discern accurately what is truly of God in the consoling movements of our hearts. Again some examples will assist us.

A man ceases to apply himself to his work and feels a peaceful sense of rest. A woman expresses to a difficult fellow worker words she has long held within; having done so, she feels a kind of satisfaction. Another person decides a vocational change and feels a welcome freedom from long-sustained responsibilities. In these situations the persons involved experience an elevation of heart; they experience consolation. Is this consolation a sign of the good spirit and a confirmation that they are faithfully following God's will in what they are doing? In the brief description of these examples nothing indicates that the consolation involved is necessarily *spiritual*, that is, arising from faith and strengthening that faith. Further details may reveal that this is or is not the case. The important point here is that discerning persons must be able to recognize the difference between what is spiritual and what is nonspiritual consolation. This ability permits them, on the one hand, to avoid drawing spiritual conclusions from non-spiritual movements and, on the other, to gain strength as God desires from genuinely spiritual consolation. We will return to this distinction as we continue our commentary on Ignatius's rules.

Forms of Spiritual Consolation

In explaining what he intends by spiritual consolation Ignatius does not proceed by way of definition but rather offers a series of examples of spiritual consolation. In effect Ignatius says to us: "This is an experience of spiritual consolation, this is another, this is yet another," and continues until, in understanding each, a meaning also emerges from them all and we grasp his sense of spiritual consolation. The list is extensive though not exhaustive, as other descriptions of spiritual consolation in Ignatius's writings witness.[6] We will consider briefly each of the experiences of spiritual consolation Ignatius describes in this rule.[7]

"When the Soul Comes to Be Inflamed with Love of Its Creator and Lord"

Ignatius writes: "I call it consolation when some interior movement is caused in the soul, through which the soul comes to be *inflamed with love of its Creator and Lord*." We have noted Raïssa Maritain's description of her prayer: "Suddenly, keen sense of his nearness, of his tenderness, *of his incomprehensible love* which impels him to demand our love, our thought. *Greatly moved*, I wept very sweet tears." And Thérèse: "I cried when I thought how God used this image in order to teach us *his tenderness toward us*. All through my life, *this is what he has done for me*! He has hidden me totally under his wings!" Both Raïssa and Thérèse, in a given moment, are "inflamed with love" of their Creator and Lord. The experience lasts for a time, and its spiritual benefit remains when the experience itself has passed. These are exquisite experiences of this first form of spiritual consolation.

Such spiritual consolations are recognizable in the life of those who seek God. These are the graced times when faithful people feel their hearts lift up in love of God. A woman attempts to pray with the Psalms and perseveres in the midst of distractions. Then she encounters a phrase that speaks to her heart and assures her that God is with her in her struggles. Her heart warms with a sense of love for her faithful God. Or again, a man has been worried about a difficult situation to be faced at work this day. He has faced it and matters have gone well. The experience reveals to him afresh that the infinite God knows and loves him. As he drives home, his heart expands in a happy sense of love for the God who is so close to him in time of need. In church on Sunday the singing is particularly alive and speaks to the heart of a woman in the congregation. The words of faith, the beauty of the sacred melody and the sense of communion she feels with the worshiping assembly raise in her heart a warm sense of love for the God who pours out his goodness upon her. In each case, the person's heart is "inflamed with love of its Creator and Lord."

Such experiences differ both in *duration* and *intensity*. Raïssa is "inflamed with love" of God throughout the hours of her morning prayer. Thérèse, too, is richly "inflamed with love" of her Lord as she stands in the garden. The warmth of this experience remains with her less intensely but truly throughout the entire day as the "heavenly expression on her face" and her words reveal when she meets her sister that evening. Spiritual consolation may be felt for just a brief moment; it may endure throughout a period of prayer or a service of worship; it may continue for several days or weeks at a time. The *duration* of spiritual consolation will vary in each instance of such consolation.

Spiritual consolations will vary also in *intensity*. At times these will be powerfully felt, as in the experiences of Raïssa and Thérèse we have quoted. At other times a person will experience a quieter warmth or just a gentle lifting of the heart in love toward God. Such variations in duration and intensity characterize all forms of spiritual consolation. They lie within the loving providence and wisdom of a God who knows how to give good gifts to his children (Luke 11:13).

"And, Consequently When It Can Love No Created Thing on the Face of the Earth in Itself, But Only in the Creator of Them All"

This second description of spiritual consolation presupposes the first and highlights a consequence of the inflaming of love of God in the heart: "the soul comes to be inflamed with love of its Creator and Lord, and, *consequently. . . .*" This enkindling of love of God within us causes our love for all other persons and things to harmonize with that central love: "And, consequently . . . it can love no created thing on the face of the earth *in itself,* but *only in the Creator* of them all."

A young man clearly senses God's call to ordained ministry and is pursuing his theological training in the seminary. Something within him, however, remains attached to the places and persons he has left in order to pursue God's call. One day he spends an hour in the seminary chapel in prayer. As he prays, his heart is "inflamed with love of its Creator and Lord." He feels God very close to him and senses a deep response of love for God well up in his heart in return. He knows with utter clarity that God's love is what his heart most deeply desires. Within the experience, he senses a new freedom regarding his attachment to all he has left behind. His love for those places and persons is no less strong, but now he can love them in the God whose love he perceives so profoundly. Now his love for all such "created things" ceases to burden his response to God's call. His heart is "inflamed with love of its Creator and Lord" and "consequently . . . it can love no created thing on the face of the earth in itself but only in the Creator of them all."

Often enough dedicated persons undergo a similar type of interior conflict. Their hearts have chosen God's love and his service, and yet experience a struggle between desire for that service and attractions toward certain places, relationships, occupations, institutions, and similar "created things," which, if followed, would distance them from the God they wish to follow. In the gift of this second form of spiritual consolation such struggles fade. Their hearts do not love these "created things" the less but rather with a new freedom, now consonant with their love of God. A weight is lifted, and their whole being is integrated into their response to God's call.

"When It Sheds Tears That Move to Love of Its Lord"

The type of spiritual consolation Ignatius next mentions manifests the involvement of the *whole* person in spiritual consolation. It is the enfleshed human person who experiences spiritual consolation, and the movements of the heart, at times, find bodily expression in the tears that accompany and complete the experience.

Tears may express many things. Ignatius specifies which tears are expressions of spiritual consolation: "tears *that move to love of its Lord.*" As in every spiritual consolation, the focus remains the conscious sense of love of God; these tears express the heart's movement toward God in love. Thus Raïssa writes: "Suddenly, keen sense of his nearness, of his tenderness, of *his incomprehensible love* which impels him to demand our love, our thought. Greatly moved, *I wept very sweet tears.*" These tears are motivated by and are the physical expression of a heart moving toward God in love. The same is true in the experience of Thérèse: "*I cried* when I thought how God used this image in order to teach us *his tenderness toward us.*" When Blaise Pascal encounters God in the powerful interior experience that he entitles "Fire," he writes: "Joy, joy, joy, *tears of joy.*"[8]

Ignatius lists three God-centered motives for such tears, two specific and one more encompassing: "whether out of *sorrow for one's sins*, or for the *passion of Christ our Lord*, or because of *other things directly ordered to his service and praise.*" Such tears "out of sorrow for one's sins" are not bitter, destructive tears of self-condemnation; they are the healing tears of the woman at the feet of Christ (Luke 7:36–50), tears that express an unburdening of the heart in the presence of infinite mercy and welcome. Such tears give freedom and peace to the human heart.[9] Another kind of tears expresses the heart's love for and sharing in the suffering of the Savior. Such tears physically manifest a growing love for the self-giving, crucified Redeemer, who reveals his love in his passion.

Finally, these tears may arise from "other things" not further specified except by their general focus: they are "directly ordered to his service and praise." Such "other things" might include the sufferings of the followers of Christ, the wounds of the church the Lord so loves (Eph 5:25), the progress of evil in the world, and similar concerns.[10] These tears, like the others, express a loving sorrow that confirms the person in love for God.

Such, then, are the blessed tears of spiritual consolation. Faithful people remember with gratitude such experiences in their lives, the times when tears have welled up in their eyes as they sensed God's closeness and love. They know the difference between these tears and other tears; these are God-centered, healing, strengthening tears. Again, we are on holy ground.

"Finally, I Call Consolation Every Increase of Hope, Faith, and Charity"

Ignatius now discusses spiritual consolation in relation to the three theological virtues, characterizing it as an *increase* in these three key virtues. Faith, hope, and charity are habitually present in the dedicated person as a legacy of baptism. Yet they may *increase* at given times in ways perceptible to the person.

A man of faith is at prayer. He seeks to turn his heart toward God but finds himself battling distractions, with little consciousness of God's presence to him. Then he recalls the promise of Jesus: "Behold, I am with you always. . . ." As he reflects on these words, his heart lifts with a vivid sense of God's personal closeness to him now as he prays. At this moment something changes in his experience of faith. A faith-based conviction of God's presence has constantly been operative in him and has sustained him even in his distracted prayer. Now, however, there is a *perceptible increase* of this faith. His faith in God's personal presence to him has become more vivid and more deeply felt. The experience increases, that is, gives new strength to his faith and provides him with new energy to serve the Lord.

If he examines his experience in prayer this man can identify the moment when this "increase" of faith began.[11] His experience *before* he prays with the words of Jesus "I am with you always" is different from his experience *after* praying with these words. Before he prays with them his faith is real but less felt; after he prays with them he is conscious of a livelier sense of faith in God's presence—he *feels* an *increase* in faith. He can also recognize the *duration* of this increase, whether for a brief moment as he prays, for the entire remaining time of prayer, or throughout the rest of the day. At some point this more vivid sense of God's presence will pass. The spiritual strengthening given through the experience, however, remains in his heart. And, finally, the person can also perceive the *intensity* of this increase of faith. His sense of faith in God's presence may increase gently, more strongly or even overpoweringly. Such experiences of perceptibly increased faith, says Ignatius, are spiritual consolation.

Something similar may also occur with regard to *hope*. A woman is facing difficult circumstances in her family life. She has been praying for help and doing all she can to improve relationships among the family members. Though problems remain, there has been some encouraging progress. This day things seem to have returned to the former pattern, and she finds her hope for real change waning. In meeting her children after school she encounters a friend who is, like her, a wife and mother. As they talk she senses this woman's confidence in God's abiding providence in her life. Returning home, her heart lifts to God in renewed trust that his providence will also guide her life and those of her family. She experiences an *increase* of *hope* that God will be with her in her efforts and is fortified in her resolve to love her family.

The same type of perceptible increase also takes place in regard to *charity*. In such spiritual experiences we feel the love of God more vividly within us and find increased strength to love those around us. In each case, faith, hope, and charity, persons who are spiritually aware will note an *increase* in their hearts that energizes and facilitates progress toward God.

"And All Interior Joy That Calls and Attracts to Heavenly Things"

A final form of spiritual consolation consists of joy. These are the experiences in which our hearts rise in happiness before God with a joy that "calls and attracts to heavenly things and to the salvation of one's soul." This joy, Ignatius tells us, spiritually refreshes the heart, "quieting it and giving it peace in its Creator and Lord." Once more, as in rule 2, Ignatius speaks of the "quieting" and peace-instilling action of the good spirit.

A clergyman has prayed and worked diligently to prepare his Sunday homily. As he preaches, the message comes from his heart and touches the hearts of his listeners. Later, as they are leaving, a number of his people tell him how helpful they found his words to them. When all are gone he resumes the activity of the day, but his heart turns to God in quiet joy. He finds himself increasingly grateful for his calling and drawn to the means that strengthen it: prayer, study, and pastoral service to his people. He is confirmed in dedication to his ministry and is drawn to seek further spiritual growth. He experiences a joy in God that *calls* and *attracts* him to "heavenly things."

There is an "upward" direction in such experiences of spiritual joy. In the joy we feel, we find ourselves attracted to "heavenly" things: to God's personal calling to us, to the Scriptures, to prayer, worship, the service of others, and to all things relating to God and his saving work in our lives. These things "call" us and we sense the attraction of them. Walter Hilton describes the devout person who in prayer,

> Finds all the powers of his soul unite, and the love of his heart is raised above transitory things, aspiring and *moving upward* towards God by a fervent longing and *spiritual delight*. . . . During this time nothing seems more *delightful* to him than to pray or think about the comfort he discovers there.[12]

In the "spiritual delight" of this prayer the person experiences an "upward" movement toward God. "Nothing seems more delightful" than prayer and dwelling upon the comfort of prayer; in this joy, the person is called and attracted to heavenly things.

A younger member of Thérèse's Carmelite community recounts an experience of prayer one day when she was profoundly discouraged and seriously considering leaving the community:

> "I will never have the strength to be a Carmelite," I said to myself; "it's too hard a life for me." I had been kneeling for several minutes

in this state of agitation and sad thoughts when, all of a sudden, without having prayed or even yearned for peace, I felt an extraordinary change in my soul. I didn't recognize myself anymore. My vocation seemed to me beautiful, loveable; I had seen the value of suffering. All the privations and the fatigues of religious life seemed to me infinitely more desirable than mundane satisfactions. I left prayer absolutely transformed.[13]

In this experience of prayer sadness disappears and peaceful joy returns. And in her elevation of heart this woman feels the call and attraction of "heavenly things" in her life. Her vocation to Carmelite life now seems "beautiful" and "loveable." She remembers once more a lesson already learned about the spiritual value that suffering can have. Even the more difficult aspects of her religious life seem desirable as a response of faithful love to a loving God. The good spirit works in her heart "quieting it and giving it peace in its Creator and Lord." She has experienced spiritual consolation in a very blessed way.

Committed people know this spiritual joy with its accompanying attraction to the things of God. They have felt it, perhaps in certain periods of their lives, perhaps in ongoing daily living. The fruitfulness of such joy-filled spiritual consolations is evident and they are a great gift of God for the journey.

Such are the various forms of spiritual consolation Ignatius outlines in his third rule. It is important to note that Ignatius is speaking of the *ordinary spiritual experience* of any person sincerely seeking God. This is not a description of remote mystical phenomena beyond the comprehension of all but a few. Dedicated followers of the Lord will recognize in their personal experience many and more probably all these forms of spiritual consolation. Ignatius understands this to be the way a loving God *ordinarily* works in the hearts of his children.[14]

What will happen in our spiritual lives if we become aware of God's "ordinary" presence to us in the spiritual consolations he pours upon us? What will happen if we are "within" enough to be aware of and identify these spiritual consolations as a loving God gives them to us day by day? Then, like Ignatius, we will increasingly "find God" during the hours of the day.[15] Then what may seem a beautiful but distant teaching of faith, that is, that God is ever with us, will cease to be abstract, and, with wonder, we will personally know its truth. Through awareness of the spiritual consolations stirring in our hearts we will know that our God is for us, as for the pilgrim people in the desert, a "pillar of cloud by day" and a "pillar of fire by night" (Exod 13:21–22), a God who always walks by our side, leading us along the way.

4

⤳

Spiritual Desolation (Rule 4)

⤳

Ah! there was a heart right!
There was a single eye!
Read the unshapeable shock night
and knew the who and the why.
—Gerard Manley Hopkins

The Time of Trial

In his fourth rule Ignatius discusses spiritual desolation, the counterpart of the spiritual consolation he described in the previous rule. Consideration of spiritual consolation, given the uplifting nature of this interior movement, is welcome and heartening. Reflection on spiritual desolation, however, is more daunting, at least initially. Yet in all discernment of spirits few considerations are more valuable and more ultimately encouraging than those Ignatius's offers on spiritual desolation. The clear understanding of such spiritual desolation to which he guides us in the fourth rule begins already to diminish its power to dishearten us. We will introduce this rule with two examples.

Alice is a dedicated woman of faith, active for years in her parish. Sharing the life of the parish is a source of spiritual strength for her and brings her joy in the Lord. More recently she has moved to a new town and joined the local parish. Here, too, Alice has sought involvement in the parish community but in her new setting has found this involvement more difficult to achieve. A year passes amid struggles and she begins to question the value of her efforts. A point comes when,

> Alice sees herself as a pretty complete failure and feels altogether discouraged. . . . Recently, even in her own personal prayer, she has experienced feelings of emptiness, of being abandoned by God. She feels that God is no longer near and she becomes overwhelmed with

58

frustration. She wonders if she isn't altogether losing her faith in God's loving care. She does continue to be faithful to community worship and to her personal times for prayer, but it all seems hopeless and meaningless.[1]

Alice experiences a state of discouragement, and in her discouragement feels that God is far from her. She continues to be faithful to common worship and personal prayer but the joy is now gone: "it all seems hopeless and meaningless."

Jane is a dedicated religious woman in her late thirties. She has come to a retreat center to make a retreat with the assistance of her spiritual director. During the first days of her retreat Jane has experienced great peace and a happy sense of God's closeness to her. On the third day of her retreat the joy she feels in God's loving presence moves her to increase her time of prayer. The following is a description of the next days of her retreat:

Day 4: Jane gets up with a bad headache, feeling exhausted and under strain. She cannot pray well. All joy has evaporated. She is tired and sad and moody. Finally in the evening she tells the director about her action of the previous day and its results. The director advises cutting down on prayer time and resting more.

Day 5: She follows the advice, prays less but still has no enthusiasm and is filled with gloom.

Day 6: At her morning prayer she becomes very much disturbed. She begins to doubt the Lord's presence to her even in the opening days of the retreat. Probably, she thinks, she should attribute everything to her overactive imagination. Who is she to be given a taste of the sweetness of the Lord? She begins to grow discouraged at the thought that she is not meant for a deep prayer life. Her desire for God is just an illusion. The rest of the day is one of disquietude, confusion, and a sense of discouragement.[2]

Jane, in different circumstances, has reached a point similar to the position of Alice. Her peace and awareness of God's love are gone. She now doubts that she ever was truly close to the Lord even in the earlier days of prayer when God had seemed so present to her. She has become discouraged and confused regarding her very desire itself for God.

In every spiritual journey, according to the varying circumstances of each person, such experiences of trial may and do occur. If it is not understood and resisted, the potential of such discouragement to cause spiritual harm in persons seeking God is clear. Ignatius terms such experiences *spiritual desolation* and dedicates his fourth rule to instructing us regarding them. All who seek to grow spiritually will readily grasp the great need to be aware of, understand, and appropriately respond to such discouraging spiritual movements.

A Specifically Spiritual Desolation

In his fourth rule Ignatius continues to describe "the different movements which are caused in the soul" (title of the rules): the movements of the heart that comprise the "matter" we discern in discernment of spirits. In the preceding rule he explored the first of these movements, spiritual consolation. Now he centers on the second, directly contrary to the first, that is, *spiritual desolation*. The fourth rule reads:

> *Fourth Rule.* The fourth is of spiritual desolation. I call desolation all the contrary of the third rule, such as darkness of soul, disturbance in it, movement to low and earthly things, disquiet from various agitations and temptations, moving to lack of confidence, without hope, without love, finding oneself totally slothful, tepid, sad, and, as if separated from one's Creator and Lord. For just as consolation is contrary to desolation, in the same way the thoughts that come from consolation are contrary to the thoughts that come from desolation.

As earlier in describing spiritual consolation, so now in treating of spiritual desolation Ignatius does not define but rather offers a series of examples of such desolation. And here once more the principle of *contrariety* is powerfully present: "I call desolation *all the contrary* of the third rule." Spiritual desolation will be precisely the opposite of all that we have seen in the last chapter regarding spiritual consolation. This principle indicates that we could largely write the fourth rule simply by taking the third rule and stating its contrary: if spiritual consolation consists in quiet of heart, spiritual desolation will consist in disquiet; if spiritual consolation is joyful, spiritual desolation will be sad, and so the opposition could be continued. Comparison of the two rules as Ignatius composed them confirms this parallelism in contrasting qualities.[3]

As in the preceding rule, the series of examples is prefaced by a title: "The fourth is of *spiritual desolation*." This rule will discuss *desolation*, and a desolation that is *spiritual* in nature. As with consolation, so with desolation Ignatius distinguishes between what is spiritual and what is nonspiritual.

Ignatius employs the term *desolation* according to the familiar usage of the word: a condition of affective heaviness that instills sadness and depletes energy for living. The adjective *spiritual*, as throughout the rules, signifies that which is directly and immediately referred to faith and the pursuit of God's will. Thus, the phrase *spiritual desolation* indicates an affective heaviness (and so "desolation") directly impacting our faith and pursuit of God's will (and so "spiritual"). Alice not only "feels altogether *discouraged*" (affective heaviness), but, in her discouragement, feels "abandoned *by God*" (direct reference to faith). Jane not only experiences "disquietude" and "discouragement" (affective heaviness) but also, in her discouragement, begins "to doubt the *Lord's* presence to her," to think that "she is not meant for a deep *prayer life*," and that "her desire *for God* is just an illusion" (direct references to faith). These are experiences of specifically *spiritual desolation*.

Just as we experience movements of consolation both on the *nonspiritual* and the *spiritual* levels, so desolation may be experienced on either level as well. If we overextend ourselves and do not provide for sufficient nourishment, exercise, and rest, our physical energies will diminish. To the extent that this process continues we will feel an increasing heaviness in facing life: we will experience *physically* based *nonspiritual desolation*. The same is true of our emotional energies. If we are disheartened and, to some degree, depressed, while this depressed condition endures, psychological heaviness will color all we encounter in life; we will experience *psychologically* based *nonspiritual desolation*. Neither level of desolation mentioned here has immediate and direct reference to faith, and, in this sense, neither is spiritual. Obviously, "nonspiritual" does not mean of no significance.

As was true of nonspiritual consolation so also *nonspiritual desolation* is frequently a *springboard* for *spiritual desolation*. A man pushes himself to the maximum for a number of months, without proper rest or exercise. As he grows increasingly weary he finds relationships at work and at home becoming heavier to sustain (nonspiritual desolation). A time soon comes when prayer, too, has become heavier and God seems farther away than before (spiritual desolation). A woman has struggled in certain relationships and finds herself anxious and depressed. She takes no steps to cope in a healthier way with what becomes an ongoing condition of depression (nonspiritual desolation). The day then comes when her energy toward her habitual spiritual practices wanes and, for a time, she loses hope of growing in love of God (spiritual desolation).

Thus nonspiritual desolation, viewed from the perspective of the spiritual life, is more than a humanly heavy movement in need of healing: it also constitutes a fertile source of spiritual desolation and so a potential hazard for the spiritual journey. The less we do to overcome *physical* (tiredness) or *psychological* (depression) nonspiritual desolation, the more likely we are to experience spiritual desolation as well. If we are tired or depressed, the step to discouragement in our God-given calling, to diminishing fidelity in prayer or in God's service generally, is very small. From the perspective of the spiritual life and specifically in regard to avoiding spiritual desolation, it is imperative that we be wise stewards of all dimensions of the humanity God has given us.

Forms of Spiritual Desolation

The fourth rule is comprised of two parts. The principal section of the rule outlines various *forms of spiritual desolation*. The second section refers more briefly to the *thoughts* that arise from both spiritual consolation and spiritual desolation. In keeping with the structure of the rule we will examine first the different forms of spiritual desolation and then, in a later part of this chapter, Ignatius's teaching concerning the thoughts related to both spiritual consolation and spiritual desolation.

In the main body of the rule Ignatius simply names various forms of spiritual desolation, one after another. We will consider them here in the order in which he lists them.[4]

"Darkness of Soul"

If the good spirit gives "inspirations" (rule 2) that communicate light and clarify the way toward God, the enemy, conversely, instills a *darkness* of soul with precisely the contrary effect. Here the person feels helplessly trapped in confusion, unable to comprehend what is occurring spiritually. Mingled with this inability to understand is the affectively heavy sense that things are going badly and will continue to worsen. This darkness-instilling action of the enemy is operative in Jane's anxiety about her "overactive imagination," her fear that her desire for God is just "an illusion," and in the "confusion" she feels, together with disquietude and discouragement. She is *in the dark*, a confusion mixed with trouble of heart. When we find ourselves caught in an anxiety-filled darkness in relation to our life of faith, then we are experiencing this first form of spiritual desolation.

"Disturbance in It"

In her morning prayer Jane "becomes very much disturbed," and the rest of the day is spent in "disquietude." And we have seen Ignatius write to Teresa Rejadell that the enemy tries "to upset you" and to "interfere with . . . your peace of mind." This *disturbance* of the heart illustrates the troubling, unsettling, restless quality that characterizes spiritual desolation. When, like both Alice and Jane, we have lost our former peace in seeking the Lord and our hearts are upset and *disturbed*, then we are in spiritual desolation.

"Movement to Low and Earthly Things"

In the joy of spiritual consolation there is an "upward" call and attraction "to heavenly things" (rule 3). In the heaviness of spiritual desolation there will be exactly the contrary movement; here there will be a "downward" attraction toward "low and earthly things." Persons in spiritual consolation are drawn to God and the things of God: prayer, the Scriptures, worship, service of others in response to God's call, sharing in the life of the church, and similar God-centered matters. Persons in spiritual desolation, on the contrary, *feel* no attraction to prayer and to God's service but are drawn toward "lower" and more "earthly" things: material comforts, gratification of the body in various ways, memories of such things from the past, immersion in empty trivia, diversion through the media, the Internet, busyness, superficial conversation, and similar occupations.

Certainly many "earthly" things serve to provide a healthy relaxation that strengthens us humanly and so in our service of the Lord; this is not what Ignatius intends here in speaking of "movement to low and earthly things." He is speaking, rather, of the "downward" pull arising from the heaviness of spiritual desolation toward "low" things that weaken our progress toward God. An example will illustrate the point.

John has dedicated his life to the Lord for years following a time of conversion in his early thirties. The faith that gives meaning to his work, daily prayer, participation in the church and family life as a response to God's love is the most important thing in his life; to all this, in the love he feels for God, his heart is consistently drawn. His former self-centered and self-indulgent lifestyle has long ceased to attract him. But now prayer has been dry for some weeks, and John is afraid that something has gone wrong. God seems distant and he fears that he has somehow failed the Lord. He begins to doubt the authenticity of his entire life of faith, and, though he perseveres in his effort to pray and to serve, his heart is increasingly heavy and troubled. This day John feels lonely and finds that he has no desire for his customary prayer. He would rather postpone or simply omit the prayer. He considers channel surfing on television or visiting different Web sites and chat rooms on the Internet, and the thought seems welcome to him. In the heaviness of this moment his feelings of attraction for his life of faith weaken, and certain of his former patterns of self-indulgence, long distasteful to him, now begin to attract him again. John experiences a movement, in time of spiritual desolation, toward what is *low and earthly*.

"Disquiet from Various Agitations and Temptations"

Once again we encounter the characteristic "disquieting" quality of the enemy's action, already mentioned in rule 2. Here Ignatius pinpoints a further trait of spiritual desolation; within the heaviness of the desolation the person experiences a restless flow of *agitating movements*, mixed with *temptations* that *disquiet* the person.

Helen goes about the work of the day feeling sad, far from God, unable to focus in prayer or *feel* any interest in spiritual matters. As the day wears on, the heaviness increases. She continues her activity, but her heart churns with upsetting, agitated stirrings. She finds herself tempted to avoid prayer, to give up her ongoing effort to love a difficult family member, to allow herself to speak sharply to another. She is tempted also to seek certain gratifications that she knows, from long experience, will only increase her sense of heaviness. This churning stream of *agitating stirrings* and *temptations* is accompanied by a sense of *disquiet*; their very presence troubles Helen and undermines her peace. Persons who experience such agitation, temptations, and disquiet of heart are undergoing spiritual desolation.

"Moving to Lack of Confidence, without Hope, without Love"

Here, too, spiritual desolation shows itself the exact contrary of spiritual consolation. In spiritual consolation the person experiences an "increase of hope, faith, and charity." In spiritual desolation there is a contrary movement toward *lack* of *confidence, hope,* and *love.* The lack experienced in spiritual desolation does not signify the loss of faith, hope, and love as abiding virtues in the heart of the baptized. What decreases is the conscious, *felt* experience of these three virtues.

Jane "begins to *doubt* the Lord's presence to her even in the opening days of the retreat." She fears now that "her desire for God is just an *illusion.*" Alice "wonders if she isn't altogether *losing her faith* in God's loving care." John "begins to *doubt* the authenticity of his entire life of faith." These are experiences of movement toward a *lack of confidence* within a time of spiritual desolation. In the darkness of the desolation the person finds doubts and questionings such as these arising: You think you've grown in love of God; look at you now, unable to pray, thinking such kinds of thoughts. You've just been fooling yourself. . . . You were so sure of God's love for you; where is that closeness now? How can God love someone who fails as repeatedly as you do? You felt so convinced of your calling; now you feel helpless to move forward in it. How can you be so confident that you read well the signs of God's will when you chose this calling? You have never made very much spiritual progress in all these years; are you really certain that God is asking you to take these new steps in prayer now? In spiritual desolation we sense doubts welling up within, moving us to *lack of confidence.*

Persons in spiritual desolation may also find themselves *"without hope."* Jane is discouraged "at the thought that she is *not meant* for a deep prayer life." She asks herself, *"who is she* to be given a taste of the sweetness of the Lord?" Alice "sees herself as a pretty *complete failure,"* and though she "does continue to be faithful to community worship and to her personal times for prayer, it all seems *hopeless* and meaningless." Spiritual desolation presses the person to *lose hope* of any real progress toward God.

Close behind this loss of hope is the urging to discontinue the effort itself toward spiritual growth.

Walter is in the habit of praying for a half hour each morning before work. This morning as he rises, the spiritual desolation of the preceding day still weighs on his heart. Though he begins his prayer as usual, he does so burdened with the sense that his efforts will be in vain. As the first minutes of distracted, dry prayer unfold, the feeling that the entire period of prayer will be fruitless continues to grow. Walter is now on the verge of simply ceasing to pray. He is, in Ignatius's sense here, *without hope* in a time of spiritual desolation. Examples of similar stirrings of hopelessness with respect to undertakings in the parish, in the family, or in the spiritual life more broadly could easily be multiplied. Clearly *it is crucial* that persons seeking God be aware of, understand, and reject the debilitating insinuations of such spiritual desolation.[5]

Persons in spiritual desolation, finally, feel as though they are *without love*. In spiritual consolation the heart experiences a "warm" perception of God's love. In spiritual desolation, on the contrary, the heart finds itself "cold," unable to sense God's loving presence; it *feels* as though it is "without love." This feeling does not signify that such dedicated persons in fact have no love of God but is, rather, a classic indication of spiritual desolation. Within the time of desolation, however, this perception can seem very real. To name such experiences as spiritual desolation is an invaluable step toward liberation from the lie they suggest.

"Finding Oneself Totally Slothful, Tepid, Sad"

The adverb "totally" is powerful here. Ignatius applies it to three further forms of spiritual desolation; persons in such desolation may experience themselves as entirely *slothful*, *tepid*, and *sad*. These three attitudes seem to dominate and appear to these persons to describe *totally* their state of heart.

Ruth has been experiencing spiritual desolation for the past week and has found her desolation deepening over the past few days. For several years she has participated in a Bible study group and has always found in these meetings rich nourishment for personal prayer and an encouraging sense of communion with others who share her love of God. Ruth consistently looks forward to these meetings and participates in them willingly. This week, however, she feels no energy toward the study of Scripture and toward sharing with the others. In this time of desolation she has almost to force herself to attend the Bible study. Ruth is, in Ignatius's sense here, wholly *slothful* with regard to an activity that brings her closer to God. She feels completely *without spiritual energy* with respect to the meeting.

Ruth does attend the Bible study in spite of her lack of attraction for it. The meeting is tasteless for her. The Scriptures do not come alive for her this time as they have in the past. She joins in the common prayer and contributes to the sharing but without affective involvement. She does her best "to get through it" as the group expects, but her heart is distant and unengaged. Ruth is, again in Ignatius's sense here, totally *tepid* in carrying out a habitual practice of her spiritual life. She is faithful but feels *no fervor* as she participates in the Bible study.

As the burdensome days of desolation continue, Ruth increasingly feels a sense of sadness. There is little "interior joy which calls and attracts to heavenly things" now in her life of faith. Often God seems far away and her spiritual life, formerly Ruth's greatest cause of happiness, is now a source of heaviness. She fears that she has regressed spiritually and that her spiritual condition may continue to worsen. In her time of spiritual desolation Ruth has become *sad* in her life of faith. This sadness, Ignatius tells us, is an experience of spiritual desolation.

Persons seeking God may recognize these or similar experiences in their own spiritual journey. It is important to observe that none of these three attitudes: *slothfulness, tepidity,* and *sadness*, is an indication that Ruth's love of God has diminished. They do not signify that Ruth has ceased to be a dedicated woman of faith. All three are, rather, experiences of the trial of spiritual desolation. If Ruth is aware of and understands this, she will find it easier to resist the feelings of slothfulness, tepidity, and sadness and persevere faithfully until they pass and peace returns. If she is not spiritually aware and does not understand this, the harm these three attitudes can cause is all too evident.

"And, as if Separated from One's Creator and Lord"

Linked to the sadness is the feeling of distance from God. When doubts arise in Jane's heart they revolve precisely around this point; she "begins to doubt *the Lord's presence to her* even in the opening days of the retreat." It is striking that the doubt concerns not only her present but also her past experience. God, she fears, was not truly present even in those earlier experiences of prayer when she had felt so joyfully certain of that presence. In the same way, Alice, in her spiritual desolation, feels *"abandoned by God"* and "feels that *God is no longer near.*" Persons in desolation tend to feel *separated* from their Creator and Lord. The happy consciousness of God's closeness that they formerly felt has vanished, and God seems remote. Now they cannot sense the Lord's presence to them.

Ignatius advisedly qualifies this feeling of separation with the words "as if." Though they *feel* separated from God, persons in spiritual desolation are not *in fact* separated from the God who is ever "Emmanuel," "God with us." Ignatius is highlighting a fundamental characteristic of spiritual desolation; while it endures, any felt consciousness of God's loving presence is weakened or absent, and such persons feel *as if* they were separated from God.

Ignatius's words "as if" prompt a crucial observation about spiritual desolation in general. Such desolation insinuates an *identity* between the heavy *feelings of desolation* and the person's *real spiritual condition*. Thus, in spiritual desolation thoughts such as these will arise: You are now feeling a movement toward "low and earthly things," toward various forms of self-indulgence; this is *the kind of person you are*, too weak to overcome what holds you back from God. You are troubled by various agitations and temptations this day; this is *who you are*, a person without spiritual peace, unable to rise above temptation. You feel no hope that your prayer will be fruitful today and feel little desire to pray; this is *who you are spiritually*, a person who does not love prayer. You feel sad and as if separated from God; this, too, is *who you are in fact*, a person far from God.

The lie of spiritual desolation includes a false equation between what the person *feels* in desolation and what the person *is* spiritually. If we accept this lie, discouragement and decline in progress toward God are not far away. If, however, we understand that such feelings indicate rather the trial of spiritual desolation, that God's call is to be faithful and thus *grow* spiritually through the trial, then an energizing liberation takes place in our hearts. The bonds of the lie are broken, and we are set free to follow the Lord with courage.

Such are the experiences of spiritual desolation Ignatius describes in his fourth rule. A person may experience one or several of these forms of spiritual desolation in combination. All the forms of spiritual desolation described possess in common the quality of *heavy affectivity* in relation to our *life of faith*. Like spiritual consolation, spiritual desolation also varies in *duration* and *intensity*. A movement of disquiet may touch a person's prayer only briefly or may characterize an entire time of prayer, a morning, a day, or days at a time. Desolation may be quietly disheartening, more intensely though bearably present, or may seem unendurably dark. Subject to God's grace, much will depend on whether the person is aware of, understands, and works to reject the desolation, that is to say, on whether this is a person of *discernment*.

In the letter to Teresa Rejadell already quoted Ignatius discusses first spiritual consolation and then spiritual desolation. He introduces his comments in the following manner:

> I will call your attention briefly to two lessons which our Lord usually gives or permits. The one of them he gives, the other he permits.[6]

Two points are worthy of note here. Ignatius affirms that *God gives* the first lesson, that is, spiritual consolation. With equal clarity he teaches that *God does not give* the second lesson, that is, spiritual desolation, but simply *permits* it to be given by another agency, that is, by the enemy. God gives spiritual consolation; God *never* gives spiritual desolation. God, however, does permit the enemy to give us spiritual desolation at times for reasons that lie within his loving providence.

And, remarkably, Ignatius utilizes the word *lesson* identically for both spiritual consolation and spiritual desolation. That spiritual consolation be considered a "lesson" from God, illuminating the path that leads to God, is clear. That Ignatius should also describe spiritual *desolation* as a "lesson," that is, as an experience able to impart spiritually valuable insight, intimates why God may permit the enemy to visit us with this trial. Ignatius understands that when we faithfully resist spiritual desolation we "learn" spiritual lessons highly useful for our spiritual journey. Later in his rules, especially in the ninth, Ignatius will instruct us further regarding what God's loving reasons for permitting spiritual desolation may be.

The "Thoughts That Come from" Consolation and Desolation

Having outlined various forms of spiritual desolation in the first part of rule 4, Ignatius turns, in his concluding sentence, to a new though related issue: the *thoughts* that come from both spiritual consolation and spiritual desolation. An experience from the spiritual journal of Cardinal Stefan Wyszynski will assist in understanding the teaching contained in this final part of rule 4.

The brief incident in question took place in 1953 in a period of high tension between the church in Poland, of which Wyszynski was then the leader, and the government. Wyszynski was taken at night from his residence by the government authorities, driven to an abandoned Franciscan friary and left alone in the room allotted to him. Understandably, his heart was filled with anxious questions: what would happen to him? What would happen to the church he so loved?

He describes what then follows:

> I glanced around the room, which showed signs of having been recently lived in by one of the Capuchin Fathers.
>
> I was alone. On the wall over the bed hung a picture with the inscription: "Our Lady of Rywald, comfort the distressed." This was the first friendly sign, and it brought me great joy. After all, what happened was that with which I had so often been threatened: "to suffer dishonor for the sake of the name of Jesus" [Acts 5:41]. I had feared that I would never share this honor which had befallen all my seminary colleagues.[7]

Prior to this moment in his room Wyszynski's heart had been heavy, carrying the responsibility of church leadership in a time of personal and ecclesial vulnerability. As he entered the room he was conscious of being left to himself, alone. Then a brief sequence of grace took place, articulated according to three elements. We will briefly examine each of these elements in the light of the final sentence of Ignatius's fourth rule.

The first element was external: a picture that recalled a biblical figure, accompanied by a prayer. The second was internal: as Wyszynski gazed on this picture and made the prayer his own, an affective change took place within him. The sense of loneliness faded and something "friendly" warmed his heart. His anxiety also disappeared, and he experienced "great joy." Clearly this was an awareness of presence and a deep joy based on faith and expressive of faith; this was *spiritual consolation*. Finally, out of the joy of spiritual consolation a new set of *thoughts* was born. What had been simply troubling was now understood in the light of Scripture; he was sharing the experience of the first apostles who rejoiced to suffer for the name of Jesus. What formerly had been a source of anxiety, now, in this moment of strengthened faith, appeared even as an "honor" which he "had feared" he might never share with his companions of seminary years. The sense of presence, the great joy, the biblically based understanding of his situation, the sense of the honor shown him in sharing the lot of his own colleagues: all this completely changed his heart and energized him to live this difficult moment with courage and faith.

Three elements, then, emerge: an external reality that serves as an *instrument of the good spirit*; an experience of *spiritual consolation* with its happy affectivity; a series of energizing *thoughts* that *arise from the spiritual consolation*. In the final sentence of rule 4 Ignatius highlights the third of these elements: the *thoughts* that *arise from* the spiritual movements in our hearts. He writes: "For just as consolation is contrary to desolation, in the same way the *thoughts* that come from consolation are contrary to the *thoughts* that come from desolation." Here, too, we encounter an element of great significance in Ignatius's teaching on discernment of spirits.

As is clear from his choice of the words "consolation" and "desolation" and from the exemplifications of these that Ignatius gives in rules 3 and 4, both spiritual consolation and spiritual desolation are *affective* experiences, uplifting or disheartening respectively. The language of the heart has predominated thus far in Ignatius's discussion of both.

Now, however, Ignatius explains that the affective experience of spiritual consolation and spiritual desolation is linked to a conceptual content, that there are "thoughts that come from" these two kinds of spiritual movements. More is involved in spiritual consolation and spiritual desolation than affectivity alone; the affective stirrings give rise to *thoughts*. These thoughts are not merely concomitant with the affective stirrings but are specifically thoughts *that come from* the affective stirrings themselves.[8] A link can be identified between the affective stirrings and the consequent thoughts: the second *come from* the first. Thus, as he stands alone in his room, from his experience of joy-filled spiritual consolation a new and faith-based set of thoughts arise within Wyszynski.

Faithful people will experience this same pattern of thoughts arising from affectivity in their daily spiritual lives. A woman feels deep spiritual consolation as she drives home from work, and she is filled with an awareness of God's great love for her. In the joy of this consolation she finds herself thinking of new ways to respond to God's love in her daily family relationships; out of the *affective* experience of spiritual consolation arise new and graced *thoughts*. Clearly these thoughts are not just simultaneous with the spiritual consolation but rather *come from* it, issuing directly from the experience of the consolation itself.

A man feels disheartened and far from God as he tries to pray. In his discouragement he finds himself thinking of postponing or abandoning his practice of daily prayer; out of the *affective* experience of spiritual desolation arise new and harmful *thoughts*. Again, these thoughts are not merely simultaneous with the spiritual desolation but rather *come from* it as from their immediate source. Many and widely diverse thoughts pass through our consciousness in the day. Among these, discernment of spirits is concerned specifically with those thoughts that *come from* spiritual consolation and spiritual desolation.[9]

And, affirms Ignatius, here, too, the principle of contrariety holds. If the affective experiences of spiritual consolation and spiritual desolation are directly contrary, the same contrast will be true also of the thoughts that arise from them: "just as consolation is contrary to desolation, *in the same way* the thoughts that come from consolation *are contrary* to the thoughts that come from desolation."

A further application of the above examples will clarify this point. As she drives home in the warmth of spiritual consolation the woman *thinks* of new ways to show love to her family. Some days later, however, she is disheartened and feels far from God. Now in spiritual desolation, she struggles to believe that she can truly progress in love in her family relationships and begins to think of simply abandoning the new attempt to love. The thoughts that come from her spiritual desolation are *directly contrary* to the thoughts that came from her earlier spiritual consolation.

The disheartened man thinks of postponing or abandoning his practice of daily prayer. Later his prayer changes and is filled with a rich consciousness of God's deep love for him. In his time of spiritual consolation he finds himself thinking of ways to ensure more firmly the presence of this blessed prayer each day. The thoughts that come from his spiritual consolation are *directly contrary* to the thoughts that came from his earlier spiritual desolation.

What is only implicitly affirmed in rule 4 will become explicit in rule 5: the thoughts that arise from spiritual consolation are to be accepted; those that come from spiritual desolation are to be rejected. Ignatius will provide us with effective tools to this end as his rules continue.

In rule 4 Ignatius presents the set of difficult movements he calls spiritual desolation. These are, in themselves, heavy and unhappy experiences. Yet, in outlining them for us with such clarity Ignatius has done us a service of enormous value. As noted, it is when we are unaware of and do not understand the nature of spiritual desolation that we are most susceptible to its harmful deception. Once we comprehend clearly, in practical and usable terms, the nature of spiritual desolation, we are on the road toward freedom from its tyranny. This is the service Ignatius renders us with his fourth rule. Ignatian discernment of spirits opens the gateway to hope; it is a proclamation of liberation to those who were held in bondage (Luke 4:18).

5

⟿

Spiritual Desolation: A Time for Fidelity (Rule 5)

⟿

When the morning's freshness has been replaced by the weariness of midday, when the leg muscles quiver under the strain, the climb seems endless, and suddenly, nothing will go quite as you wish—it is then that you must not hesitate.
                                                          —Dag Hammarskjöld

Guidelines for Action

The title of the rules and the first four rules themselves are essentially *instructive*. Ignatius's goal thus far has been to familiarize us with the field in which discernment of spirits occurs. In his title Ignatius establishes the basic paradigm of such discernment: be aware, understand, take action. The first two rules outline the action of the two spirits with respect to the fundamental direction of the person's spiritual life: moving away from God (rule 1) or toward God (rule 2). In the third and fourth rules Ignatius describes the two interior movements we are to discern: spiritual consolation (rule 3) and spiritual desolation (rule 4). At this point we are initially equipped to "be aware" and to "understand" the movements of which we have become aware. We know what it means to be "within" and spiritually aware, and we can begin to understand which interior movements are spiritual consolation and which are spiritual desolation.

Ignatius has not yet concluded the task of instructing us regarding discernment; more of such instruction lies ahead in the rules to follow. With the fifth rule, however, a shift occurs and the rules become predominately *normative*, providing guidelines for action.[1] As we become increasingly capable of noticing and understanding spiritual consolation and spiritual desolation, the third step in discernment rises ever more insistently to the fore; we desire counsel regarding how we may effectively take the spiritual

72

action toward which the deepened awareness and understanding are directed. Consequently, we increasingly look to Ignatius for guidelines concerning how to accept faithfully the work of the good spirit in spiritual consolation, and how to reject efficaciously the work of the enemy in spiritual desolation.

It is especially to this last point that Ignatius directs the remainder of the rules, that is, how to reject effectively the disheartening action of the enemy in spiritual desolation. Clearly, if we compare the action of the good spirit with that of the enemy, the first is by far the primary spiritual reality. In the history of salvation, communal and personal, the grace-giving action of God is the essential reality; thus the fundamental issue in discernment of spirits will always be to accept the work of God in time of spiritual consolation, to be strengthened by it as God intends, and so respond ever more fully to that divine love. And Ignatius will have further guidance to offer to this end.

Nonetheless, because Ignatius writes these rules with an eminently practical purpose in mind, he dedicates the majority of them to assisting us in rejecting the pitfalls of spiritual desolation. In the spiritual situation these rules envisage, the person's need for assistance in overcoming the discouraging lie of spiritual desolation is greater than the need for help in accepting God's work in spiritual consolation. This latter is welcome and encouraging, and we readily receive it into our hearts. There are, in fact, some concerns to be addressed with respect to spiritual consolation, but they are fewer than those regarding spiritual desolation.[2] The greater difficulty lies in the trap of spiritual desolation and its power to debilitate—if we are not aware of it, do not understand it, and do not concretely know how to reject it.

The potential for spiritual harm in spiritual desolation is evident in the discouragement of Alice, Jane, John, and the others we considered in the previous chapter. For most dedicated people, as they progress on their spiritual journey, this is the principal obstacle in growth toward God: the weakening induced by the discouragement and disheartening insinuations of spiritual desolation. Assistance toward achieving increased freedom from this obstacle is one of the greatest gifts that our spiritual tradition can offer us. And, as this freedom grows, not only does spiritual desolation hinder us less; it is itself progressively transformed, as God intends, into a "lesson" capable of further solidifying our progress toward God. The crucial issue, from the perspective of human initiative in the spiritual life, will be how we respond to the spiritual desolation when it comes. In a practically oriented set of rules, therefore, the guidelines useful to this end will predominate.

In terms of the basic paradigm of discernment this signifies that the central focus will henceforth be the second half of the third step: *how to reject* the work of the enemy in time of spiritual desolation. We may represent this through recalling that basic paradigm and highlighting Ignatius's point of emphasis at this stage of his rules:

> Be aware
> Understand
> Take action (accept/*reject*)

From this point forward Ignatius will present us with a wealth of practical counsel on how to overcome the deceptions of the enemy in spiritual desolation.

The next four rules (rules 5 to 8) discuss rejecting such desolation when we are *already within the time of spiritual desolation* itself. They indicate what we should *not do* in time of spiritual desolation (rule 5) and what we *should do* in time of spiritual desolation (rules 6, 7, and 8). In this chapter we will consider the first of these.

In Time of Desolation Make No Changes

The fifth rule reads as follows:

Fifth Rule. The fifth: in time of desolation never make a change, but be firm and constant in the proposals and determination in which one was the day preceding such desolation, or in the determination in which one was in the preceding consolation. Because, as in consolation the good spirit guides and counsels us more, so in desolation the bad spirit, with whose counsels we cannot find the way to a right decision.

The rule contains two parts; the first gives us a guideline and the second explains the reason for the guideline. We will examine first the guideline and then the reason for it.

Ignatius begins the rule by specifying clearly in what precise situation this rule applies; this is a directive for persons who are "in time of desolation." As we have noted, experiences of spiritual desolation may vary in duration: a brief moment, an hour, a day, or weeks at a time. The norm given in this rule applies to persons who are *now* in such a *time of spiritual desolation.* Thus, this rule would apply to Jane when enveloped in spiritual desolation on the sixth day of her retreat, or to Alice in the weeks of her spiritual desolation following upon the year of seemingly fruitless activity in her new parish. It applies to any persons who can say of themselves: "I am now experiencing spiritual desolation." Such spiritual desolation would include any of the forms of desolation described in the fourth rule.

The guideline is simple and absolute: in time of spiritual desolation *never make a change.* In life we make many changes on many different levels of our being and action; of which "changes" exactly is Ignatius speaking here? As always in discernment of spirits, Ignatius has in view the spiritual life and what concerns it; these changes, then, will be changes with direct pertinence to our life of faith and pursuit of God's will.

If there is "a time of spiritual desolation," there is also a time *preceding* the time of spiritual desolation. Neither Jane, for example, before the fourth day of her retreat, nor Alice, earlier in the year, was yet in spiritual desolation. Ignatius presumes that persons now "in time of desolation," made various decisions regarding their spiritual life before this time of desolation began. Such are, he says, "the *proposals and determination* in which one was the day *preceding* such desolation," or "the *determination* in which one was in the *preceding* consolation." When these persons were not yet in spiritual desolation, and when they enjoyed the inspiration of the good spirit in spiritual consolation, they resolved upon certain steps in their spiritual life. In their time of peace and light, before the heaviness of spiritual desolation had begun, these persons planned ways of growing in regular prayer, decided to make retreats or join Bible study groups, proposed new means of living their God-given calling, or similar spiritual steps. *These* are the *proposals and determination* that they must never change in time of spiritual desolation.

A parenthetical but important note is called for at this point. For a proper understanding of rule 5 and in order to avoid potentially harmful misapplications of Ignatius's counsel never to make changes in time of spiritual desolation, it is key to note clearly that Ignatius is speaking here of a time of *spiritual* desolation—not of a time of *nonspiritual* desolation—and of not making changes in proposals regarding our *spiritual* life. If a man is exhausted from the pace of life he has maintained or if a woman is deeply depressed because of a harmful relational situation (examples of nonspiritual desolation), healthy changes may indeed be necessary, even urgently so. Ignatius's fifth rule must not be invoked in such cases to advise these persons simply to persevere in nonspiritually harmful situations; such a misapplication of this rule would obviously lead to injurious consequences. This observation indicates once more that the distinction between what is spiritual and what is nonspiritual must always be kept in mind for all correct discernment of spirits.[3]

Ignatius knows from experience that it is precisely such strengthening "proposals and determination," decided upon in earlier times of spiritual tranquility and consolation, that the enemy will attempt to undermine in time of spiritual desolation. If, for example, in a time of spiritual consolation a man has proposed to spend some minutes each day reading and praying with Scripture, "in time of desolation" he will find himself moved to "make a change," that is, to give up his earlier "proposals and determination"; he will be moved to abandon the practice of daily prayer with Scripture. The tactic of the enemy in the darkness of spiritual desolation is to suggest that we reverse the decisions taken in preceding times of light; into this trap, says Ignatius, we must never fall. Rather, we must remain *firm and constant* in such proposals throughout the time of spiritual desolation. Spiritual desolation is a time that calls us to *constancy and fidelity*.

The following is an account written by a person making the Ignatian Spiritual Exercises. We will explore it carefully in the light of the rules discussed thus far and particularly of the rule presently under consideration.[4] The narrative concerns both affectivity and thought in prayer, as well as small decisions and how discernment is involved in these. It will advance us one step further toward the type of reflection involved in gaining understanding of our interior movements. This woman writes:

> During the first part of the prayer, I *could not settle down* to pray.

As an exercise in learning, a question may be immediately raised: is this a *spiritual* or a *nonspiritual* movement, and is it, therefore, matter for discernment of spirits? Obviously, it is not consolation, whether spiritual or nonspiritual. Is it spiritual desolation? A certain level of disquiet is evidently present, and it occurs while this person is at prayer. Nonetheless, we know too little thus far to specify whether this is nonspiritual, physically or psychologically based disquiet, or whether it is truly spiritual desolation, tending directly toward weakening this woman's life of faith. At this point we need simply to note this disquiet during prayer and remain alert for further information that may assist us in understanding whether it is spiritual or nonspiritual.

She continues:

> I was sitting in my room, but the *thought* kept going through my mind that maybe I should be in the chapel. I *felt restless*, while my *mind* was having a debate about where I would most find the Lord's presence.

Both affectivity and thought are evident here. This woman *feels* "restless"; mingled with her restless feelings is a recurring *thought* suggesting a change of place for her prayer. Apparently she had decided, before beginning her prayer, to do so in her room. Now she finds herself thinking of moving to the chapel where, perhaps, she would pray better. A debate about this question absorbs her mind.

What might we suggest to this woman at this point? Her prayer is consumed by a restless concentration on the issue of place. Would she do well to resolve the debate by changing her place of prayer? Would she be better advised simply to set this debate aside and continue to pray where she is? Again, we know too little to be sure. If we could clearly identify her disquiet as spiritual desolation, then rule 5 would give us an equally clear answer: she should make no changes in time of spiritual desolation but remain firm and constant in the decision she made *before* the spiritual desolation began. Again, we need to watch the further unfolding of her experience.

And she writes:

I finally decided to stay in my room, but I was still *feeling restless*. I next started wondering *how* I would pray. I did not resonate with Ignatius's meditation at this point in the Exercises. I would, I *felt sure*, do better with a different way of meditation, yet I wanted to learn Ignatius's way. So my *thoughts* went on. The inner debate just *aggravated* my *feelings of restlessness*. Throughout, I was asking the Lord *where* and *how* he wanted me to pray, but my *restlessness* and *inner debate* were leading to *confusion*.

This woman does, in fact, resolve the debate with the choice to remain firm in her earlier decision; she opts to remain in her room. Nonetheless, though she has settled this question, the restlessness remains. Immediately a second debate begins: should she pray according to Ignatius's teaching on meditation or follow another way of meditating? As her restlessness continues, she considers changing her former decision regarding *how* to pray. She feels "sure," even, that her prayer will improve if she makes this change.

What would we now advise this woman? Should she adhere to Ignatius's way of meditating as she had planned? Would she do better to change in a way she feels "sure" will assist her to pray better? Our answer must once more be the same: if this is truly spiritual desolation then she should make no change but should continue to pray with Ignatius's form of meditation as she had planned. Again, we must remain watchful for further indications of the nature of the movements she experiences. Something, however, does begin to feel suspect in this series of restlessly proposed and re-proposed changes.

Although this woman has decided not to change the *place* of her prayer, as her restlessness deepens, this first debate reopens and is added to the second: "Throughout, I was asking the Lord *where* and *how* he wanted me to pray." And while all this is happening, her sense of disquiet increases: "The inner debate just *aggravated* my feelings of *restlessness* . . . my *restlessness* and *inner debate* were leading to *confusion*." Restlessness, inner debate about changes of place and method, growing feelings of restlessness, a decision made and then revoked, all of this leading to "confusion." What would we suggest to this woman at this point? Should she make changes? Should she adhere to her earlier decisions?

Now the moment of insight occurs:

Suddenly I *recognized* what was going on (because of our class on discernment) and *prayed against it*. Suddenly the *inner debate stopped* and I *felt strongly attracted* to a particular scriptural passage. The prayer time went well: I was *peaceful* and able to allow the Lord to reveal the meaning of the Scripture passage and its application to my life. The challenge of the Scripture to my sinfulness was *peaceful*, with a *strong sense* of the Lord's *loving acceptance* and *transforming power*.

"Suddenly I recognized what was going on." A graced-inspired moment now arrives when this woman moves from the first step in discernment— she is clearly very *aware* of the movements within and able to describe them in great detail—to the second step: "suddenly I *recognized*." Now she *understands* the spiritual meaning of this swirl of interior movements and related thoughts. Evidently, though she does not tell us so explicitly, she perceives this restless debate and its consequent confusion to be of the enemy, and therefore to be rejected. She *takes action*, setting herself "against it" through prayer. And her turning to God in prayer is effective; the inner debate now ceases and a time of warm and energizing spiritual consolation follows. What transforms this woman's prayer is not making changes suggested in growing restlessness of heart and inner debate but rather a fruitful exercise of discernment of spirits: awareness, understanding, action.[5]

"Never": A Categorical Norm

"In time of desolation *never* make a change." The adverb is categorical, and the norm admits of no exceptions: in time of spiritual desolation no change should ever be made to spiritual proposals decided before the desolation began. At times, dedicated persons may wonder whether they should or should not make certain changes in their previous decisions regarding prayer, the service of God, apostolic initiatives, and other aspects of their spiritual life. If they recognize that they are now in a time of spiritual desolation, then they need consider no further; in such a time they should *never* change these earlier proposals. It is enough for them to know that they are in spiritual desolation and all doubts regarding making such spiritual changes are resolved. Such changes should not be made.

David is the pastor of a dynamic parish. A number of the leaders in the parish ask him to guide them in a weekend retreat. David considers and prays about this request for several weeks, recognizes the great good it could accomplish for those requesting it, and decides to direct the retreat. The decision awakens pastoral energy in David; he senses with quiet joy that his ability to serve his people is growing. He finds the preparations spiritually enriching, both his own personal preparation in prayer and his sharing in the planning with the parish leaders. With them he looks forward to the approaching time of retreat together.

Three days before the retreat weekend David is obliged to handle a difficult matter in the parish. Several of those involved are unhappy with his response to the situation and tell him so openly. David feels discouraged and finds himself doubting his ability as pastor to deal with such issues in ministry.

That evening, with this burden in his heart, David begins his customary time of personal prayer. He is disheartened, distracted, and unable to feel the presence of God with him in prayer. A troubling question enters his heart concerning how capable he really is of exercising strong parish leadership. The approaching retreat comes to mind, and David now wonders whether he did well to accept the commitment. He is unsure that it was wise to undertake a similar role of spiritual leadership for the leaders of the parish when he finds himself so deficient in handling the ordinary ministerial matters of parish life. He begins to fear that the retreat will be a failure and that his parish leaders will be disappointed both in the retreat and in him. Perhaps, he thinks, it would be better not to risk weakening the existing situation of strong lay leadership in the parish through a disappointing retreat experience. As David continues to reflect, it becomes increasingly clear to him that the most prudent course is to find an appropriate way to postpone the retreat for some weeks at least. Certainly in his present state he could not lead it well, and there seems little point in holding the retreat now when it is unlikely to bear much fruit.

What can be said about David's conclusion? Should David hold the retreat as planned? Would he, in fact, be wiser to postpone the retreat as now seems wiser to him? What would we advise David to do?

Rule 5 provides us with a roadmap through such uncertainties. Two questions must be asked. First, as David prays this evening, is he in a time of spiritual desolation? The answer is evidently yes. While at prayer he experiences heavy affectivity; he is disheartened and feels far from God, "as if separated from his Creator and Lord." He is moved to "lack of confidence" regarding his ability to live his God-given calling as pastor.

Second, is David, in time of spiritual desolation, considering a change in a spiritual proposal made before the desolation began? Again the answer is clearly yes. The decision to lead the retreat has matured over several months, was born of peaceful prayer, and has been a consistent source of energy and spiritual consolation throughout the time of preparation.

"In time of desolation *never* make a change." Rule 5 gives an unequivocal answer in precisely such situations; David should completely disregard the thought of postponing the retreat and should go forward with the retreat as scheduled. Regardless of how compelling the thought of change appears in time of spiritual desolation, the categorical "never" provides all the clarity that David needs. Spiritual desolation, as we have said, is the time of the lie, and its "wisdom" is never to be followed. On the contrary, David should remain "firm and constant" in the proposal taken before the time of desolation began.

Frequently enough committed people find themselves considering changes concerning their life of faith and pursuit of God's will. If they look "within" and perceive themselves to be in spiritual desolation, they then know that they should not make the change in question but should remain firm and constant in their former decisions as long as the spiritual desolation endures. Such decisions range from small matters, like the woman deciding on whether to change the place and method of her prayer already begun, to the largest, as, for example, decisions concerning vocational changes in life. Any such changes made in time of spiritual desolation will be harmful. As Ignatius will indicate in the following rule, in time of spiritual desolation we should never change our former spiritual decisions but should work instead to change the *spiritual desolation itself*. When peace and spiritual consolation have returned, then questions of change may be profitably addressed. We will return to this point later in this chapter and in the next.

Ignatius in Desolation

In his *Spiritual Diary* Ignatius recounts an experience in which, in time of spiritual desolation, he is moved to change a decision already taken. Examination of what he writes will further solidify our understanding of rule 5; it will also permit a glimpse into the heart of Ignatius himself as he shares in our same spiritual struggles. He is our brother on the journey and writes of what he, like us, has experienced.

In the early months of 1544 Ignatius was concerned with determining the manner of gospel poverty his Society of Jesus would embrace. He set aside forty consecutive days to seek clarity from God regarding one specific issue of poverty—whether, as was the current practice, the Society should accept fixed revenues for the churches it administered or whether this practice constituted a departure from the full evangelical poverty that God willed of the Society.[6] He decided to celebrate Mass on each of these forty days, seeking light from the Lord.

In fact, over the course of the forty days Ignatius clearly understood that the Lord did not want this exception to the Society's general practice of full gospel poverty. He received the answer he sought. Now he has reached March 12, the last of these forty days and is about to celebrate the final Mass. He is hoping to receive a spiritual consolation that will confirm the decision he has reached. He writes:

In the customary prayer I *felt great devotion* and from midway on there was much of it, *clear, lucid* and as it were *warm*. Once in the chapel, as I saw some going down the stairway in a hurry and at a great pace, I did not feel ready to celebrate the mass and I returned to my room to prepare myself. Composing myself *with tears*, I returned to the chapel.[7]

Ignatius prepares for his Mass with personal prayer, filled with a warm sense of devotion. Apparently, however, the stairway in the house runs close by the chapel and the bustle of those going down it distracts Ignatius enough so that he returns to his room to prepare more fully for the Mass. This time of prayer too is graced with warmth and tears. Ignatius now feels ready to celebrate the Mass and returns to the chapel. He continues:

> During a part of the mass I *felt great devotion*, sometimes with *movements to tears*. During the other part I *struggled* many times with what I would do to finish, because I was not finding what I was seeking. . . .

The situation begins to change during the Mass. In part, the same warm prayer, moving him to tears, continues. Nonetheless Ignatius does not experience the confirming spiritual consolation he had sought in this final Mass and a struggle begins. Lacking the consolation for which he had hoped, Ignatius becomes unsure of how to finish his forty-day search for God's will regarding poverty. He writes further:

> When the mass was finished, and afterward in my room, I found myself *totally alone* and *without help* of any kind, *without power to relish* any of my mediators[8] or any of the Divine Persons, but so *remote* and so *separated* from them, as if I had never felt anything of them, or never would feel anything again.

Unmistakable signs of spiritual desolation abound here. Alone in his room, Ignatius experiences a great sense of distance from God; he feels isolated and without spiritual help of any kind. The warmly devout prayer and the tears he earlier experienced have disappeared completely. Two additional qualities of spiritual desolation now appear and merit our close attention: the manner in which *present* spiritual desolation attempts to define the *spiritual past and future* as well, and the *universal negatives* directed toward self found in spiritual desolation.

Remarkably, Ignatius's present spiritual desolation casts its shadow over both the past and the future: "as if I *had never felt* anything of them, or *never would feel* anything *again*." In the present heaviness of spiritual desolation, Ignatius, who has experienced so deeply and so often the great love of the Lord, now reads his past in a different—and falsified—way. It now appears to him that he *has never* felt anything of God in the past and that he *will never* feel God's loving presence again in the future. Spiritual desolation claims power over the past and the future; it shows us a past without God and a future remorselessly bound in lasting desolation. A further characteristic of the deception of spiritual desolation is starkly evident here.

The universal negatives of spiritual desolation are also worthy of note:

"I had *never* felt *anything* . . . I *never* would feel *anything* again." The negatives are universal both with respect to time—at no point in the past or in the future—and with respect to spiritual experience—Ignatius feels that he never has and never will feel *even the slightest* sense of God's closeness. In his letter to Teresa Rejadell, Ignatius explains this quality of the enemy's action in time of spiritual desolation:

> If he sees that we are weak and much humbled by these harmful thoughts, he goes on to suggest that we are *entirely forgotten* by God our Lord, and leads us to think that we are *quite separated* from him and that *all* that we have done and *all* that we desire to do is *entirely* worthless.[9]

Once again the assumption of power over past and future, here with regard to our efforts to love and serve God: "that *all* that we have *done* and *all* that we desire to *do* is *entirely worthless*." And the universal negatives: the *universal* "all" and "entirely," linked with the *negative* "worthless." An alert eye for spiritual desolation's false assumption of power over the spiritual past and future as well as for any form of self-directed universal negative will assist us greatly in recognizing and overcoming the distortions such desolation suggests.

Ignatius, then, is alone in his room and undergoing a time of intense spiritual desolation. From the desolation a series of diverse thoughts now arises, as his account relates:

> Rather, *thoughts* came to me sometimes *against Jesus*, sometimes *against another Person*, being so *confused* with different *thoughts*, such as to leave the house and rent a room so as to avoid the noise, or to attempt a fast, or to begin the masses over again, or to put the altar on a higher floor. *In nothing could I find peace* since I desired to finish at a time when my soul was in consolation and completely at rest.

Some of these thoughts are directed against the persons of the Trinity, the persons whom Ignatius most loves, and we can readily imagine the distress that such thoughts must cause him. Others of these thoughts suggest various changes as solutions to the heaviness of the moment. We enter here into the spiritual territory specifically contemplated by the fifth rule.

One thought invites Ignatius "to leave the house and rent a room so as to avoid the noise." This "thought" would have the leader of the community abandon the house of the community in order to overcome his inner trouble. A second thought prompts Ignatius "to attempt a fast," another "change" of a spiritual nature.[10] It is striking that yet another thought proposes that he "begin the masses over again." On this fortieth day Ignatius has completed the sequence of Masses seeking God's will and has received his answer clearly. Now, as Ignatius is on the verge of concluding this process as planned and in a time of spiritual desolation, a thought arises suggesting that the entire process has been a failure and should be completely redone. The final thought is a milder version of the first: to move the chapel to a place of greater quiet within the house. As these different thoughts pass through his mind, Ignatius summarizes the state of his heart: "In nothing could I find peace."

In light of rule 5, how should Ignatius act with respect to the changes suggested by these thoughts? Above all, should he accept the prompting to set aside his preceding clarity regarding God's will and begin the series of forty Masses once more? The answer in rule 5 is unmistakable: "in time of desolation *never* make a change" but rather remain "firm and constant" in the determination chosen before the desolation began.

In point of fact, Ignatius quickly realizes that the root of his desolation is his great desire for a confirming experience of spiritual consolation during the final Mass. Having renounced any "control" of God's work in his heart, he finds that the darkness gradually recedes and consolation again fills his heart. He concludes the forty-day process in peace, remaining firm in the decision reached earlier.[11]

The Reason for the Norm

In the concluding sentence of rule 5 Ignatius explains the reason for the categorical "never" regarding changes in time of spiritual desolation:

Because, as in *consolation* the *good spirit* guides and *counsels* us more, so in *desolation* the *bad spirit*, with whose *counsels* we cannot find the way to a right decision.

In rule 4 Ignatius underlined the conceptual element that accompanies the affective experience of spiritual consolation and desolation: "For just as consolation is contrary to desolation, in the same way the *thoughts* that *come from* consolation are contrary to the *thoughts* that *come from* desolation." Thoughts arise from each of these two spiritual movements and, like the movements themselves, are directly contrary to each other. Here in rule 5 Ignatius further explains that "in *consolation* the *good spirit guides and counsels* us more," whereas "in *desolation* the *bad spirit*" guides and *counsels* us more.[12]

During spiritual consolation the good spirit is guiding and counseling us. The time of spiritual consolation is thus the time to "accept" the work of God, to be open, to listen, to receive the thoughts and inspirations arising from the consolation itself.[13] When new spiritual steps are necessary, *this* is the time to review our earlier proposals and make the appropriate changes.

In time of spiritual desolation, however, the bad spirit is at work, "with whose *counsels* we cannot find the way to a right decision." There are counsels, too, in time of spiritual desolation: Jane begins to think that she is not meant for a deep prayer life; David decides it is better to postpone the parish retreat; Ignatius considers reopening a search for God's will already complete, and similar harmful suggestions. The thoughts that arise out of spiritual desolation, the "guidance" and "counsel" of the bad spirit we then receive, if followed, will always lead to spiritual diminishment. With the enemy's counsels "we *cannot* find the way to a right decision." In such desolation, like David and the others, we see as if through a warped mirror; the mirror reflects all the elements of the scene before it, but reflects them all in a distorted way.

At times, within the experience of spiritual desolation, these counsels will seem overwhelmingly evident; in desolation David, for example, recognizes with great "clarity" that the retreat must be postponed. We will "understand" that we would be foolish to continue with the prayer we had planned, that various spiritual initiatives already decided upon would be better omitted or altered. If such counsels arise in time of spiritual desolation we know them to be the lie of the enemy and know they are simply to be rejected. Our spiritual call is rather to remain 'firm and constant" in what we had proposed before the desolation began.

It is difficult to exaggerate the good this single rule has worked in the lives of countless dedicated persons over the centuries since Ignatius formulated it. At times it will be the one light that shines in the confusing darkness, revealing clearly the call of the Lord to unchanging fidelity in time of spiritual desolation. Knowledge and practical application of this guideline will bless us repeatedly on the spiritual journey.

6

⤿

Spiritual Desolation: A Time for Initiative (Rule 6)

⤿

> *To fight aloud is very brave,*
> *But gallanter, I know,*
> *Who charge within the bosom,*
> *The cavalry of woe.*
> —Emily Dickinson

The Changes That We Should Make

The sixth rule, after briefly repeating the teaching of the fifth, adds a new guideline as a counterpart to it:

Sixth Rule. The sixth: although in desolation we should not change our first proposals, it is very advantageous to change ourselves intensely against the desolation itself, as by insisting more upon prayer, meditation, upon much examination, and upon extending ourselves in some suitable way of doing penance.

If the former rule told us what we *should not* change in spiritual desolation, the present rule now indicates the changes that we *should* make in time of spiritual desolation. This rule reiterates the norm that in spiritual desolation "we should not change our first proposals," that is, the spiritual choices decided before the desolation began. But here Ignatius teaches further that spiritual desolation is not only a time for fidelity to the spiritual past; it is also—and energetically so—a time for spiritual initiative in the present. Spiritual desolation is, indeed, a time to "charge within the bosom, the cavalry of woe."

The instruction of the preceding rule that we should make no changes to our spiritual proposals in time of spiritual desolation does not mean that we must otherwise passively await the cessation of the desolation: that the best we can hope for is to resist harmful change while enduring, resignedly, the desolation itself. In spiritual desolation there *is* a change to be made, a change that will prove to be "very advantageous" spiritually. We are not to change our proposals but rather to change *ourselves*, to change ourselves *intensely*, and to change ourselves precisely *against the desolation itself*: "although in desolation we should not change our first proposals, it is very advantageous to *change ourselves intensely against the desolation itself.*" We may hope to accomplish more than solely avoiding collaboration with the enemy's urging to change existing spiritual plans; Ignatius invites us to *act* intensely against the very desolation itself.

We must not pass by this point too quickly. At times dedicated people who undergo spiritual desolation, when God seems far away and their hearts are heavy as they serve the Lord, sincerely believe that God has chosen them to bear this unhappy lot and wills that they simply accept this burden. However consciously, their understanding is essentially the following: "I wish to dedicate my life to the Lord and am trying to live this commitment faithfully. For days (weeks, months, years . . .) I have felt burdened and sad spiritually. God seems far away and I do not experience the warmth of grace in my heart. God permits this, and so, apparently, is calling me to carry this heaviness day after day in my life. My task is just to bear it as best I can." When endured in this good-willed but resigned manner, the spiritual desolation is likely to persist and, often enough, to deepen. The captives have not been set free. . . .

There *are* situations of suffering that God does call us to bear, even at length. In spite of our best efforts, we may face difficult conditions of health, burdensome responsibilities, relational trials, and similar struggles that cannot be substantially altered and must simply be born with God's help. This is the *cross* that, Jesus tells us, will always be part of discipleship (Luke 9:23) and that leads us, as it led Jesus, to resurrection and newness of spiritual life. Ignatius, however, is not addressing such situations here. In rule 6 he is referring specifically to *spiritual desolation,* and his teaching is clear: we are *never* called merely to endure such desolation passively until it somehow fades.[1] God's call in time of spiritual desolation is *always* to take active steps to resist and reject the desolation itself. This is what Ignatius intends in presenting the call to "change ourselves intensely against the desolation itself."

Thus, returning to cases already mentioned, Alice must not simply carry the weight of spiritual desolation helplessly as the weeks pass, hoping that somehow it will lighten; nor must Jane simply bear with resignation the spiritual desolation that darkens her retreat. Both, as the sixth rule explains, must *change themselves intensely against the desolation* that burdens them. To do so, says Ignatius, will serve to their great spiritual advantage. Again, the same buoyant note of hope, characteristic of the whole

Ignatian teaching on discernment, is sounded. *This* is the approach that sets the captives free.

Spiritual Means for a Spiritual Struggle

Ignatius now outlines the various *spiritual means* that serve to change ourselves against spiritual desolation when we experience it: "as by insisting more upon *prayer, meditation*, upon *much examination*, and upon extending ourselves in some *suitable way of doing penance*." He names four such means and urges us to resist spiritual desolation "by insisting more" on these during the time of such desolation.[2] Spiritual desolation is thus, in Ignatius's understanding, the time for *intensifying* certain of our spiritual practices that may assist us in our confrontation with desolation.

Each of these practices is valuable at any time in the spiritual life; in this rule, however, Ignatius has one specific context in mind—persons in time of spiritual desolation—and how these means may be advantageously employed to sustain us in that precise setting. The principle of contrariety applies once more; each of these means will hearten us to move directly contrary to the harmful suggestions of spiritual desolation.

Prayer

The first of these spiritual means, Ignatius writes, is *prayer*. This may be understood as prayer of *petition*.[3] Alice and Jane, in the cases mentioned above, are experiencing spiritual desolation. Another woman feels far from God one afternoon, and her heart is oppressed. A pastor finds himself "totally slothful, tepid, and sad" as he begins his parish duties on a certain day and senses how easily he could omit part of his service toward his people. In each case Ignatius's first counsel is simply *to pray*: to turn to the God who says, "Ask and it will be given to you" (Matt 7:7), and beg his help in resisting and overcoming the desolation.

Often, in spiritual desolation, and more so when it is intense, we experience a sense of helplessness. The enemy insinuates the inevitability of defeat: Alice feels trapped in hopelessness; Jane is caught in darkness and confusion; the woman fears that she has lost God; the pastor is reminded of past failures in similar circumstances and "knows" that he will be vanquished again today. At such times the first spiritual means is to pray: to petition our God and those who intercede for us with God in the communion of saints (*SpirEx*, 232) for the assistance we need in our time of trial.

As simple as this may appear when expounded on the written page, the concrete reality in time of spiritual desolation may be very different. In the pain and distress of desolation, and when spiritual things have lost their sense of attraction, prayer may be far from our minds; and because we feel ourselves "as if separated from our Creator and Lord," the actual turning to God in prayer may require conscious effort. Such *turning toward God* in prayer directly counters the sense of *separation from God* induced by spiritual desolation.

Experience reveals the profound efficacy of such prayer of petition in time of spiritual desolation. Through this prayer God already seems less remote and we feel less alone. Through it, the sense of growing distance from God begins to reverse, and expectancy of spiritual defeat gives way to new stirrings of trust that, in God, we will be victorious. God, who hears the cry of the poor (Ps 34:6), does not leave us without his strengthening grace when we call upon him.

Meditation

This counsel, too, is more than a recommendation of meditation as a generally helpful spiritual practice. Ignatius continues to address persons afflicted by spiritual desolation; to them he proposes a particular kind of meditation directed toward replenishing their spiritual energy in a situation of special vulnerability—the time of spiritual desolation.

Such meditation focuses on the sustaining truth of God's faithful love as a source of hope in time of distress. Spiritual desolation is a time of confusion and darkness; this meditation enkindles a light of faith to illuminate the darkness. Spiritual desolation disquiets the person; this meditation opens the heart to the Lord's gift of peace (John 14:27). Spiritual desolation diminishes faith, hope, and love; this meditation nourishes our trust, invigorates our hope, and confirms us in God's love.

Alice, after her frustrating year in her new parish, is immersed in a desolate sense of hopelessness and separation from God. One afternoon she is alone for a half hour in her home. She sits by the window, takes her Bible in hand, opens to Psalm 23, and reads slowly: "The Lord is my shepherd; there is nothing I shall want. . . . He guides me along the right path; he is true to his name." She closes the Bible, looks out at the landscape before her and repeats these words over and over. As she does so, she finds that her heart begins to lift a little, and tears come to her eyes. Quietly, she knows that God has not forgotten her, that she will want for nothing, that even now the divine Shepherd is guiding her "along the right path." She trusts that, in a way not yet evident to her but very real, God's love is at work in her present struggles. She rises and resumes the activity of the day with new hope. This is the *meditation* in time of spiritual desolation to which Ignatius refers in this rule.

Jane has reached the sixth day of her retreat and is deeply oppressed by spiritual desolation. She feels that her desire for God is an illusion and that she is not meant for a deep life of prayer. Her heart is filled with confusion and discouragement. Jane goes out walking in the evening and, as she walks, consciously recalls past times of similar discouragement in her life. She considers these times, one after another, and reflects on how God not only protected her during them but, in each case, transformed these difficult experiences into times of fresh spiritual beginnings. Though she continues to feel the heaviness of desolation, a movement of trust gently stirs in her heart that God, through the present darkness, is working new life in her once more. Jane returns to the house less burdened and more ready to continue her retreat. This, again, is the *meditation* in time of spiritual desolation that Ignatius has in view.

Such meditation centers on those truths of faith, those words of Scripture, those memories of our own life history, and similar considerations that reveal God's loving fidelity to us and so instill new spiritual vitality when our hearts are heavy. The transforming power of such meditation, practiced *in the time of spiritual desolation itself*, is evident. Such meditation in time of spiritual desolation, like prayer of petition in the same circumstances, may require a certain effort. When we experience spiritual consolation or, more generally, a tranquil heart, the attraction to meditation may be spontaneously felt; such will not be true in spiritual desolation. Here a decision to use this means—to meditate, in the time of darkness, on the strengthening truths of faith—is necessary. This is a decision and a courageous act that bear rich fruit in prevailing over spiritual desolation.

Much Examination

Ray has long placed faith at the center of his life and in recent years, especially, has grown closer to the Lord. He rejoices in seeing that, as a result of this spiritual growth, his love for his wife and children has deepened and their family bond is now stronger. Each day as he rides the commuter train to work he dedicates a few minutes to reading from Scripture. Today on his way to work he finds himself distracted and unable to read with attention or to reflect fruitfully. He arrives at work and the busyness of the morning envelopes him, but he is also vaguely conscious of a certain interior malaise. While his fellow workers have no direct awareness of his deepening faith in the Lord, they have noticed a change in Ray recently and appreciate his ready smile and willingness to help; today, however, he struggles even to be patient with them and only wishes the working hours to end.

The lunch hour arrives. As the hour begins, Ray normally takes a few minutes, alone in his office, to lift his heart to God in prayer. Today he feels no desire to pray and does not; instead he finds himself considering taking his meal in a place nearby where he knows the surroundings and the conversation is not conducive to his life of faith. Ray is on the point of leaving the office with this intention when suddenly he stops. He is aware that his heart is troubled; his distracted prayer on the train, his lack of willingness to assist his companions in the office, his omission of habitual prayer as his lunch hour began, and now his readiness to follow what he knows is a temptation with potentially harmful consequences—all of these signal that something is spiritually amiss. Ray senses that he must address this.

He sits down at his desk in the silence of his office and asks the Lord's help to understand what is occurring within him. He remembers how only the day before he was happy and energetic in his service of the Lord, of the others at work, and of his family. As he reflects, he is able to pinpoint the moment the change took place. Before leaving home this morning, preoccupied with his preparations for work, he unthinkingly brushed aside a request for attention from his little son. His wife was present, and Ray saw the hurt in her eyes, mirroring the hurt in those of his son. Rushed and impatient, he responded to neither and left for work. Ray perceives that this was the moment when he lost his peace; this was the origin of the malaise he has felt since and which has burdened everything thus far in the day: prayer, relationships at work, even his present decision regarding where he will take lunch.

This new sense of clarity lightens his heart, and he grasps clearly what he must do. He calls his wife and expresses his sorrow for his impatience that morning and for the hurt he caused her and his son. Her joy in their conversation lifts his heart further. He prays as usual in his office. He rejects the thought of taking lunch in the inappropriate place and eats with his office companions as usual. Now he finds that his smile again comes easily and that his habitual willingness to assist the others has returned.

Clearly Ray has experienced a time of spiritual desolation; he gives up his prayer, feels no energy for serving the Lord, and is prey to temptation. The key to overcoming his desolation was precisely what Ignatius recommends in his rule at this point: *much examination* in time of spiritual desolation, until we understand what is at work in the desolation and so can adopt the appropriate measures to reject it.

In the case just described, the enemy utilizes the emotional unhappiness remaining in Ray after a brief but relationally important experience earlier in the day; this emotional unhappiness serves as a springboard for spiritual desolation. If Ray or anyone in similar circumstances simply allows the spiritual desolation to persist without stopping to examine it, it is likely to increase and may lead to great spiritual harm. The spiritual desolation continues to deepen until the moment when Ray *does* examine it and becomes aware of its cause. At that moment it is stripped of much of its power, and Ray understands exactly how to reject it.

Like prayer and meditation, this examination *in time of spiritual desolation*—precisely when we are immersed in the painful ordeal itself and are least inclined to be "within"—will not happen spontaneously. We must decide to face and examine the spiritual desolation. In a very real sense, it will appear easier and seem more welcome to find escape in diversion. At such times we may immerse ourselves in busyness, the media, or various gratifications of a more or less healthy nature; all of them, in this case, serve as a way to be "without" when being "within" seems too uncomfortable. Unhappily, we generally discover that on the other side of the diversion, when the busyness and the gratifications have terminated, the spiritual desolation remains. The "aspirin" has worn off without truly healing the pain in its source. In fact, the longer we delay confronting it, the more this pain tends to increase.[4]

The "much examination" that Ignatius counsels here directly counters such flight into diversion. In the time of the spiritual desolation itself we interiorly stop and ask: What is happening in my heart? Am I in spiritual desolation? How did this begin? What was its cause? How has it developed? What action will help me to reject it? Though this may be initially difficult, the rewards are quickly immense. As we begin to find answers to our questions, what may have seemed an all-encompassing and unbearable heaviness is reduced to a manageable concern, an experience of spiritual desolation; and, with lightened hearts, we can begin to adopt effective spiritual measures to overcome the darkness.

Toner writes:

> By reflection on my state of desolation, I set *myself-in-desolation* apart from *myself-reflecting-on-myself-in-desolation*. . . . By doing this, I have made space in my consciousness for something besides desolation with its causes and consequences. In that space I can now reconnoiter, maneuver my attention and reason and will, and thus attack and weaken or even destroy the sources of desolation.[5]

The passage from "myself-in-desolation" to "myself-reflecting-on-myself-in-desolation" is the transition Ray makes during his lunch hour as he moves from simple and unhappy immersion in spiritual desolation (*myself-in-desolation*) to a conscious examination of the desolation (*myself-reflecting-on-myself-in-desolation*). With this passage, as Toner notes, the sense of driven helplessness vanishes. Whenever we find ourselves immersed in spiritual darkness and disquiet, this is the time when *much examination*, when the change from "myself-in-desolation" to "myself-reflecting-on-myself-in-desolation" will begin to set us free from bondage, and free to follow the Lord.[6]

"Extending Ourselves in Some Suitable Way of Doing Penance"

As with the preceding three spiritual means, so this fourth, which consists in "some suitable way of doing penance," applies specifically to the time of spiritual desolation and is undertaken as a means to reject it. As we have said, the interior discomfort of spiritual desolation invites an escape into external diversion and gratifications of various kinds, an escape that protracts and may even deepen the desolation. The call to *extend ourselves* in some *suitable* way of doing *penance*" encourages us yet again to oppose directly a tendency of spiritual desolation; in place of an "unsuitable" indulgence that prolongs our unhappiness, Ignatius proposes a "suitable" penance that energizes in a spiritually healthy way and aids in overcoming the desolation itself.[7]

The penance is suitable when it counters the precise tendency to flight we feel in the spiritual desolation and permits us to act against the specific form of desolation we are undergoing. When, for example, Ignatius considers the inclination a retreatant may experience in time of spiritual desolation to shorten the time of prayer as planned, that is, to change a spiritual proposal in time of desolation, he writes:

> It is to be noted that, as in time of consolation it is easy and requires only a slight effort to remain in the contemplation the full hour, so in time of desolation it is very difficult to complete the hour. For this reason the retreatant, in order to act against the desolation and conquer the temptations, should always stay somewhat more than the full hour, so as to accustom himself not only to resist the adversary but even to overthrow him. (*SpirEx*, 13)

If, in desolate prayer, when God seems far away and our efforts useless, there is a tendency to resolve the heaviness by ending the prayer sooner than planned, then, says Ignatius, the "suitable" remedy is to do exactly the opposite. In the first place, we should reject the tendency to shorten the prayer and should continue for the full time as planned before the spiritual desolation began. In fact, says Ignatius, rather than shorten the prayer we may even *lengthen* it, perhaps just a minute or two, beyond the time originally planned. In this way we habituate ourselves "not only to resist the adversary but even to overthrow him." Ignatius offers in this paragraph one illustration of the small but well-directed acts of courage that "act against the desolation" and fortify in us the ability to resist and overcome the enemy.

What form might such suitable ways of doing penance take in our various experiences of spiritual desolation? As so often in the spiritual journey, once again the importance of the injunction to "know thyself" is evident. The greater our awareness of our particular vulnerabilities in time of spiritual desolation, the more accurately we will choose the suitable gestures to counter efficaciously its urgings to surrender. For one person it may simply be the delaying of an impulse toward self-indulgence; as hope grows through one small victory, the next is already prepared.[8] For another it may be a smile when one feels little inclined to smile or to smile at this particular individual; it might be the choice to serve a person in need when this calls for patience, or the restraining of impatient words, or other steps of this nature. Each small act of resistance engenders further courage . . . and thus, step by step, the desolation is vanquished.

The Fruit of Spiritual Initiative

Ignatius repeatedly utilizes the language of courageous initiative in the short text of the rule we are examining. We are to change ourselves *intensely*[9] against the desolation; we are to *insist*, and to insist *more* upon each of the four means outlined; we are to *extend* ourselves in some suitable way of doing penance. Against the lie which insists that we are too weak to overcome spiritual desolation, Ignatius reveals here his great confidence in our capacity, sustained by God's loving assistance and through use of the means described, to stand firm in the hour of the test. When in time of spiritual desolation we resist actively—we humbly turn to God and beg for help; we meditate on God's faithful love; we examine the desolation and gain deeper understanding regarding its causes and remedies; when we make small, "suitable" gestures of courage that counter its destructive tendencies—then, Ignatius affirms, we have found the road that leads surely through the darkness of desolation into the light of God's love.

A doubt may arise even as we read: can we really live with such courage when burdened and confused by spiritual desolation? Is such spiritual initiative truly possible? Ignatius believes that it is. This courage is born at the point where God's grace and human effort intersect. Certainly, the practice of each of these spiritual means requires courage, but this courage is itself more than the fruit of human effort alone. Perhaps it is not by chance that in portraying these four means Ignatius begins, first of all, with humble supplication in *prayer*. In contending with spiritual desolation we know that, as Jesus tells us, "Without me you can do nothing" (John 15:5); we know, too, that, with Paul, we may confidently say: "I can do all things in him who strengthens me" (Phil 4:13).

Experience teaches Ignatius that by humbly and sincerely striving to use the means he proposes in this rule, we will grow in the ability to use them and so become increasingly able to face spiritual desolation without fear. Although this list of means is not exhaustive and Ignatius will suggest a number of further means in the rules that follow, nonetheless, the sixth rule already begins to equip us solidly to resist spiritual desolation. Through its teaching, our feet are already set on the road to spiritual freedom.

7

⌐

Spiritual Desolation: A Time for Resistance (Rule 7)

⌐

JOAN. His friendship will not fail me, nor His counsel, nor His love. In His strength I will dare, and dare, and dare, until I die.
—George Bernard Shaw, *Saint Joan*

The Thinking That Strengthens Our Resolve

The seventh rule, like the fifth and sixth, focuses on persons in time of spiritual desolation and continues to provide guidelines on how to resist and overcome such desolation. The preceding two rules dealt with *changes*: unhealthy changes to be avoided (rule 5) and healthy changes to be practiced assiduously (rule 6). Ignatius now widens the field of such resistance and tells us that we can resist in time of spiritual desolation not only by what we choose to *do*—prayer, meditation, examination, and suitable penance—but also by how we choose to *think* in the time of the spiritual desolation. The decision to think about spiritual desolation during the time itself when we are in desolation *from the perspective of God* whose mysterious and loving providence allows us to undergo this struggle, can awaken a faith-based understanding capable of fortifying our determination to resist the desolation itself.

Ignatius's seventh rule reads in the following way:

Seventh Rule. The seventh: let one who is in desolation consider how the Lord has left him in trial in his natural powers, so that he may resist the various agitations and temptations of the enemy; since he can resist with the divine help, which always remains with him, though he does not clearly feel it; for the Lord has taken away from him his great fervor, abundant love, and intense grace, leaving him, however, sufficient grace for eternal salvation.

94

"Let one who is in desolation *consider*": the whole guideline revolves around a particular way of thinking about the experience of spiritual desolation precisely while we are immersed in its darkness. The *consideration* Ignatius recommends centers on *God* and on what God is working in us through permitting this time of spiritual desolation: "consider how the *Lord* has left him *in trial* in his *natural powers, so that he may resist. . . .*" This strengthening consideration includes, then, three related elements: persons in spiritual desolation should consider that such desolation is a *trial* permitted by the Lord; they should consider the *nature* of the trial; and, finally, they should consider the divine *purpose* in allowing this trial to occur. We will discuss each of these in order.

A Trial

"Let one who is in desolation consider how the Lord has left him *in trial.*" Spiritual desolation, seen from the standpoint of God, is a *trial.* Persons in spiritual desolation, who consider this truth *while* they are enduring the desolation, find themselves crossing a spiritual threshold. Prior to or without such consideration, they can only be guided by their spontaneous response to such desolation; the desolation appears to have no meaning or value and appears to be simply an unhappy burden that leaves them disheartened and confused. When their response to spiritual desolation is *un*considered, the desolation may easily cause some measure of bitterness or submerge them in sadness and hopelessness.

Spiritual desolation, when it appears as purely futile distress, is especially difficult to bear, and those who undergo it will all the more easily fall prey to its harmful promptings. Through the *consideration* Ignatius proposes, such persons cross the threshold *out* of this spontaneous sense of heavy meaninglessness and *into* awareness that there is, in fact, a God-intended meaning in their experience of desolation. Once their darkness has acquired meaning in God, these persons gain new energy to resist and reject the desolation itself.

Blessed Angela of Foligno recounts an experience of deep and prolonged spiritual desolation:

> During this period I was in a state of great stress, for it seemed to me that I felt nothing of God, and I also had the impression that I was abandoned by him; nor was I able to confess my sins. On the one hand, I thought that perhaps this had happened to me because of my pride, and on the other hand, I perceived so clearly the depths of my many sins that it did not seem to me that I could confess them with adequate contrition or even so much as say them. It seemed to me

that there was no way in which I could bring them out in the open. Nor could I even praise God or remain in prayer. It seemed to me that all that was left of God in me was the conviction that I had not suffered as many trials as I deserved and, similarly, that I did not want to fall away from his grace by sinning for all the good or evil or sufferings that the world has to offer, nor did I want to assent to any evil. I was in this intense and terrible state of torment for more than four weeks.[1]

This is the classical language of spiritual desolation: "I *felt nothing* of God," and "I also had the impression that *I was abandoned* by him." Angela, at this point in her life a woman deeply in love with God, painfully adds: "*Nor could I* even *praise God* or *remain in prayer*," and "It seemed to me that *all that was left of God in me* was the conviction that I had not suffered as many trials as I deserved." She finds herself in an "*intense* and *terrible* state of *torment*," which persists for four weeks.

Angela knows well that neither "for all the good or evil or sufferings the world has to offer" would she even consider any action that would diminish God's grace in her. Her heart is solidly set on God, and she is firmly aware of this even in the deep distress of her spiritual desolation; yet this conviction does not remove her inner trouble. While she is thus afflicted, Angela struggles to understand the reason for her desolation. Two possible reasons enter her reflections, both of them self-directed. She writes, "I thought that perhaps this had happened to me because of my *pride*." This thought implies that one specific fault—her pride—is the explanation of her present pain. The other is more broad; her acute consciousness of her *sins* in general awakens a sense of helplessness in her. Angela feels that she cannot "confess them with adequate contrition" nor "even so much as say them" and that "there was no way in which I could bring them out into the open." During these four weeks she feels trapped in the remorseless grip of spiritual desolation, deprived of any conscious sign of hope to lift her heart.[2]

"Let one who is in desolation consider how the Lord has left him in *trial*." If Angela, *while submerged* in her four weeks of interior pain, can move beyond her spontaneous reaction of fear and helplessness and *consider* that this is a *trial* that *God* permits in a loving providence guiding her life, then she will cross the threshold described above. The heaviness of the spiritual desolation may not lift immediately or totally, but she will be strengthened to endure what she now knows, in faith, to have meaning in the eyes of an infinitely wise and loving God.[3] She will perceive that her trial, like the trials of God's people throughout the history of salvation (Judith 8:25–27), has redemptive meaning and lies within a divine pedagogy of love.

We may say something similar in the cases of Alice and Jane. Alice, in spite of her best efforts to serve in her new parish, finds herself in spiritual desolation and "all seems hopeless and meaningless." If Alice consciously *considers* that the *Lord* is at work in her life even now, permitting the spiritual desolation as a trial, while the pain of desolation may not pass immediately, she will be heartened to bear it with greater hope. Though in the present moment she cannot clearly perceive *how* this is so, she will grow in trust that God's love is truly at work in her, permitting this distress in order to lead her to new life. That increased trust will be a light shining in the surrounding darkness. If Jane, on that deeply desolate sixth day of her retreat, can *consider* that this spiritual desolation is not simply meaningless affliction but is rather a *trial* that the *Lord* is permitting her to undergo, then she will grow in a similar strength to bear it without faltering.

Such consideration in time of spiritual desolation—that this is a trial situated within the loving providence of God—though clearly valuable, may not be easy when we are immersed in the sorrow of desolation and may require a conscious choice to reflect on the level of a faith that we cannot easily *feel* in the moment. Until repeated exercise of this rule causes such consideration to become more habitual, our first thoughts will tend to be more confused and focused on the pain itself. The constantly renewed choice to *consider* that presently experienced spiritual desolation is a trial permitted by God will lead to increasing spiritual stability in our times of darkness; in this way, as Ignatius tells Teresa Rejadell, spiritual desolation is transformed into a lesson for growth.

The Nature of the Trial

When Angela describes her experience of spiritual desolation, she speaks both of what she feels is *taken away* from her and of what *remains* in her. Any ability to sense God is stripped away: "I *felt nothing* of God." The same is true of any awareness of God's presence to her: "I also had *the impression* that *I was abandoned* by him." Angela feels utterly without power to overcome sin: "*nor was I able* to confess my sins . . . it did *not seem to me* that I could confess them with adequate contrition or even so much as say them. It *seemed* to me that there was *no way* in which I could bring them out in the open." All strength, even to praise God or simply to pray, has been taken from her: "Nor could I even *praise God* or *remain in prayer.*" Angela is penetratingly aware of all that has been *taken away* from her in her time of spiritual desolation. She is painfully conscious, too, of what *remains* in her during her time of sorrow:

> It seemed to me that *all that was left of God in me* was the *conviction* that I had not suffered as many trials as I deserved and, similarly, *that I did not want* to fall away from his grace by sinning for all the good or evil or sufferings that the world has to offer, *nor did I want* to assent to any evil.

All spiritual consolation, any warm consciousness of God and sense of spiritual energy has been stripped away. All that remains is her own conviction that she has not yet suffered as she deserves and her firm will never to separate herself from God's grace. We sense, as we read, that Angela feels utterly left to herself spiritually. She is aware that *her* conviction and *her* will are operative, but she feels no sense of *God working* in her. This, says Ignatius, is the nature of the trial: "the Lord has taken away" from the person the "great fervor, abundant love, and intense grace," that is, the spiritual consolation the person formerly enjoyed, and now the person is "left" by the Lord "in trial *in his natural powers*." Like Angela, persons in spiritual desolation *feel* no assistance or presence of the Lord with them; they *feel*, rather, that all that remains in them is the use of their "natural powers": their ability to think (mind), to choose (will), to call certain truths to mind (memory), to envisage spiritual realities (imagination), and all the human "powers" given to them by the Creator.

Thus, for example, when persons in spiritual desolation attempt to pray, there is no sense of any "great fervor, abundant love, and intense grace" in their hearts. Like Angela, they feel utterly dry and spiritually lifeless as they pray. They feel that all that remains to them is the use of their natural human powers; they can *choose* (natural power of will) not to shorten the prayer; they can *read* and *think* (natural power of intellect) about a text from Scripture; they can *picture* a Gospel scene (natural power of imagination), and carry out other such exercises of their "natural powers." They feel no warmth in doing this and are conscious of little fruit. The disquiet, the sadness and agitation, the various temptations typical of spiritual desolation invade them; and their hearts feel "as if separated from their Creator and Lord." This, says Ignatius, is *the nature of the trial*. The same trial could characterize times of community worship, of service to others, or of any daily efforts to love the Lord when we are in spiritual desolation. As Angela's narrative, and as spiritual experience in general suggests, this trial can be very difficult to bear.

The Purpose of the Trial

Let us imagine, now, that Angela, Alice, Jane, or any other dedicated person experiences this trial at different points in their spiritual lives. Each time this trial occurs it will be painful; the degree of pain will vary depending on the differing intensity and duration of the experiences of desolation, but these will always be spiritually distressing. Let us imagine further that each time they undergo this trial they humbly strive to resist and reject the spiritual desolation; they seek to remain faithful to their earlier proposals and employ the appropriate spiritual means to overcome the desolation. As they persevere in this struggle with all their victories and failures, gradually something wonderful takes place; they discover that the power of this trial to afflict them is diminishing, that their awareness, understanding, and action in rejecting the spiritual desolation now begins more quickly and achieves its effect more surely. By undergoing these trials with persevering fidelity, they become increasingly able to bear them without harm.

Alice, for example, perseveres in her time of spiritual desolation. She does not give up her prayer and desire to serve. She resists the desolation through petition, meditation, examination, and suitable gestures of penitential courage, together with all the other means that Ignatius suggests toward rejecting spiritual desolation. The desolation passes, and Alice discovers new opportunities for service that God now provides in the parish and beyond. Spiritual consolation returns, and her prayer is filled with God's presence once more.

When, as it eventually will, spiritual desolation returns, Alice will again feel its burden, but this time she will be less likely to believe that all is "hopeless and meaningless." She has been here before spiritually, and she knows, *through concrete personal experience*, that this darkness is not the end of hope and meaning in her spiritual life. Rather, it is a trial permitted by the Lord. She now knows by experience that, if she sincerely seeks to resist the spiritual desolation as best she can, God will see her through it, the trial will pass, spiritual consolation will return, and, through this trial, God will give her new growth in grace. *By resisting*, Alice is *learning to resist*. When Alice experiences this trial and resists not once or twice only but as often as the spiritual desolation arises, her learning is consolidated and her capacity to resist is all the more firmly established. An impediment that is for many the major impediment to spiritual growth, that is, the discouragement of spiritual desolation, is losing its capacity to hinder her progress toward God.

And this, says Ignatius, is *God's purpose* in allowing the trial itself:

Let one who is in desolation consider how the Lord has left him in trial in his natural powers, *so that he may resist* the various agitations and temptations of the enemy.

Ignatius tells us that the reason why God leaves us in this trial, feeling bereft of all divine help and with only our human powers to sustain us, is so that, in undergoing this trial, we may have *the opportunity* to resist "the various agitations and temptations of the enemy" that arise in its course. Rooted spiritual capabilities (virtues), as classical theology teaches, develop through repeated exercise of their acts. Repeated *experience* of and repeated *resistance* to the trial of spiritual desolation is the normal path, in God's design for the human person, toward freedom from subjugation to such desolation. When humbly and courageously resisted, spiritual desolation becomes, indeed, a crucial spiritual lesson, teaching hope and guiding the person toward spiritual maturity in ways that spiritual consolation alone could not accomplish.

A key reflection regarding the entire spiritual life emerges here. As dedicated people look back over their lives, over how they have lived their calling, over a period of service in their families, in ministry or at work, over a week of prayer or over this day's prayer, they may tend to judge that the times of peace and spiritual consolation were the fruitful times, and that the times of spiritual desolation were the emptier, less fruitful or even lost periods of time in terms of spiritual progress. They are grateful for the times of light and consolation and recognize God's love and action in them. The times of spiritual desolation, past or present, may, however, leave them uneasy or saddened; these appear as spaces "outside" the workings of God's grace, and some sense of regret is associated with them.

Much begins to change when such dedicated persons recognize what Ignatius affirms here: that God's loving providence does not include only "half" of our experience—spiritual consolation, yes, spiritual desolation, no—but rather is *always* active in our lives, both in giving us spiritual consolation and in permitting us to experience the trial of spiritual desolation. When spiritual consolation is embraced and spiritual desolation resisted, each movement permits its own kind of growth. *Both* are necessary, in the measure God's loving wisdom disposes, and both are, as Ignatius tells us, lessons. Through both, we come to "the full stature of Christ" (Eph 4:13).

When "You Can't" Becomes "I Can"

At this point in Ignatius's text we encounter one of the most hope-filled statements in the entire series of rules. God, he says, permits the trial of spiritual desolation so that a person may have the opportunity to resist:

Since he can resist with the divine help, which always remains with him, though he does not clearly feel it; for the Lord has taken away from him his great fervor, abundant love, and intense grace, leaving him, however, sufficient grace for eternal salvation.

Persons in spiritual desolation, like Angela of Foligno, feel deprived of the "great fervor, abundant love, and intense grace" they formerly rejoiced to experience. They *do not feel* God's grace at work in them; they *do feel*, on the contrary, "the various agitations and temptations of the enemy," burdening their hearts and enveloping them in darkness. They appear to themselves utterly left alone, with only their fragile "natural powers" to assist them in their hour of trial. Often, in time of spiritual desolation, such persons will feel that they *cannot* persevere, that they *cannot* escape the desolation spiritually unscathed.

The reality, Ignatius reminds us, is quite different. Though they do not "clearly feel it," since the Lord has taken away their "great fervor, abundant love, and intense grace," nonetheless the "divine help . . . always remains" with them, supplying "sufficient grace for eternal salvation."[4] Persons in spiritual desolation, then, must "consider" what they cannot "clearly feel" in the darkness of the desolation: that God *always* gives us *sufficient grace* not only to pass safely through the trial but also to grow spiritually toward our eternal salvation through resisting. If Angela and all who suffer spiritual desolation consider that the Lord says to them, as to Paul in his struggle, "My grace is *sufficient* for you" (2 Cor 12:9; *emphasis added*), they will be encouraged to resist the more firmly.

This consideration brings Ignatius to a categorical affirmation vibrant with hope; since God always provides sufficient grace to withstand the trial of spiritual desolation, persons immersed in such desolation and seeking to resist can know with certitude that they *can resist*. Angela, in her four weeks of trial, Alice, when "all seems hopeless and meaningless," and Jane, whose heart is filled with "disquietude, confusion, and a sense of discouragement" on her sixth day of retreat, and others in time of spiritual desolation may feel that the burden is too great to bear, that they *cannot resist* the desolation and that they must inevitably be overpowered by it. In their time of trial they are to consider with faith and know with full assurance what they cannot feel: that they *can resist* because of the divine help that always remains with them.

Certainly, there are situations of *nonspiritual* desolation that surpass our physical and emotional energies and that we cannot face and should not try to face by dogged resistance alone. If our physical or emotional resources are depleted and we are overly tired or experience depression, the primary need is for wise measures to replenish those resources. Having done so, we will the more effectively face the situation at hand.

Ignatius, however, is not speaking here of nonspiritual but specifically of *spiritual* desolation. He is presuming that our physical and emotional energies as, for example, appears to be true of Alice and Jane, are essentially healthy. In this case, the "I can't" arises not from a true lack of human resources but rather from the *spiritual discouragement* induced by the enemy in time of spiritual desolation. Ignatius's sixth rule, anchoring us solidly in faith, invites us to reject the enemy's whispered "You can't," and to assert with unwavering faith, "I can," because "I know that sufficient divine help is always with me."

Alice may feel that she *cannot* persevere any longer in her effort to serve the Lord. Jane may feel that her retreat has become unendurable, that she *cannot* persevere to the end and that she must leave the retreat house this day. A religious may feel that she *cannot* bear another day of life in common with the others or that she *cannot* continue in her work. A pastor in his parish may feel that he *cannot* continue any longer in his parochial ministry and must plan to resign. Dedicated persons at prayer may feel that the prayer period is endless this day, is intolerably demanding, that they *cannot* persevere, and that they must give up the effort now. In these and all such cases, presuming that the origin of this feeling has been accurately understood to be *spiritual* desolation, Ignatius confidently replies: "You can!" Though you do not feel God's loving presence now, you can, because God's grace is *always* sufficient in time of spiritual desolation. The transition from a faltering "I can't" to a courageous "I can," with God's sustaining help, creates the freedom for persevering resistance and breaks the power of spiritual desolation.[5]

"Remembering" and "Forgetting"

In all this there is a remembering/forgetting dynamic at work. In spiritual desolation the enemy leads us to *forget*; our task at such times is to *remember*. Ignatius advises Teresa Rejadell that the enemy "places obstacles and impediments in the way of those who love and begin to serve God our Lord," and

> *fails to remind us* of the great comfort and consolation which our Lord is wont to give to such souls, who, as new recruits in our Lord's service, surmount these obstacles and choose to suffer with their Creator and Lord.[6]

In time of spiritual desolation, the enemy veils, "fails to remind us," of the great comfort and consolation God gives to faithful and dedicated people. Ignatius explains to this woman that the enemy "goes on to suggest that we are *entirely forgotten* by God our Lord."[7]

Teresa of Avila, in describing certain of her "very bitter trials of soul," writes that during these experiences "all the favors the Lord had granted me *were forgotten*. There remained only a memory to cause pain; they were *like a dream*."[8] In her time of trial *all* of the earlier favors of the Lord— and these were extraordinarily abundant—were *forgotten*. No more than a "memory" of them remains, but a memory that casts them as unreal and dreamlike; this memory, in fact a denial of their truth, does not comfort but only causes pain. Fiorito comments: "We may note how Saint Teresa says that one of the tactics of the bad spirit, when he attacks us, is to cause us to forget. . . ." The enemy "knows that in remembering the graces received, we find strength against his present temptations; and, for this reason, he tries to lead us to forget."[9]

Persons in spiritual desolation will experience this inducement to "forget," characteristic of the enemy's action. At such times, when wrapped in the sad darkness of desolation, the enemy will "fail to remind" them of God's faithful love as they have already experienced it on their spiritual journey. Alice in her hopelessness and Jane in her discouragement may easily fail to recall God's unwavering fidelity throughout their lives. If they, and all who experience spiritual desolation, are not aware of this tactic, they may not see beyond the feelings of heaviness and spiritual isolation that burden their hearts; they will indeed *forget* the "steadfast love" of God (Ps 117:2), in which, like Paul, they can say: "I can do all things in him who strengthens me" (Phil 4:13).

In such times of spiritual desolation, then, our part is to *remember*, as Ignatius writes to Teresa Rejadell, "the great comfort and consolation which our Lord is wont to give to such souls" who seek to love and serve, to remember the truth that the enemy obscures: that we are not alone, and that *we can resist*, because divine help—sufficient grace—is always richly present to us. This "remembering" fortifies us, as it does the whole people of God (Deut 32:7; Ps 105:5; Ps 143:5), to progress with courage on our spiritual journey.

Through striving to resist in time of spiritual desolation we become increasingly able to resist. Simultaneously, our awareness also grows that God is *always* with us and that his providence is *always* at work in our lives: palpably in time of spiritual consolation and in an unfelt but very real and sustaining way in time of spiritual desolation. Ever more deeply we know that at every moment of our journey we may in truth say, like Jesus: "I am not alone" (John 16:32).

8

∽

Spiritual Desolation: A Time for Patience (Rule 8)

∽

> *On the bleakness of my lot*
> *Bloom I strove to raise.*
> *Late, my acre of a rock*
> *Yielded grape and maize.*
> —Emily Dickinson

> *Patience achieves everything.*
> —Teresa of Avila

Endurance in Time of Trial

Elisabeth Leseur, a married woman of deep faith and prayer, describes several weeks of great interior struggle in her spiritual diary for October 18, 1902. She writes:

Cowardice, weakness, awkwardness in my demeanor with others—things that can harm the ideas I cherish; acute physical suffering and deep moral suffering; in the midst of this a will unshakably turned to God, a plenitude of confidence in him and love for him; daily duties performed at whatever cost by great effort, without fervor, but still performed; then, little by little, calm returning to me, and divine strength penetrating me again; new and energetic resolutions, the hope that God will help me to do my duty, all my duty—that is the tale of these last weeks and of my soul during this time.[1]

There is clearly nonspiritual desolation here, physical and emotional suffering, and indications of spiritual desolation as well. Elizabeth experiences "deep moral suffering" and accomplishes her God-given tasks only with

104

"great effort." She is faithful in spite of the fact that she is "without fervor," the classic language of spiritual desolation.

She faces this difficult time with remarkable courage, without giving way to her affliction, and remaining firmly faithful to God and to her daily call: "in the midst of this *a will unshakably turned to God*," and "daily duties performed *at whatever cost* by *great effort*, without fervor, but still performed." And this enduring fidelity in trial bears fruit in a return of spiritual consolation: "then, little by little, calm returning to me, and divine strength penetrating me again." Energy and hope well up once more within her: "new and energetic resolutions, the hope that God will help me to do my duty, all my duty." Through patient and faithful perseverance in a time of struggle, Elizabeth remains completely unharmed by the darkness and experiences the gradual return of spiritual consolation.

A year later, on November 3, 1903, she undergoes a parallel experience:

> More than two months in the dejection of almost continual physical suffering, and with terrible anxiety on Juliette's account; the miserable belief that my illness will last as long as I do, always impeding my life. Complete resignation, but without joy or any inner consolation. The resolve to use my misfortunes for the good of souls. To fill my life with prayer, work and charity. To maintain serenity through everything. To love more than ever those who are the dear companions of my life.[2]

Nonspiritual desolation is again manifest, and elements of spiritual desolation also appear. Here, too, Elizabeth confronts her inner affliction with patient courage. Even though she is "without joy or any inner consolation," she accepts with "complete resignation" the trial God permits her to undergo; and this resignation is not merely passive but is linked to "the resolve to use my misfortunes for the good of souls." Elizabeth determines, during the ordeal, "to fill my life with prayer, work, and charity," and, as an interior attitude, "to maintain serenity through everything." Above all, her two months of darkness become a time in which she chooses "to love more than ever" those whom God has given her as companions.

In these two passages Elizabeth demonstrates in a sublime way the disposition most necessary if we would resist in time of desolation: a faithful patience that *will not surrender* in time of trial but which actively and courageously perseveres until the trial passes and peace of heart returns. This *patience* in time of spiritual desolation is the focus of Ignatius's eighth rule.

Ignatius's text reads:

> *Eighth Rule.* The eighth: let one who is in desolation work to be in patience, which is contrary to the vexations which come to him, and

let him think that he will soon be consoled, diligently using the means against such desolation, as is said in the sixth rule.

The rule describes a two-fold call to persons in time of spiritual desolation: a call to *work* toward something (maintaining an attitude of patience) and a call to *think* of something (that consolation will soon return). This thinking is, in its own turn, linked to action; it is to be accompanied by the diligent use of the means outlined in the sixth rule: prayer, meditation, examination, and suitable penance. The thinking and related action described in the second part of the rule assist in the "working to be in patience" proposed in the first part of the rule. We will now look more closely at the first and then at the second part of this rule.

Patience: The Key Virtue in Spiritual Desolation

A person who is undergoing spiritual desolation, says Ignatius, is to "*work* to be in *patience*."[3] The vocabulary itself is highly indicative of the effort involved in fulfilling this guideline. The *patience* of which Ignatius speaks, as its etymology denotes, is the virtue proper to persons undergoing a trial; they do not flee the trial but carry the burden faithfully, enduring the trial as long as it persists.[4] Elizabeth's courageous response to her interior sense of burden illustrates precisely the patience Ignatius intends; she does not give way in the affliction but chooses to stand firm in her love and service as long as the trial continues.

This *patience* signifies more than simply "going forward" when circumstances make it relatively easy to do so: for example, completing the full time of prayer when spiritually consoled or serving others when such service feels rewarding and spiritually energizing. Faithful prayer and loving service in time of spiritual consolation *are* fruitful ways to progress spiritually, but they are not the "patience" of which Ignatius speaks in the eighth rule.

Here, as for Alice, Jane, Angela, Elizabeth, and for all persons in spiritual desolation, when everything—interior darkness, sadness, a sense of hopelessness, lack of fervor, inability to sense God's love—urges us simply to relinquish our efforts to love and to serve, we do not yield; we go forward with *patience*, enduringly faithful to the task at hand. We finish the prayer or the retreat in spite of the dryness; we continue to serve even though God seems far away; we remain faithful to a commitment to love though we feel no fervor in doing so; we go forward in the effort to love in the family, within a parish group or in the workplace, in spite of the sadness we feel.

This understanding of persevering patience renders Ignatius's choice of a verb fully comprehensible; we are to *work* to persist in such patience when in spiritual desolation. Elizabeth exemplifies fully the "work" involved in maintaining this patience in time of desolation: "daily duties performed *at whatever cost* by *great effort*, without fervor, but still performed," and "The *resolve* to use my misfortunes for the good of souls. To fill my life with *prayer, work* and *charity*. To *maintain serenity* through everything. To *love* more than ever. . . ." Effort and resolve, service performed whatever the cost, prayer, work, charity, the endeavor to maintain serenity through it all, the attempt to live with greater love in time of darkness than in time of peace; this is the portrait of a person *working* to remain faithfully patient in a time of spiritual desolation.

Such work is the spiritual equivalent, for example, of the marathon runner who feels the fatigue of many miles already run but does not cease running till the race is fully completed; of the family member who cares for another family member through an extended illness, faithful to the task notwithstanding the effort required, until the illness is healed; of the student at the end of the semester, studying for one examination after another, who faithfully continues to study, at the price of prolonged effort, until the last examination is completed. When, in like manner, we remain faithful to prayer, to service, to our spiritual commitments, and to our calling in general in spite of the urgings of spiritual desolation to admit defeat, we are *working* to remain *patient*. Persons who respond to spiritual desolation in this way will not only not be harmed by it but will also grow greatly through this effort to stand firm while the desolation lasts.

The Thought That Builds Patience

In rule 7 Ignatius advised persons in spiritual desolation to *consider* that such desolation is a trial permitted by the Lord for their spiritual growth; by resisting they become increasingly able to resist. This consideration serves to hearten them and to fortify their strength in resisting spiritual desolation. Now, once more, Ignatius invites persons in spiritual desolation to adopt a certain type of *thinking* that will further assist in resisting the desolation: "and let him *think* that he will soon be consoled."

Earlier we mentioned how spiritual desolation claims power over both the spiritual past and future. Ignatius, as we have seen, in his time of spiritual desolation, feels "remote and separated" from the Divine Persons, "as if I had never felt anything of them or never would again." The enemy falsely claims such power and instills a conviction that the present affliction will remain unaltered into the future. In Dostoevsky's words, present desolation is often accompanied by a feeling of "something permanent, eternal, foretelling hopeless years of this cold and deathly misery."[5]

When Jane begins her sixth day of retreat in deep spiritual desolation, she feels, though she may not be reflectively aware of this, that the rest of the day and, indeed, the rest of the retreat will continue in just such desolation; this feeling greatly contributes to the almost unbearable quality of the desolation. In her spiritual desolation Alice's sense that her efforts not only are now but will also remain "hopeless and meaningless" adds notably to the pain she feels. This same presumption of power over the future characterizes spiritual desolation in general and is a major factor in the burden such desolation imposes on those who experience it.

When persons in spiritual desolation begin a time of prayer, they will frequently feel "convinced" that the entire period of prayer will be similarly desolate; this feeling forms a significant part of the urging simply to abandon the prayer itself. When dedicated persons experience spiritual desolation as they begin a day or an undertaking of service, they will likewise often feel convinced that the entire day or the entire undertaking will be filled with the same heavy emptiness. If they give credence to this assumption they are only a short step away from weakening their efforts or relinquishing their service entirely.

Thus the power of Ignatius's injunction that persons who are in spiritual desolation *think* that they "will *soon* be *consoled*" is clear. They are to think, to choose to reflect, that the enemy does not possess power over the future, that the future, as all things, is in the hands of a God whose plan of salvation directs everything in our lives (Rom 8:28). Ignatius's brief phrase is packed with vibrancy and hope; the false insinuation that the current desolation will inevitably characterize the future is met with the thought that *consolation will return*, that the desolation will be broken in the future, and that once more these persons will experience the warmth of God's love and closeness. And not only will it return; Ignatius, with a kind of spiritual boldness, invites persons in spiritual desolation to reflect that the spiritual consolation will return *soon*.

When Alice dejectedly feels that her spiritual desolation will endure for weeks and months, Ignatius invites her to think about the truth: that this "permanent, eternal . . . hopeless" perspective is utterly false and that spiritual consolation will return to her *sooner* than the desolation suggests, sooner than she has dared to hope. When Jane sadly feels that her spiritual desolation will color all the remaining days of her retreat, Ignatius urges her to think instead of the truth: that her present "disquietude, confusion, and . . . sense of discouragement" will be changed into spiritual consolation *sooner* than her present desolation implies, sooner than she, too, has dared to hope. Our earlier comments on such thinking in time of spiritual desolation apply once again here: this thinking will not occur spontaneously but will require conscious effort, an effort made easier precisely by our repeated choices to adopt such thinking.

Nonetheless, however heartening it may be, thinking alone is not sufficient of itself; it must be joined to action and, when it is so joined, achieves its full effect in breaking the grip of spiritual desolation. Ignatius writes: "let him think that he will soon be consoled, *diligently using the means* against such desolation, as is said in the sixth rule." These are the four means with which we are familiar: prayer, meditation, much examination, and suitable penitential gestures of courage. Spiritual consolation will return sooner than the darkness of spiritual desolation suggests, but, Ignatius seems to say, it will return still sooner if we diligently use the spiritual means at our disposal.

There is a kind of spiral of grace here. When persons in spiritual desolation *think* that the desolation will not characterize the future forever but that spiritual consolation will soon return, then, fortified by this thinking, they will gain increased energy to employ the four means mentioned in the sixth rule. And when they *diligently use* these four means, the thinking of which Ignatius speaks will become all the more possible. Those persons, who with humble trust in God's sufficing grace, think and act in this way, are solidly set on the path to overcoming spiritual desolation. We touch here the mystery of divine grace and human effort working together; such persons may say with Paul: "his grace to me has not been ineffective. Indeed, I have toiled harder than all of them; not I, however, but the grace of God that is with me" (1 Cor 15:10).

A simple scenario will serve to illustrate how rule 7 applies in practice. Anthony habitually dedicates an hour to prayer in church on Saturday mornings. The preceding week has been a time of spiritual desolation, and, as he rises this Saturday morning, Anthony feels little inclination to spend his habitual time in church. As he prepares to go he increasingly considers simply omitting his customary practice this Saturday. Prayer has been dry and seemed fruitless throughout the week; Anthony feels sure that it will be so again this morning and is unwilling to endure a full hour of such empty prayer.

As he is considering this, Anthony senses that something is wrong. He stops to examine what is happening within; now, "myself-in-desolation" has become "myself-reflecting-on-myself-in desolation." Through this transition Anthony achieves new clarity. He realizes that this is not a time to change his former spiritual proposal (rule 5—no changes in time of spiritual desolation) but that he must strive to resist the spiritual desolation itself. As he continues to prepare, he asks God for help to pray faithfully in church this morning. Anthony thinks of Paul's words that, though "we do not know how to pray as we ought," "the Spirit too comes to the aid of our weakness" (Rom 8:26). He finds comfort in the thought that the Spirit, the Consoler, assists us in our weakness when we seek to pray. He remembers past Saturdays of prayer that began in total dryness but later, within the hour, became times of rich experience of God. Anthony goes to the church and faithfully completes his customary hour of prayer, finding in it a peace that sustains him throughout the day.

Anthony has *worked* to remain *patient*, not to surrender but to persevere faithfully in a time of spiritual desolation. He has *thought*, as Ignatius teaches, that spiritual consolation will return *soon*, sooner than the desolation suggests, perhaps even during the hour of prayer itself. And he has *diligently used* several of the four means indicated in rule 6; he begins with examination and then turns to prayer of petition and meditation on helpful truths of faith. God's grace and Anthony's wise spiritual efforts to resist the desolation are effective, and his spiritual journey moves faithfully forward.

Spiritual Consolation and Desolation: A Normal Alternation

The counsel in rule 8 that persons in spiritual desolation think of the spiritual consolation soon to return invites us to note an Ignatian view of spiritual experience in general. For Ignatius, the ongoing alternation of these two spiritual movements is *a normal pattern* of every spiritual life. Neither spiritual consolation nor spiritual desolation lasts forever; each will eventually give way to the other. Having experienced spiritual consolation, we are not to be surprised that spiritual desolation should arise once more; and when, as Ignatius tells us in this rule, we are in spiritual desolation, we should think ahead to the inevitable return of spiritual consolation, thereby depriving the present desolation of much of its power. Spiritual consolation followed by spiritual desolation, this spiritual desolation followed once again by spiritual consolation, the spiritual consolation followed in turn by further spiritual desolation: this is the normal alternation experienced by every disciple of the Lord down through the centuries and today.* Both spiritual consolation and spiritual desolation lie within God's loving providence, the first given and the second permitted by God; and both are a "lesson" through which God offers us spiritual growth.

Julian of Norwich gives us a striking illustration of this alternation in her book of *Showings*. She writes:

> And after this he revealed a supreme spiritual delight in my soul. In this delight I was filled full of everlasting surety, powerfully secured without any painful fear. This sensation was so welcome and so spiritual that I was wholly at peace, at ease and at rest, so that there was nothing upon earth which could have afflicted me.[6]

---

* In life itself, because the duration and intensity of each movement vary, the alternations will not be so symmetrically proportioned. Longer and more intense periods of one movement may follow briefer and less intense experiences of the other, and vice versa. There will also be times of calm when neither movement is present. Ignatius describes this experience of the heart in which neither spiritual consolation nor spiritual desolation is present as a "tranquil time when the soul is not agitated by various spirits and uses its natural faculties freely and tranquilly" (*SpirEx*, 177).

Very clearly, Julian experiences profound spiritual consolation here. But Julian's experience of spiritual consolation is short lived. She continues in her account:

> This lasted only for a time, and then I was changed, and abandoned to myself, oppressed and weary of my life and ruing myself, so that I hardly had the patience to go on living. I felt that there was no ease or comfort for me except faith, hope, and love, and truly I felt very little of this.

Faith-filled people will empathize fully with Julian's somewhat plaintive expression regarding her former spiritual consolation: "This lasted only for a time. . . ." Now her spiritual consolation has passed and is replaced by intense spiritual desolation.

Then a further alternation occurs, and the spiritual desolation is changed once more into spiritual consolation:

> And then presently God gave me again comfort and rest for my soul, delight and security so blessedly and so powerfully that there was no fear, no sorrow, no pain, physical or spiritual, that one could suffer which might have disturbed me.

The alternations repeat again and again:

> And then again I felt the pain, and then afterwards the delight and the joy, now the one and now the other, again and again, I suppose about twenty times. And in the time of joy I could have said with St. Paul: Nothing shall separate me from the love of Christ; and in the pain I could have said with St. Peter: Lord, save me, I am perishing.

In humbly describing her own experience here, Julian has described the experience of every person who seeks the Lord; such persons, like Julian, feel spiritually up and then down, high and then low, energized and then faltering, joyful and then sad. . . . The ongoing alternation of spiritual consolation and spiritual desolation, with their differing durations and intensities, and interspersed with quiet times when neither is felt—this is to be expected as normal spiritual experience.

Julian, in fact, understands that God allows these alternations for a reason:

> This vision was shown to teach me to understand that some souls profit by experiencing this, to be comforted at one time, and at another to fail and to be left to themselves. God wishes us to know that he keeps us safe all the time, in sorrow and in joy.

Ignatius's teaching in his eighth rule offers a kind of spiritual liberation in this same vein. When dedicated people undergo spiritual desolation, as they inevitably will, they may assume that they are "the only ones" who experience these repeated fluctuations, that others, more spiritually rooted than they, progress in an affectively linear fashion, always desirous of the things of God, always able to sense God's nearness in prayer, rarely or never feeling without hope or far from God. The fact that they themselves, after periods of feeling spiritual energized, find themselves feeling so disheartened and so distant from God, seems to them evidence of their weakness and lack of spiritual progress.

Much can change when, like Ignatius and Julian, they understand that such alternations of spiritual consolation and desolation are *normal* spiritual experience, common to *all*. God's loving call to growth reaches them in *both* spiritual consolation and spiritual desolation. God calls them to grow both through the light and energy received in spiritual consolation, and through the strength they will develop by resisting in time of spiritual desolation. The more they become *people of discernment*—aware of what is stirring spiritually within, able to understand this, able to accept what is of the good spirit, and able to reject what is of the enemy—the greater will be the fruit of spiritual consolation in their hearts and the less will be the duration, intensity, and harm of spiritual desolation in their lives. Ignatius offers them his rules with their *instruction* concerning these spiritual realities and their *guidelines* for action in response to them precisely to assist them in this all-important endeavor.

9

⤴

Why Does God Allow Spiritual Desolation? (Rule 9)

⤴

Yet take Thy way, for sure Thy way is best:
Stretch or contract me, Thy poor debtor:
This is but tuning of my breast,
To make the music better.
                    —George Herbert

God's purpose is to make the soul great.
                    —John of the Cross

"It Is Better for You That I Go" (John 16:7)

In his ninth rule Ignatius now faces a question that arises, at times with great intensity, in the hearts of dedicated people undergoing spiritual desolation: Why does a God who loves me permit me to experience this pain? In time of spiritual desolation this question is always real, sometimes even urgent, all the more so when the desolation is deep and prolonged: "I will say to God, my rock: 'Why do I go mourning, oppressed by the foe?'" (Ps 42:9). Is there a faith-filled person who has never raised this cry to God from the depths of spiritual desolation? Ignatius's rules would remain fundamentally incomplete were he not to address the pressing need for spiritual understanding in time of desolation.

Some first intimations of an answer are already present in what we have seen thus far. In the seventh rule Ignatius has told us that spiritual desolation is a *trial* permitted by God so that, by resisting, we may learn to resist. We have also heard Ignatius describe spiritual desolation to Teresa Rejadell as a *lesson* through which invaluable learning is gained. Ignatius now dedicates his ninth rule to an explicit and detailed consideration of the question, "Why?" As throughout these rules, his treatment of the issue will not

113

be simply speculative but will be eminently practical; in outlining the reasons why God permits spiritual desolation, his purpose is to assist us in more effectively resisting and rejecting it.

Jules Toner aptly introduces this rule by applying to spiritual desolation the words of Jesus to his disciples on the eve of his passion: "But I tell you the truth, it is better for you that I go. For if I do not go, the Advocate will not come to you" (John 16:7).[1] Jesus has told his followers that he will soon depart from them, and, because they love him, his words fill them with sadness. Like many in spiritual desolation, feeling "as if separated from our Creator and Lord," they focus only on the loss of the Lord and are saddened. We sense that they have barely heard and scarcely understood Jesus' repeated mention of the gift of the Consoler, the Advocate, who, through Jesus' departure, will soon come to them (John 14:16, 26; 15:26). Sorrow over that approaching departure consumes their hearts, and they do not look beyond it.

Jesus, who loves his own and loves them to the end (John 13:1), now seeks to lighten their affliction by explaining to them why *it is better for them* that they experience this temporary separation from him; unless he distances himself from them in his time of passion and death they will not receive the transforming gift of the Spirit, so essential for all that lies ahead in their mission. Toner writes:

> He is trying to get their minds *off the sorrow* of anticipated separation and *on to the reasons for it*, reasons springing from his love and the Father's love for them. If they could only grasp why Jesus is going away, then they could deal with their sorrow; and they could also respond to Jesus' departure in such a manner as to cooperate with what he was doing, and grow through it in the way his love intended.[2]

The same is also true for us. If, in time of spiritual desolation, we can shift our attention from the sorrow we feel to consideration of the *reason* why God, in his love for us, permits us to experience this "separation," then the sorrow itself will be lightened, trust will grow that a gift is being offered to us through the pain, and we will be strengthened to resist the desolation. The purpose of Ignatius's ninth rule is to assist us, in time of spiritual desolation, to achieve this change of interior focus: away from immersion in sorrow and toward understanding of the redemptive reason for the sorrow.

"There Are Three Principal Causes"

The ninth rule reads:

Ninth Rule. The ninth: there are three principal causes for which we find ourselves desolate. The first is because we are tepid, slothful, or negligent in our spiritual exercises, and so through our faults spiritual consolation withdraws from us. The second, to try us and see how much we are and how much we extend ourselves in his service and praise without so much payment of consolations and increased graces. The third, to give us true recognition and understanding so that we may interiorly feel that it is not ours to attain or maintain increased devotion, intense love, tears or any other spiritual consolation, but that all is the gift and grace of God our Lord, and so that we may not build a nest in something belonging to another, raising our mind in some pride or vainglory, attributing to ourselves the devotion or the other parts of the spiritual consolation.

The governing word in this text is "cause": "there are three principal *causes* for which we find ourselves desolate." "Cause," in this context, signifies *God's motive* in withdrawing spiritual consolation from us and in allowing the enemy to oppress us with spiritual desolation. "Cause" here does not indicate origin (the causing agent) but rather *finality* (the purpose for which the desolation is permitted to occur). In the ninth rule, this is God's finality: God's saving purpose in allowing us to undergo the trial of spiritual desolation. This rule views spiritual desolation from the perspective of God and invites us to understand why we are experiencing it from that saving perspective.

It is important to note that spiritual desolation, *of itself*, does not produce growth; indeed, if not resisted, it will cause spiritual harm in varying degrees. The experience of spiritual desolation becomes fruitful *when we resist it*. The persevering effort to resist spiritual desolation, as described in these rules, is the necessary condition that God's motives in allowing this desolation be fulfilled.[3] If, for example, Alice as she struggles in her new parish and Jane as she undergoes her desolate days of retreat simply surrender to their spiritual desolation, obviously only harm will result. If, on the contrary, they humbly and courageously use the means proposed to resist it, *then* God's purpose in allowing the desolation will be accomplished.

Ignatius speaks of "three *principal* causes" for which God allows spiritual desolation. The adjective indicates that the list of causes given here is not intended to be exhaustive and that God may have other redemptive motives as well in permitting us to experience spiritual desolation.[4] The modifier "principal" signifies, however, that the three causes mentioned here are of special importance among the different causes for which God may permit spiritual desolation. Precisely because they are the principal causes, therefore, they will merit our close attention.

God, first, permits us to experience spiritual desolation as a means of healing us from our faults; in this case, the gift God wishes to give us is *conversion* and the spiritual growth consequent upon it. Second, God permits such desolation as a trial; the gift he wishes to give us here is spiritual *learn-*

ing. Third, God permits spiritual desolation so that we may perceive the complete gratuity of spiritual consolation; the gift he wishes to give us here is a spiritually rich *humility*.[5] We will examine each of these three.

Our Faults and the Gift of Conversion

"The first is because we are tepid, slothful, or negligent in our spiritual exercises, and so through our faults spiritual consolation withdraws from us." We will approach this first cause through two illustrations of how it may be operative in God's working in the hearts of faithful people.

Patrick has chosen to make a retreat of several days as part of a group in a local retreat center. God is at the heart of his life, and he chooses the retreat because he desires to grow closer yet to the Lord. During the first days Patrick dedicates himself fully to prayer in common with the group and personally with Scripture. He is attentive to God's work in his prayer and enjoys the atmosphere of silence in the house that aids him in focusing on God. These days prove spiritually blessed, and he experiences abundant spiritual consolation.

After a time, however, Patrick begins to weaken somewhat in his application to the process of the retreat. He is now less careful to maintain his quiet focus on God; he occasionally shortens prayer time and ceases to be as spiritually alert in noting God's workings in his heart. A time comes when the spiritual consolation of the earlier days fades and is replaced by small stirrings of spiritual desolation. This disquiet moves Patrick to review his situation in the retreat. In the course of this review he becomes aware of his negligence in prayer and in attentiveness to God's workings in the preceding days of his retreat. Patrick determines to renew his earlier dedication to the retreat, does so, and finds that the spiritual desolation disappears and spiritual consolation returns.

The same dynamic may also take place in daily living. Catherine has grown closer to God and has progressed in her life of prayer over the last several years. She is faithful to Sunday worship, prays frequently with Scripture, and faithfully attends a weekly prayer meeting. Catherine frequently senses the Lord's presence, and her prayer brings her peace in the midst of life's busyness. At a certain point, however, her dedication to prayer diminishes a little. She continues to pray but with lessened regularity and diligence. For Catherine, too, a moment comes when she no longer experiences the same peace in her prayer, no longer senses God's presence as readily as before, and begins to feel some disturbance in her relationship with God. This interior trouble serves as a kind of spiritual wake-up call. Catherine compares her former relationship with God before she relaxed her habitual prayer with her present unhappier circumstances and decides to resume her customary prayer with renewed fidelity. The spiritual desolation disappears, and Catherine is conscious once more of God's closeness. She recovers her peace in God and finds new vitality in her life of faith.

In both instances the pattern is the same; persons genuinely seeking God have become, with greater or lesser awareness of the fact, negligent in some aspect of their spiritual exercises—their life of prayer in its various facets. As a consequence, their former spiritual consolation wanes, and spiritual desolation enters in its place. When such persons *discern* their situation— are aware of it, understand that they are in spiritual desolation, and take wise steps to reject it—then God's "cause" in permitting the desolation is fulfilled. The spiritual desolation has alerted them to a need for *conversion* in that area of their spiritual exercises, and, having made the appropriate changes, they are once more solidly set on the path of spiritual progress.

The persons of the ninth rule are persons whose fundamental direction of spiritual life is toward God and away from sin; they are "persons who are going on intensely purifying their sin and rising from good to better in the service of God our Lord" (rule 2). They may, nonetheless, become "tepid, slothful, or negligent" in some *particular* aspect of their spiritual exercises, as in the examples of Patrick and Catherine given above. In this case, such persons may be *progressing* toward God in *general* but *regressing* in a *particular* aspect of their spiritual life. God, in order to heal them in this particular area, may withdraw spiritual consolation and permit spiritual desolation to replace it.

This first cause of spiritual desolation in the ninth rule describes an action of the good spirit similar to that which we saw in the first rule. There, in the case of persons "going from mortal sin to mortal sin," the good spirit adopted a "stinging and biting" action through the use of reason, arousing in such persons an acute distress of conscience so that they would be moved to desist from serious sin and turn back to God. Here, though now on a much more refined level, God once again allows spiritual discomfort—the removal of spiritual consolation and its replacement by the disquiet of spiritual desolation—as an inducement to conversion and spiritual newness in a particular area of regression in those whose spiritual life remains otherwise faithfully directed toward God.[6]

An example from Ignatius's *Spiritual Diary* will assist in further clarifying this first cause of spiritual desolation and will serve to illustrate the sensitive spiritual levels on which this dynamic may operate. On April 2, 1544, Ignatius wrote:

> Later, at another time, when much consoled, I thought that I was satisfied, that is, I thought that it was better not to be consoled by God our Lord, if the lack of his visitation was due to my not having disposed myself or helped myself throughout the day, or in giving place to some thoughts that distracted me from his words in the sacrifice [the Mass] and from his divine majesty, and so I thought it would be better not to be consoled in the time of my faults, and that God our

Lord orders this (who loves me more than I love myself), for my greater spiritual benefit, so that it is better for me to walk straight, not only in the sacrifice, but throughout the day, in order to be visited.[7]

This paragraph reveals what discernment of spirits can become, with faithful daily application, in the lives of those who love the Lord; such words show us a person continually alert to the love and workings of God within his heart. For Ignatius, at this point in his life, a constant discerning awareness gives his relationship with God all the richness of ongoing daily interaction characteristic of every genuine relationship of love.

"Later, at another time, when much consoled": Ignatius writes now out of the peace and joy of deep spiritual consolation. The light and the warmth of present consolation assist him in understanding the fluctuations of spiritual consolation that have preceded this moment. He affirms that he is "satisfied," that is, able to understand now the reason for, and so be at peace with, the absence of consolation he has just experienced.

Ignatius comprehends that the lack of this spiritual "visitation" by God was "due to *my not having disposed myself or helped myself* throughout the day, or in giving *place to some thoughts that distracted me* from his words in the sacrifice [the Mass] and from his divine majesty." The love between Ignatius and his God has grown so deep, so habitual, and Ignatius is so deeply desirous of living constantly in communion with God that he is aware even of small moments of distraction from God during the day and in the celebration of the Eucharist. When his attention, even occasionally, slips away from God, he senses that God loves him too much to fail to recall him and does so by quietly withdrawing spiritual consolation.

As he reflects, Ignatius grasps God's cause in withdrawing such spiritual consolation: "and so I thought it *would be better not to be consoled in the time of my faults*, and that God our Lord orders this (who loves me more than I love myself), *for my greater spiritual benefit*." These words in his *Spiritual Diary* mirror his description of the first cause in his ninth rule: "The first is because we are tepid, slothful, or negligent in our spiritual exercises, and so through our faults spiritual consolation withdraws from us." Ignatius, who is so sensitively attuned to God's constant workings in his heart, does not even need spiritual desolation to alert him to his momentary distraction from God's presence; the withdrawal of spiritual consolation alone is enough. Through this he realizes the Lord's purpose and resolves to renew his habitual seeking of the Lord throughout the day.

What follows is an expression of great spiritual beauty. Ignatius, having understood why God has removed spiritual consolation from him, now reveals his image of the God who acts thus in his heart: "God our Lord orders this (*who loves me more than I love myself*)." "Who loves me more than I love myself": these striking words bring us to the heart of the first cause described in the ninth rule. Ignatius recognizes that he himself would not wish to be deprived of spiritual consolation and that the God who loves him knows this well. He also recognizes, however, that God loves him *more* than he loves himself and, in this "more," perceives the "cause" for which the God of love has removed from him the spiritual consolation earlier enjoyed. Through withdrawing spiritual consolation, God offers Ignatius an opportunity to become aware of and to overcome even his minor faults and so be restored to the constant union with God his heart so seeks.[8]

"Who loves me more than I love myself." When, like Ignatius, dedicated people discover the God who loves them more than they love themselves and understand the withdrawal of spiritual consolation and the experience of spiritual desolation in the light of this healing love, then they have understood the first cause for which God permits spiritual desolation. Aided by such understanding they will find strength, like Ignatius, to make the changes that will bring them once more close to God.

A Trial and the Gift of Learning

God's second cause in permitting spiritual desolation, Ignatius writes, is that the trial of such desolation reveals valuable truths about our spiritual condition: "The second, to *try* us and *see* how much we are and how much we extend ourselves in his service and praise without so much payment of consolations and increased graces."

In the sixth rule Ignatius spoke of spiritual desolation as a *trial* permitted by God so that, by resisting, we may increasingly learn to resist desolation. In his ninth rule Ignatius returns again to consideration of spiritual desolation as a trial, focusing once more on the gift God desires to give us through this trial: here, that through it, we may learn spiritual lessons that will fortify us in the struggle against desolation.

A comparison adopted by Daniel Gil aptly illustrates the trial that Ignatius describes in this ninth rule. In this trial God ceases to give "so much payment of consolations and increased graces." When this occurs, "we encounter a situation like that of a soldier who is not given his pay: the mercenary gives up the battle, the patriot continues to fight."[9] Two groups of soldiers are joined in an army; some are mercenaries fighting simply for pay, others are patriots fighting to defend the country they love. A time comes when resources diminish and payment can no longer be given. At this point the mercenaries simply lay down their weapons and give up the struggle; they are fighting for pay only, and, without this pay, they will not continue to fight. The patriots, however, persevere faithfully in the struggle even without pay, since their hearts are firmly fixed on their cause independently of whether or not they are given payment.[10]

In like manner, Ignatius affirms, God allows us to experience spiritual desolation in order "to try us and see *how much we are* and *how much we extend ourselves* in his service and praise *without so much payment* of consolations and increased graces." If we take Ignatius's words just as written, God would appear to be saying: "Here is a dedicated person, faithful to prayer and loving service. Let us see whether this person is a spiritual mercenary or patriot. Let us see whether in time of spiritual desolation, when one is no longer rewarded with spiritual consolation, this person will give up the effort to pray and to serve, or whether this person will persevere even without the 'payment' of spiritual consolation." God *tries* us in this way by permitting us to experience spiritual desolation. Through this trial something is *seen*; through it a clear sense of our spiritual identity ("how much we are") and of how perseveringly we will serve in the time of trial ("how much we extend ourselves") emerges. Such learning is spiritually fruitful in many ways.

In chapter 2 we cited the experience of Lucia's interior turmoil while driving home from her grace-filled retreat; in a time of intense spiritual desolation she finds many "reasons" to doubt the authenticity of the retreat just concluded. After this time of struggle she calls her retreat director and, in conversation with the director, finds the answer to her fears and a further confirmation of God's gift during her retreat. Now Lucia writes to the director:

> So it was truly the grace of God that prompted me to make that phone call, and your words and prayers revealed the truth to me. I realize now more than ever how much God loves me, how much I need him; and I am more determined than ever to "keep my eyes fixed on Jesus," to follow him, to serve him, to do his will.[11]

The *learning* consequent upon this trial of spiritual desolation is evident in the "more" that characterizes this woman's spiritual reality following her time of desolation; after her time of desolation she has "more" spiritually than she had before the time of desolation. Through the trial she has learned two key spiritual truths in a new and deeper way: "I realize now *more than ever* how much God loves me." She has also learned more fully than before "how much I need him." Such learning "in the flesh" of these basic truths reveals why God permits her trial of spiritual desolation as she returns home from her retreat.

This "more" is not limited to understanding alone; a further gift is given her on the level of the will. She is "*more determined* than ever" to focus on Jesus: to keep her eyes fixed on Jesus (Heb 12:2), to follow Jesus, to serve Jesus, and to do his will. Again, the spiritual growth resulting from her trial of spiritual desolation is manifest.

We may note that this learning and growth occur as God intends *because Lucia resists* the spiritual desolation. She does not surrender to the thoughts that arise in her spiritual desolation, and she has the courage to share all this with her director, thus breaking the grip of the spiritual desolation.[12] Because she does this, the spiritual desolation does not diminish the grace of her retreat. On the contrary, her trial of spiritual desolation achieves the purpose for which God allowed it; Lucia learns powerful spiritual lessons and grows in her will to love and follow Jesus Christ. God's cause in permitting the spiritual desolation has been fulfilled.

Another person also gains new learning through the trial of spiritual desolation and writes:

> I realize through this desolating experience how powerless I am over my compulsive tendency to work so hard and my great need for God's strength in this area of weakness. God's constant love for me is enabling me to see in a deep way how lovable I am. It is helping me to appreciate my own giftedness in working with the homeless.[13]

Again a "desolating experience" leads to learning: "I *realize* through this desolating experience. . . ." The learning in this instance is increased self-knowledge, that self-knowledge which creates the opportunity for new freedom from bondage. Here the learning centers on a "compulsive tendency" to work too hard and on "God's constant love for me." This love permits the person "to see in a deep way how lovable I am." The learning that emerges from the experience of desolation is profound: clear awareness of captivity to a tendency toward excess, a sense of God's personal love, and, consequently, a new ability to love self in a spiritually healthy way. The "desolating experience," this person says, is also "helping me" to appreciate a God-given gift in working with the poor. Once more, we can hear Jesus gently say to this person, with great love: "It is better for you that I go."

The learning that comes through spiritual desolation when it is resisted, as these examples indicate, can take many directions.[14] Such desolation may disclose to us our own limitations in a way that will put us on guard against ill-considered spiritual steps; it may reveal to us precisely where we can most helpfully pursue spiritual growth. Through resisting in time of spiritual desolation we may also, to our happy surprise, learn that we need not fear desolation as we formerly did: that, with God's help, we can come through the trial spiritually unscathed and even confirmed in our spiritual progress. Indeed, as Toner affirms, without the trial of such desolation we would likely remain spiritual children.[15] Spiritual desolation when resisted produces learning and moves us solidly toward spiritual maturity. For this cause, Ignatius tells us, a loving God permits us to experience this trial.

In the life of Francis of Assisi we read of a Franciscan brother who was struggling with temptations that he felt helpless to resist. He knew that Francis was well aware of his inner conflict and one day, when alone with Francis, begged this holy man for help, saying:

Pray for me, kind Father, for I am sure that I will be immediately freed from my temptations if you will be kind enough to pray for me. For I am afflicted above my strength and I know that this is no secret to you.

We can imagine how consoling Francis's answer must have been to this brother in his time of trouble:

St. Francis said to him: "Believe me, son, for I think you are for that reason more truly a servant of God; and know that the more you are tempted, the more will you be loved by me." And he added: "I tell you in all truth, no one must consider himself a servant of God until he has undergone temptations and tribulations. Temptation overcome," he said, "is in a way a ring with which the Lord espouses the soul of his servant to himself."[16]

The tribulation that this brother thought an indication of his spiritual deficiency Francis knows to be rather the sign that this brother is a true servant of God. In his love for this oppressed man Francis reveals the very heart of God: "and know that the more you are tempted, the more you will be loved by me." Such temptations and tribulations, Francis says, have even a spousal significance; when they are resisted and overcome, through them, God espouses the human heart ever more intimately in love. This is the encouragement that Ignatius would give us in describing God's second cause in allowing the trial of spiritual desolation.

Poverty and the Gift of a Humble Heart

Ignatius expresses the third cause for which God permits spiritual desolation as follows:

The third, to give us true recognition and understanding so that we may interiorly feel that *it is not ours* to attain or maintain increased devotion, intense love, tears, or any other spiritual consolation, *but that all is the gift and grace of God* our Lord, and so that we may not build a nest in something belonging to another, raising our mind in some pride or vainglory, attributing to ourselves the devotion or the other parts of the spiritual consolation.

Here, for the first time in his rules, Ignatius appears to abandon the brief, essential style he has consistently employed thus far and to explain his teaching without economy of words. The stylistic change suggests that this third cause is of special importance in Ignatius's mind.[17] The third cause does, in fact, touch a pivotal theme in the whole of Ignatius's *Spiritual Exercises:* that evangelical *humility*, rooted in evangelical poverty, is the gateway to God's grace and to following the Lord Jesus in our lives (*SpirEx*, 146).

A common thread runs through the examples mentioned above in our exposition of the second cause. After her experience of spiritual desolation while driving home from her retreat, Lucia writes: "I *realize now more than ever* how much God loves me, *how much I need him.*" The trial of those painful hours of spiritual desolation leads this woman to perceive very concretely her need for God; she learns in a powerfully experienced way through the darkness and agitation of spiritual desolation that she is not spiritually sufficient unto herself, that she needs God and the grace of God.

In a similar vein, the other person states: "I *realize* through this desolating experience *how powerless I am* over my compulsive tendency to work so hard and *my great need for God's strength* in this area of weakness." Again the actual experience of desolation awakens a keen awareness both of personal weakness and of a "great need for God's strength." For this second person as for Lucia, this awareness does not debilitate but rather deepens a confident dependence on God's loving assistance. Both are stronger spiritually for having experienced, in time of spiritual desolation, their great need for God's grace.

This, says Ignatius, is a further reason why God permits dedicated people to experience spiritual desolation. These persons recognize that in the affliction of spiritual desolation they felt more than at other times the truth of Jesus' words: "Without me you can do nothing" (John 15:5). With particular intensity, in time of spiritual desolation they "interiorly feel that *it is not ours* to attain or maintain increased devotion, intense love, tears, or any other spiritual consolation, *but that all is the gift and grace of God* our Lord."

Thus the time of spiritual desolation reveals to them with utter clarity that all spiritual growth is God's gift: that spiritual consolation, when they experience it, is purely God's gift. Having undergone the dryness and heaviness of spiritual desolation, Ignatius writes, we will "not build a nest in something belonging to another, raising our mind in some pride or vainglory, attributing to ourselves the devotion or the other parts of the spiritual consolation." Ignatius, Angela, Alice, Jane, and all who undergo spiritual desolation will not build such a "nest"; they will know deeply that spiritual consolation is purely the free gift of a loving God.

Such awareness strengthens the *evangelical humility* that leads "to all the other virtues" (*SpirEx*, 146); it deepens in these persons the poverty in spirit that gives entrance to the kingdom of heaven (Matt 5:3). This humility opens the heart to receive the further blessings of the God "who gives grace to the humble" (1 Pet 5:5). Again we can hear the Lord quietly repeat: "It is better for you that I go," better so that, through the trial of spiritual desolation, such spiritual fruit may be given.

An Implicit Norm

Although in rule 9, by contrast with the preceding four rules, Ignatius does not explicitly give us a guideline for action—he dedicates his rule to *instructing* us in the three principal causes for which God permits spiritual desolation—this rule, as Fiorito points out, does implicitly propose an important guideline for resisting desolation. If Ignatius instructs us so carefully with respect to the causes of spiritual desolation, he is plainly counseling us *to seek the specific cause* at work when we are in spiritual desolation. By so doing, we will be all the more prepared to take effective steps in response to the specific experience of desolation we are undergoing.[18]

Like the disciples in the Upper Room, as long as we focus solely on the sorrow of the desolation and do not think to seek its cause, we are unlikely to resist it efficaciously. When, however, we examine it well (rule 6) and perceive its cause, we are then readied to resist it with new energy and with new wisdom.[19] Thus, it is key that in time of spiritual desolation we consciously ask this question: "*Why* am I in this spiritual desolation? *What is the cause* of this spiritual desolation?"[20]

Persons who are physically unwell may have a vague sense of malaise but cannot take effective steps toward healing until they have understood the precise nature of the illness; once they have reached an accurate diagnosis they know exactly how to overcome it.[21] A parallel situation exists regarding the spiritual malaise of spiritual desolation. Ignatius, in rule 9, invites us to pursue an accurate diagnosis of the desolation we are experiencing: to examine it until we understand its cause. Once we have determined its cause we can adopt the appropriate spiritual remedies toward overcoming it. In this way we will begin to see the spiritual desolation as *God* sees it, as within his plan of redemption in our lives.

The difference between this effort to understand the cause of spiritual desolation and an unreflective assumption that, if we are in spiritual desolation, it is *always* due to some fault on our part, is apparent. Faithful people undergoing spiritual desolation may spontaneously conclude that, "If I am in spiritual desolation, it *must* be because I have failed the Lord in some way." Ignatius, as rule 9 abundantly indicates, does not accept such unreflective identifications and teaches that God has more than one reason for permitting spiritual desolation.

It is true that through spiritual desolation God may wish to alert dedicated persons to particular areas of negligence in their spiritual lives. If, however, such persons examine their spiritual exercises and cannot identify such negligence, they may then assume that God has allowed the spiritual desolation for reasons other than their own negligence, principally for the second or third cause of desolation as Ignatius describes these in rule 9. These persons may find great comfort in knowing that they are in spiritual desolation not because they have failed as disciples of the Lord but precisely because they *are* faithful disciples whom God is calling to grow further through the trial of spiritual desolation (Heb 12:5–13). Here once again, as throughout the rules, the captives are being set spiritually free.

10

⌒

Spiritual Consolation: A Time to Prepare (Rule 10)

⌒

You looked with love upon me
and deep within your eyes imprinted grace. . . .
—John of the Cross

Before the Trial Begins

With the tenth rule Ignatius moves from the person in spiritual desolation, the focus of the previous five rules, to "the one who is in consolation." The text is the most brief of all the rules:

Tenth Rule. The tenth: let the one who is in consolation think how he will conduct himself in the desolation which will come after, taking new strength for that time.

We have, therefore, a rule regarding *spiritual consolation.* In this rule, nonetheless, Ignatius's intention to assist us in rejecting spiritual desolation remains his primary concern. As we have said, for most dedicated people, for much of the way on the spiritual journey, spiritual desolation more than spiritual consolation constitutes the basic problem.[1] Consequently, although Ignatius now turns to spiritual *consolation* in rule 10, he does so from his primary perspective of aiding faithful persons to overcome spiritual desolation. The fundamental purpose of these fourteen rules remains constant: our great need is for assistance in overcoming spiritual desolation and its related deceptions. Rule 10, in fact, views spiritual consolation precisely as it relates to spiritual desolation: "let the one who is in *consolation* think how he will conduct himself in the *desolation* which will come after."[2]

Thus far Ignatius has instructed us concerning how to resist spiritual desolation *while we are actually experiencing* this desolation as, for example, when Alice's heart is heavy after her year of struggle in her new parish, or when Jane is discouraged on her sixth day of retreat. He has instructed us regarding how to resist spiritual desolation during "the time of spiritual desolation." Now Ignatius adds a further refinement to the effort to resist spiritual desolation and tells us there are steps we can take *before the spiritual desolation begins* that will assist us greatly in resisting such desolation when it actually comes.

We have seen that Ignatius understands the spiritual life as an ongoing alternation of spiritual consolation and spiritual desolation: spiritual consolation followed by spiritual desolation, followed by spiritual consolation, and the pattern continues. Before each time of spiritual desolation, therefore, there is always a time of spiritual consolation. Jane, for example, enjoys several days of spiritual consolation in prayer before the desolate sixth day arrives. In his tenth rule Ignatius instructs us regarding effective spiritual measures that we can take *during the spiritual consolation that precedes* spiritual desolation, which will provide increased strength for the struggle when, as it inevitably will, desolation returns.

Spiritual consolation, as we have said, like spiritual desolation, endures for a certain period of time: a brief moment, a few minutes, an hour, a day, several days or weeks, or possibly longer yet. There is *an identifiable time* when we are in spiritual consolation as, for example, the three hours that Raïssa Maritain spends in deeply consoled prayer, the day that Thérèse passes in joyful gratitude after her experience in the garden, or the initial grace-filled days of Jane's retreat. In rule 10, Ignatius centers on this *time* when we are in spiritual consolation and on how we can employ it toward better resisting the spiritual desolation to follow.

"The Two Hours So Enjoyed"

Before proceeding further, however, it is important that we address the time of spiritual consolation *in itself* and not yet in relation to the spiritual desolation that will follow. This will provide a helpful balance to our discussion of spiritual consolation and ensure that we accurately grasp its place in our spiritual life. Before spiritual consolation serves any additional purpose, however valuable, such consolation is above all a gift of God to be received with gratitude and from which to gain new energy in the ways God intends; it is God's look of love upon us, imprinting grace within our hearts.

The following quotation from Elizabeth Seton abundantly illustrates this point. Elizabeth describes, at a distance of some years, a spiritual experience that occurred in the summer of her fifteenth year in Connecticut. She writes:

> In the year 1789, when my father was in England, one morning in May, in the lightness of a cheerful heart, I jumped in the wagon that was driving to the woods for brush, about a mile from home; the boy who drove it began to cut, and I set off in the woods, soon found an outlet in a meadow; and a chestnut tree with several young ones growing around it, found rich moss under it and a warm sun. Here, then, was a sweet bed—the air still a clear blue vault above—the numberless sounds of spring melody and joy—the sweet clovers and wild flowers I had got by the way, and a heart as innocent as human heart could be, filled even with enthusiastic love to God and admiration of His works. . . .
>
> God was my Father, my all. I prayed, sang hymns, cried, laughed, talking to myself of how far He could place me above all sorrow. Then I laid still to enjoy the heavenly peace that came over my soul; and I am sure, in the two hours so enjoyed, grew ten years in the spiritual life. . . .[3]

Again, we are standing on holy ground. . . . For a period of two hours Elizabeth experiences what is clearly an intense form of spiritual consolation. Her final words beautifully describe the fundamental gift which God gives through spiritual consolation: "and I am sure, in the *two hours* so enjoyed, *grew ten years* in the spiritual life." This, most essentially, is why God gives us spiritual consolation: that, through it, our faith may deepen, our hearts grow in love, and our whole being expand in new spiritual life. This is the time, as Ignatius said in his fifth rule, when "the good spirit guides and counsels us more." Our primary task in time of spiritual consolation always remains to *accept* the blessed work of God within us through such consolation.

No other spiritual purpose must ever distract us from simply receiving God's gifts in time of spiritual consolation, not even all that Ignatius will say in his tenth rule about preparing for future spiritual desolation in time of spiritual consolation. Raïssa, during her three hours of deeply consoling prayer, must not feel obliged to set aside God's workings within her in order to prepare consciously for coming spiritual desolation; nor must Thérèse feel a similar obligation during her grace-filled moment in the garden. These and all to whom God gives spiritual consolation must let *no other spiritual task* weigh upon the freedom simply to receive and be joyfully strengthened by God's gift, while God wishes to give that gift.

A time comes for Raïssa, however, after her three intensely consoled hours, when God's consoling action remains though now in gentler fashion and she is more free to direct her thoughts as she chooses. A time comes too for Thérèse, when, after the moment of profound grace in the garden, she lives the rest of the day with a joy-filled heart. A time comes for Elizabeth, when, returning home after her two hours in the woods, she still feels the happy consciousness of God's love. And a time comes for Jane, during her first consoled days of retreat, when, after the formal times of prayer, she sits quietly in her room with her heart at peace. All these persons have already *accepted* God's gift of spiritual consolation. Now, while their hearts are filled with light and joy, they may also specifically *choose to prepare* for future spiritual desolation. If they do so, then spiritual consolation will bless them in yet another way, even beyond the great gift they have already received; through this choice to prepare, they will find themselves more ready to resist when spiritual desolation returns.

In this case, when Jane's sixth desolate day of retreat arrives she is less likely to be so helplessly discouraged and more apt to be prepared to respond in an effective way. Consequently, her desolation is likely to be less painful and pass more quickly than when it finds her unprepared. Ignatius's tenth rule aims to assist us in such preparation for resisting spiritual desolation. This is *what* Ignatius calls us to do: to prepare for future spiritual desolation during the preceding spiritual consolation. *How* are we to do this? Ignatius gives a single answer in two parts; when in spiritual consolation we may choose a way of *thinking* that will assist in *taking new strength* for resisting spiritual desolation when it returns.

The Thinking That Prepares

"Let the one who is in consolation *think* how he will conduct himself in the desolation which will come after." Once more, as earlier in rules 7 and 8, Ignatius refers to a way of *thinking*. These repeated references to "thinking" indicate Ignatius's sense of the power for resisting spiritual desolation found in choosing certain ways of thinking, whether in time of spiritual *desolation* (rules 7 and 8) or in time of spiritual *consolation* (rule 10).[4]

The "thinking" mentioned in rule 10, since it is adopted in time of spiritual consolation, does not focus on *present* spiritual desolation, as does the thinking counseled in rules 7 and 8, but rather on *future* spiritual desolation. And this thinking centers on *how we will act* in the future spiritual desolation: "Let the one who is in consolation think *how he will conduct himself* in the desolation which will come after." Jane, for example, during her first consoled days of retreat, when she is experiencing the warmth of God's love, may *think ahead* to the spiritual desolation that she knows will eventually return and to *how she will act* at that future time in order to resist it.

In discussing rules 7 and 8 we noted that the thinking to which Ignatius calls us in time of spiritual desolation—to consider that this desolation is a trial permitted by the Lord (rule 7) and that consolation will soon return (rule 8)—is unlikely to arise spontaneously within us in the darkness of desolation and that it must be consciously chosen. On her sixth day of retreat Jane will tend more easily, on the purely spontaneous level, simply to feel discouraged than she will to *think* as Ignatius suggests; she must consciously choose to employ the teaching of his rules.

Similarly, the thinking in time of spiritual consolation that prepares for future spiritual desolation is unlikely to occur spontaneously. If persons who experience the loving closeness of God respond only on the spontaneous level to their consolation, they are more likely to affirm with Julian of Norwich: "In the time of joy I could have said with St. Paul: Nothing shall separate me from the love of Christ." Persons blessed with spiritual consolation are indeed gaining strength and growing through God's loving gift. Whether the spiritual consolation will serve further to prepare in a specific way for future spiritual desolation depends on whether these persons, in addition to receiving the grace of the spiritual consolation, *also* choose to think in the way Ignatius recommends in rule 10. They are called to make this choice when, on the merely spontaneous level, this does not feel necessary. Here again, as with the earlier rules, repeated practice will lead to growing ease in applying Ignatius's guideline.

This reflection on the value of certain consciously adopted ways of thinking, both in spiritual consolation and desolation, reveals an Ignatian vision of daily spiritual living. For Ignatius, spiritual persons do not allow themselves to be borne along passively by the inevitable alternations of spiritual consolation and desolation. On the contrary, they live with *constant spiritual awareness*. They are *aware* of spiritual desolation and *choose* to think about it in certain faith-based ways while experiencing it. They are also *aware* of spiritual consolation and *choose*, while experiencing it, to think ahead to future spiritual desolation and to prepare for it. Ongoing, daily efforts to live with such spiritual awareness form the *discerning* person, living the examined spiritual life.[5]

If We Are Not Prepared

What will happen in our spiritual lives if, in time of spiritual consolation, we *do not* think ahead to future spiritual desolation and prepare? If Jane, in her first consoled days of retreat, does not think ahead to the likely return of spiritual desolation and prepare? If Julian of Norwich simply accepts her spontaneous feeling, when in spiritual consolation, that now she can say with Paul, "Nothing shall separate me from the love of Christ"?

In this case, says Toner, the spiritual desolation will come upon us "with the confusing shock of surprise."[6] It may cause "complete loss of composure"; under the impact of this confusing surprise, all our spiritual practices and plans may simply unravel.[7] We may feel, he writes, "bitterness with a tendency to accuse self falsely or to doubt God's faithfulness or to be angry with life." In fact, when spiritual desolation comes as a completely unexpected blow we may indeed feel a certain sadness or even bitterness, and find ourselves saying to the Lord these or equivalent words: "I have tried to serve you, Lord, the best I am able, and is this interior pain the only result? Is there any value to my efforts? Is all of this spiritual striving worthwhile?" Unanticipated spiritual desolation leaves us more readily prey to an unreflective equation of this desolation with some failure on our part—forgetting the various causes for which God may permit it, as we have seen in the ninth rule; when this occurs, discouragement is not far away. Spiritual desolation, if we are not prepared for it, will all the more easily take hold of and weigh upon us; it will also be all the harder to resist and overcome. In his tenth rule, Ignatius shows us the way to avoid such difficulties.

If We Are Prepared

Toner continues:

> If, on the other hand, *I do look ahead*, expecting the loss of consolation and the coming of desolation as the normal course of events, I am in a position, with God's grace, to maintain control of the situation, and to render the impetus of desolation ineffectual against my prayer, work and decisions. I am in a position to counterattack immediately with all the means for doing so.[8]

If we *have* thought ahead in time of spiritual consolation to the return of spiritual desolation and *have* prepared, the desolation will not then come with "a confusing shock of surprise"; we will be ready to resist more quickly, with the help of God's grace, which is always sufficient for our need. In this case, the desolation is much less likely to harm us.

A comparison will serve to illustrate this point further. We may imagine two people riding a city bus on the way to work, both standing and supporting themselves by clasping the vertical metal rods placed for that purpose. The first person is engaged in talking and viewing the passing sights as the bus progresses along a straight stretch of the street. Because this part of the street is without curves, the course of the bus is constant; consequently, a loose hold on the metal rod suffices to maintain his balance. At the end of the straight stretch of road, however, lies a sharp curve. Since this person's attention is engaged elsewhere he does not notice the coming change in direction until the bus is already in the curve. His loose hold on the rod no longer suffices to maintain his balance and he falls. His fall results in minor injury to himself and some small damage to the items he is carrying. He rises from his fall and continues with his planned activity, but the rest of the day is somewhat more difficult because of his fall.

The second person, like the first, also clasps the supporting rod loosely as the bus proceeds along the straight stretch of road. This person too is engaged in personal activity as the bus goes forward but, unlike the other, looks up from time to time to see what lies ahead on their route. He notes the sharp curve approaching and, before the bus enters it, grasps the rod more firmly. As the bus negotiates the curve he sways a little with the motion of the bus but remains solidly on his feet. This person expends a little extra energy in passing through the curve, but that is all. There is no fall, no injury, and no damage. His day is not further burdened by the passage of the curve as is the day of the first person.

Through his tenth rule Ignatius seeks to guide us to a point of spiritual preparation similar to that of this second person. In time of consolation the spiritual road is easier to walk and we go forward without a sense of burden. If, during the times when we find delight and ease in the spiritual life, we not only accept the present gift but also *look ahead* and *think* of *how we will conduct ourselves* in future spiritual desolation, then that desolation, when it comes, will lose much of its power to harm us. When the onset of desolation finds us already prepared, although we will need to expend spiritual energy in resisting it, we are much more likely to maintain our spiritual balance while it endures. Experience consistently reveals the power in the tenth rule, when faithfully practiced.

When commenting on the ninth rule we saw Ignatius himself sensitively practice this kind of preparation. His reflection, *in time of spiritual consolation*, about an earlier absence of such consolation clearly leaves him better prepared to understand and respond to any such future absence. When in spiritual consolation he writes: "Later, at another time, *when much consoled*, I thought that . . . it was better not to be consoled by God our Lord, if the lack of his visitation was due to my not having disposed myself or helped myself throughout the day." And from this reflection he gains new spiritual insight: "and so I thought it would be better not to be consoled in the time of my faults, and that God our Lord orders this (who loves me more than I love myself), for my greater spiritual benefit."[9]

Ignatius not only *accepts* the gift of great spiritual consolation but also, in time of consolation, *thinks* about his former experience as a *preparation* toward future times when spiritual consolation will be withdrawn: "I *thought* that I was satisfied . . . I *thought* that it was better . . . I *thought* it

would be better. . . . The power of this thinking, in time of spiritual consolation, to sharpen his response to any such withdrawals of consolation in
the future, is evident.

"Taking New Strength for That Time"

"Taking *new strength* for that time": this is the spiritual equivalent of
the wisdom of Joseph in Egypt, as recounted in the Book of Genesis (chap.
41). Joseph looks into the future and stores up resources during the seven
years of plenty, when these resources are not needed, for the seven years of
deprivation to follow when these stored resources will be vitally important
for sustaining life itself. In like manner, Ignatius tells us that in spiritual
consolation, when we are not in spiritual need, we are to take such "new
strength" for "that time" of spiritual desolation which will, at some point,
follow upon the present spiritual consolation.

Ignatius's statement is brief and he does not further develop here the
ways of taking such new strength. Toner affirms that the context of this
tenth rule explains why. In the previous five rules Ignatius has given us a
series of guidelines on how to resist spiritual desolation when we are *in
such desolation*; his counsel now regarding "taking new strength" to resist
future desolation when we are *in spiritual consolation*, Toner says, "would
surely include recalling and getting clear in our minds the practical directions given in Rules I:5–9 [rules 5 to 9] so that we will not be at a loss when
desolation comes."[10]

Toner himself proposes several such ways of "taking new strength"
toward resisting future spiritual desolation while we are in spiritual consolation. We will outline the ways he suggests, expanding somewhat upon
them and adding others to them.[11] This list of ways is indicative only, without intending to be exhaustive.

Prayer of Petition for Strength in Future Spiritual Desolation

In his sixth rule Ignatius called us to *prayer of petition* during spiritual
desolation, asking of God the help we need in the moment to resist the desolation. We may make this same prayer of petition *before* the desolation
begins, when we are in spiritual consolation; enveloped in the warmth and
light of God's closeness, we ask for the help we will need when spiritual
desolation returns once more. This prayer may take very individual forms.
We may be conscious of the ways in which spiritual desolation most easily
gains hold of us: the particular tactics "the enemy is ordinarily accustomed" to adopt in our regard. We may ask, then, for strength in these
specific areas.

Meditation on Truths That Will Sustain in Spiritual Desolation

This also is a counsel that Ignatius offered us in his sixth rule: to meditate, when in the darkness of spiritual desolation, on the truths of faith that reinforce within us the conviction of God's faithful love. This too can be done in time of spiritual consolation, *before* the spiritual desolation comes, "taking new strength for that time." Such meditation is, in fact, easier in time of spiritual consolation, when that love is not only believed but also *felt* so warmly.

Alice meditates on Psalm 23 in her time of spiritual desolation; and the words, "The Lord is my shepherd; there is nothing I shall want," lift her heart and lighten her spiritual darkness. Recalling Ignatius's tenth rule, she may also meditate on these words when in spiritual consolation, *before* the desolation begins. She is most likely to find, then, that these words sustain her more powerfully when the desolation does come; her darkness will be less dark and less lasting. She is, in this way, "taking new strength" for facing future desolation.

Consideration of the Value of Spiritual Desolation for Growth

We may choose, *when we feel God's consoling love* in our hearts, to think of all that Ignatius has said about the value of spiritual desolation for spiritual growth, if only we will resist it. When consoled, we may consider that God permits such desolation for reasons of love, that without it we would remain spiritual children, that through the trial of desolation we grow in learning, in evangelical humility, and in spiritual maturity in general. These truths are more readily grasped and accepted when considered through the light and warmth of spiritual consolation than if seen only in time of spiritual desolation. Spiritual consolation is the time of clarity, when "the good spirit guides and counsels us more." If, in our time of light, we think of the fruitfulness of spiritual desolation when faithfully resisted, this conviction is more likely to support us once desolation returns.

Reflection on Past Personal Growth through Spiritual Desolation

Spiritual desolation, by its very nature, is difficult to bear. In times of such desolation, because we are so close to it and so affected by it, we may not easily perceive that God is offering us growth through this experience. The gift given by God through spiritual desolation is often more easily seen after some time has passed; it is also more readily perceived when we feel God's love once again in time of spiritual consolation. Then we more readily grasp what we could not so easily recognize during the time of the spiritual desolation itself: how we were moved through it to take helpful spiritual decisions, to speak with a spiritually competent person, to make certain changes in our prayer, our service, and similar growth-giving spiritual actions. We may also realize, with heartfelt gratitude, that the blessing of these new spiritual steps is with us yet.

In time of spiritual consolation, we can choose to reflect on the times, over the years, when God has given us growth through the trial of spiritual desolation. If we do so, then, when spiritual desolation returns, we will stand more firmly in the trial; we will more readily trust that though we cannot see it now in the darkness of the moment, God, as in the past, is once more offering us spiritual growth. Experience teaches how helpful this reflection on past progress through desolation can be toward rendering future spiritual desolation easier to resist.

Resolution to Make No Changes in Time of Spiritual Desolation

Our point of reference here is Ignatius's fifth rule: "In time of desolation never make a change, but be firm and constant in the proposals and determination in which one was the day preceding such desolation. . . ." We have seen above the grave harm caused by such changes in our spiritual proposals made in time of spiritual desolation. We may presume that in future spiritual desolation we will again be tempted to make similar changes. If, in time of spiritual consolation, we look ahead to future spiritual desolation and put ourselves on guard against making such changes, we will the more easily avoid them when in the desolation itself. One way to put ourselves on guard consists of recalling any such changes we may have made in the past and their consequences. The resulting clarity will assist us in avoiding the repetition of such changes in the future.

Review of These Ignatian Rules

What is clear on the written page is often more difficult to identify amid the pressures and occupations of daily life. Unless we keep these rules at our spiritual fingertips we will find it difficult to project the clarity they offer onto the many particular spiritual situations we encounter in a fast-paced day. If *when we need them less*, during a peaceful time of spiritual consolation, we choose to reflect regularly on these rules, then, *when we need them more*, in time of spiritual desolation, we are more likely to remember them and to apply them effectively. The ways of ensuring such ongoing consideration of these rules are as individual as the persons who choose them: regular reading of Ignatius's text, occasional or set times of reflection on these rules, conversation with others, and the like.[12] If we wish that these rules assist us effectively in daily living, adoption of some such manner of recalling these rules *when we need them less* will benefit us greatly.

Planning for Specific Situations of Spiritual Desolation

Persons seeking God may know that in certain situations they tend to be vulnerable to spiritual desolation. Situations of living together with others, at work, in the parish, in ministry, or in their practices of prayer may trigger such spiritual desolation. They may know that in certain places, at certain times of the year, at certain hours of the day, or faced with certain kinds of stresses, they are more readily prone to spiritual desolation. Again, the age-old spiritual injunction is crucial: "Know thyself!" If, in time of spiritual consolation, in the warm consciousness of God's love, they consider these situations and plan concretely how to respond to them, they are indeed "taking new strength" for such spiritual desolation when it recurs. Specific preparation of this kind can change situations of habitual spiritual desolation into opportunities for growth, infusing new hope in our spiritual journey.[13]

A Portrait of the Tenth Rule

An example will serve to summarize what we have said in this chapter. Martha is a religious woman who has recently recovered her peace after several weeks of intense spiritual desolation. Prayer is once more a time of quiet joy, and Martha now experiences the closeness of God often throughout the day. Spiritual consolation has returned.

Martha recognizes that the issues of community life and ministry that gave rise to spiritual desolation are likely to present themselves again. She decides to do her best, with God's grace, to be better prepared should this spiritual desolation recur. In her daily prayer she asks of God an increased ability to resist such spiritual desolation in the future.

She has found Ignatius's rules helpful in her struggle against spiritual desolation and decides to place them on her desk where she will see them frequently. She also plans to use occasional free moments to focus on one or another of the rules, fixing the rule in her mind and planning how to apply it in times of desolation.

Martha's favorite scriptural text, and the text that most helps her to sense God's faithful love, is Isa 43:1–7: "Fear not, for I have redeemed you; I have called you by name: you are mine. When you pass through the water, I will be with you. . . . When you walk through fire, you shall not be burned. . . . Because you are precious in my eyes and glorious, and because I love you." She plans to read this text daily.

Sunday afternoons are generally her quietest time in the week. Martha decides to find helpful reading about these spiritual struggles and related psychological issues, and, for several weeks at least, to use this quiet time to read and learn more about this topic. Martha further resolves to discuss monthly with her spiritual director how her efforts to prepare are progressing.

In her own personal way, Martha, during a period of spiritual consolation, is employing the counsels we have described for "taking new strength" in time of spiritual consolation and so finding herself prepared when spiritual desolation returns. We can sense that when the spiritual desolation *does* return she will be more alert and more decisive in her resistance to it. The tenth rule, like the preceding rules, contributes to set the captives free.

11

⤳

Spiritual Consolation and
Spiritual Desolation: Finding Our Balance
(Rule 11)

⤳

For, upon this road, to go
down is to go up, and to go
up, to go down.
—John of the Cross

Both Spiritual Movements in a Single Rule

After a set of rules addressed to persons in time of spiritual desolation
(rules 5 to 9) and a rule for those in time of spiritual consolation (rule 10),
Ignatius now gives us a rule in which both spiritual movements appear
together. Rule 11 reads:

Eleventh Rule. The eleventh: let one who is consoled seek to humble
himself and lower himself as much as he can, thinking of how little
he is capable in the time of desolation without such grace or consolation. On the contrary, let one who is in desolation think that he can
do much with God's sufficient grace to resist all his enemies, taking
strength in his Creator and Lord.

Prior to this point in the rules Ignatius has focused on each of these two
spiritual movements individually and counseled us regarding how we are
to *think* and *act* during the one and the other. In his eleventh rule he brings
together the separate pieces and gives us a total picture of the discerning
person, able to maintain a firm spiritual balance amid the ongoing alternations of spiritual consolation and spiritual desolation.

The rule is articulated according to the same principle of contrariety that
we have seen throughout; the two halves of the rule are divided with the

138

now familiar: "On the *contrary*. . . ." Because spiritual consolation and spiritual desolation are contrary to each other, so too the *response* of discerning persons to the one will be the contrary of their response to the other. The eleventh rule describes both responses and, in placing both side by side, highlights the resulting *spiritual balance* toward which Ignatius would guide persons of discernment. We will discuss each response and then examine this balance in a concrete spiritual experience.

In Spiritual Consolation: A Humble Heart

In the first half of this rule, Ignatius speaks to those in spiritual consolation and presents to them both an *attitude* they are to seek and the *manner of seeking it*. The person in spiritual consolation is to seek a humble heart: "let one who is consoled *seek* to *humble* himself and lower himself as much as he can." Ignatius has already taught us that one principal reason for which God permits us to experience spiritual desolation is to anchor us more deeply in evangelical humility (rule 9, third cause). Now, in rule 11, Ignatius returns again to this theme and urges the one in spiritual consolation to "seek" actively this attitude, "as much as he can." Why does he insist so much on this particular spiritual quality of heart?

Certainly humility is blessed in itself and draws upon us the grace of God (1 Pet 5:5). For Ignatius, a humble heart is the rich spiritual soil from which all other virtues spring (*SpirEx*, 146); a heart that is humble is a heart completely open to embrace God's call (*SpirEx*, 167). As always in these rules, however, Ignatius is addressing specific needs in regard to discernment—awareness, understanding, taking action—of the movements in our hearts. A humble heart, he tells us, will assist us in a particular way *in time of spiritual consolation*.

In commenting above on the eighth rule, we cited a text from Julian of Norwich in which she describes repeated alternations of spiritual consolation and spiritual desolation, "again and again, I suppose about twenty times." In her times of spiritual consolation Julian expresses her strong sense of total security in God. Of her first such consolation she writes: "In this delight I was filled full of *everlasting surety*, *powerfully secured* without any painful fear . . . so that there was *nothing upon earth* which could have afflicted me." In her following time of spiritual consolation the same sense of utter security returns: "God gave me again comfort and rest for my soul, delight and security so blessedly and *so powerfully* that there was *no fear, no sorrow, no pain*, physical or spiritual, that one could suffer *which might have disturbed me*."

Julian, in fact, summarizes this entire sequence of recurring spiritual consolation with precisely this sense of spiritual security: "And in the time of joy I could have said with St. Paul: *Nothing* shall separate me from the love of Christ." Spiritual consolation carries with it a joyful feeling of security in God: this feeling is one aspect of God's gift in time of such consolation.

In Julian, this sense of complete security from all fear, sorrow, and pain and the deep feeling that nothing can separate her from the love of Christ is wedded to yet another spiritual attitude of great beauty: her heart, in the midst of her spiritual consolation, is *humble* in the sense Ignatius indicates here. Gladdened as she is by this repeated outpouring of spiritual consolation, Julian knows nonetheless that, just as the intervening spiritual desolations were not due to her sin, "*Nor did I deserve* these feelings of joy, but *our Lord gives it freely* when he wills, and sometimes he allows us to be in sorrow, and both are one love."[1] She does not, in time of spiritual consolation, presume on her own strength or spiritual progress but humbly recognizes that the spiritual consolation she enjoys is God's grace at work in her. When God's gift of love in spiritual consolation is *accepted* by a heart that remains, at the same time, rooted in evangelical *humility*, a great and solid spiritual energy for growth is set free. We sense precisely such energy in Julian.

What will happen if God's gift of security in time of spiritual consolation is *accepted* by those so blessed but *without* a corresponding effort to seek, "as much as [they] can," to maintain a humble heart? Then, like Peter on Holy Thursday evening, filled with great love for the Lord and rejoicing in the warmth of the Lord's friendship, their very sense of security may expose them to ill-considered spiritual steps with a consequent risk of spiritual collapse (Mark 14:27–31).[2] Peter will indeed come to be rooted in humility but only after his painful fall when fear overcomes the personal strength on which he presumed in his time of closeness to the Lord (Mark 14:66–72). A heart that welcomes with joy the grace of spiritual consolation and, simultaneously, seeks as much as it can to remain humble will not presume in this way on its own energies and so will be spared the pain of such failures.

In the first half of rule 11, Ignatius wishes to alert us to this risk of presuming on our own energies when warmed by the joy of spiritual consolation. In counseling us to strive to maintain humble hearts in time of spiritual consolation, he points out the way to conserve safely the work of God in us through such consolation and effectively avoid the pitfalls of naively adopted spiritual measures.

This, then, is the *attitude* that Ignatius counsels in time of spiritual consolation: a humble heart. *How* are we to attain such a heart when in the joy of spiritual consolation? Ignatius writes: "Let one who is consoled seek to humble himself and lower himself as much as he can, *thinking* of how little he is capable in the time of desolation without such grace or consolation." Again, as in earlier rules, the path toward such humility lies in the choice to *think* in a certain way, while we are in spiritual consolation.

The one who is in spiritual consolation is to think "of *how little he is capable* in the *time of desolation* without such grace or consolation." If Julian *thinks* in her time of spiritual consolation when, she writes, "I could have said with St. Paul: Nothing shall separate me from the love of Christ," that in her time of *spiritual desolation* she "could have said with St. Peter: Lord, save me, I am perishing," her heart will the more easily remain humble in her present spiritual consolation, as she rejoices in God's love. To think back, *when in spiritual consolation*, on how we conducted ourselves in past spiritual desolation—whether we remained faithful to or relinquished our prayer, whether we persevered in our proposals or made changes to them, whether we used the means to resist, worked to remain patient, thought of future spiritual consolation, or failed to do these things—will give us a true gauge of our spiritual energies and teach us of our very real need for the Lord's continuing help. In this way we are protected, *while in spiritual consolation*, from experiences parallel to Peter's in Mark 14: delight in the closeness of the Lord and good-willed but naïve presumption on our spiritual energies, followed by painful failure.

How strong were we, in fact, during the darkness and sadness of past spiritual desolation?[3] Would we have said, like Alice, that, "it all seems hopeless and meaningless"? Did we, like Jane, "grow discouraged" and feel "disquietude, confusion, and a sense of discouragement"? The choice, when in spiritual consolation, to think back to past experiences of spiritual desolation and "of how little [we were] capable in the time of desolation without such grace or consolation," is, Ignatius tells us, an effective way to root us in a fruitful humility.[4] Such humility safeguards and confirms the gift of the spiritual consolation presently enjoyed.

This *thinking*, like the earlier kinds of thinking Ignatius counsels, will not arise spontaneously; a choice must be made to think in this way: "let one who is consoled *seek* to humble himself and lower himself *as much as he can*, thinking of. . . ." Again, such thinking becomes habitual through repeated striving to put this rule into practice.

In Spiritual Desolation: A Trusting Heart

If Julian maintains a fruitfully humble heart in her *spiritual consolation*, no less does her heart remain quietly trustful in her *spiritual desolation*. Certainly, her spiritual desolation is dark and intense: "Then I was changed, and *abandoned* to myself, *oppressed* and *weary* of my life and ruing myself, so that *I hardly had the patience to go on living*. I felt that there was *no ease or comfort* for me except faith, hope and love, and truly I felt very little of this." In her repeated times of spiritual desolation, writes Julian, "I could have said with St. Peter: Lord, save me, *I am perishing*."

If there is, in spiritual consolation, a feeling of spiritual security, in spiritual desolation the exact contrary is true; here there is a sense of great spiritual *insecurity*. Julian hardly has "the patience to go on living," and cries out, with Peter, "I am perishing!" This *feeling* of abandonment and helplessness, with its accompanying insinuation of inevitable spiritual ruin, is familiar to all who have undergone spiritual desolation.

Julian, however, now becomes "myself-reflecting-on-myself-in desolation." Calmly, and in the light of faith, she ponders the meaning of both her spiritual consolation and her spiritual desolation. Though she feels the pain of the spiritual desolation, she views this with serenity and without self-blame, as part of God's providence in her life:

> This vision was shown *to teach me* to understand that some souls profit by experiencing this, to be comforted at one time, and at another to fail and to be left to themselves. God *wishes us to know* that he keeps us safe all the time, in sorrow and in joy; and sometimes a man is left to himself *for the profit of his soul*, although his *sin is not always the cause*. For in this time I committed no sin for which I ought to have been left to myself, for it was so sudden. Nor did I deserve these feelings of joy, but our Lord gives it freely when he wills, and sometimes he allows us to be in sorrow, *and both are one love*.[5]

Julian here exemplifies the second half of the spiritual balance that Ignatius describes in rule 11: she *thinks* about her spiritual desolation with faith and in a way that gives her courage to persevere while it lasts. Through this thinking, she stands firm regardless of the *feeling* that she can hardly go on living in such spiritual desolation. Ignatius, as already in rules 7 and 8, once more calls on those in spiritual desolation to *think* in this strengthening way: "On the contrary, let one who is in desolation *think* that he can do much. . . ."

Although in the second half of rule 11 Ignatius returns to ground already covered (rules 7 and 8: how we are to think in time of spiritual desolation), a brief review of his words here will be helpful. The language is charged with hope, a characteristic of all the thoughts that Ignatius counsels for the time of spiritual desolation.

The one in spiritual desolation is to "*think* that he can do *much* with God's *sufficient grace* to *resist all* his enemies, *taking strength* in his Creator and Lord." In spiritual desolation, precisely when we feel moved, like Julian, to cry out to the Lord, "I am perishing!," when we *feel* that we can do so little, then it is that we are to *think* that, on the contrary, we can do *much*. We are to think that we can do much because, though like Julian we feel abandoned, nonetheless God's *sufficient grace* is always with us: we will have all the divine help we need to *resist* in the trial. Remarkably, we are to think that God's grace suffices so that we can resist *all* our spiritual enemies, without exception. Through all of these thoughts and the actions to which they lead us, we will be *taking strength* in our Creator and Lord, a strength that sets us firmly on the path toward God.

Neither Naively "High" Nor Despairingly "Low"

Although each half of the eleventh rule contains a rich teaching in itself, the real power of this rule lies in the juxtaposition of the two halves in a single rule: "let one who is *consoled* seek . . . *thinking* of how *little* he is capable. . . . Let one who is in *desolation think* that he can do *much*. . . ." Discerning persons, in welcoming the gift of spiritual consolation and in striving to resist in time of spiritual desolation, preserve a kind of spiritual equilibrium. *Humble* in time of spiritual consolation ("lowering" them-selves when spiritually "high") and *trusting* in time of spiritual desolation ("raising" themselves when spiritually "low"), they progress faithfully through the alternations of these two contrary movements with a certain spiritual balance and maturity. This balance is the growing fruit of con-stantly renewed efforts to live in spiritual consolation with such humility and in spiritual desolation with such trust. *All that Ignatius has said thus far* in his rules is intended to assist us in achieving precisely this balance.

Ignatius's words to Teresa Rejadell aptly describe the spiritual balance he proposes in his eleventh rule:

> If we are in *consolation* we should *lower and humble* ourselves, and should *think* that soon the trial of temptation will come; if *tempta-tion, darkness or sadness* comes, we should act *contrary* to it without allowing the unpleasant impressions it causes to affect us in any way, and *wait with patience for the consolation* of the Lord, which will cast out all our troubles and darkness.[6]

The indispensable presupposition of such balance is *daily spiritual awareness*. All faithful persons will experience the continuing fluctuations of spiritual consolation and spiritual desolation; such experience alone does not form the discerning person. What makes this spiritual balance possible is the continual transition from "myself-in" to "myself-reflecting-on-myself-in" spiritual consolation and spiritual desolation.[7] As we said from the start of our reflections, the choice to live with such ongoing spir-itual awareness is the beginning of discernment and the gateway to spiri-tual freedom.[8]

Maintaining Spiritual Balance: An Experience

In these pages we have referred often to Jane in her days of retreat. We have spoken both of her first days of spiritual consolation and her later, sixth day of spiritual desolation. At this point in the rules, when Ignatius brings together both spiritual movements in a total picture, it will be helpful to examine the entirety of her retreat. A look at her eight-day experience as a whole will allow us to see this total picture in a concrete setting and to explore how the wisdom of rule 11 might assist Jane and all dedicated people who experience the alternations of spiritual consolation and spiritual desolation. It will also permit us to illustrate yet again the type of thinking and the questions that discerning persons must consider. This experience takes place in the setting of a retreat; the spiritual dynamics it contains apply equally to every setting in which committed people live their journey of faith.

The retreat opens with a note of hopeful anticipation:

Day 1: Jane begins the retreat in *peace*, with a *quiet expectation* of meeting Christ. She reflects, as directed, on chapter 55 of Isaiah and is *attracted* to verse 1: "All you who are thirsty, come to the water!" and verse 12: "Yes, in joy you shall depart, in peace you shall be brought back." She is *confident* that the Lord will nourish and refresh her for her ministry.[9]

Jane appears to begin her retreat with a gentle movement of consolation. As an exercise in discernment we may raise the question: is this spiritual or nonspiritual consolation? The "quiet expectation of meeting *Christ*," her attraction to a *scriptural text*, and her confidence that the *Lord* will nourish and refresh her, all indicate the presence of spiritual consolation. Jane's retreat continues:

Day 2: In praying over the assigned Scripture verse, "Come to me . . . I will refresh you" (Matt. 11:28), Jane experiences an inner cleansing and refreshment as if she were drawn into a fountain of fire and water. She is filled with *wonder* and *joy*. The *blissful feeling* remains with her throughout the day, and she experiences the *nearness of Jesus* as she ponders other assigned Scripture readings and listens to what the Lord is saying to her.

We are standing, once more, on holy ground. Jane's spiritual consolation has become intense, and through it she experiences "an inner cleansing and refreshment." God is pouring out his gifts upon her in her time of spiritual consolation; the whole description of this second day tells us that Jane is indeed *accepting*, drinking in fully, the grace of this spiritual consolation and that it is richly effective in her. In this, Jane is acting exactly as the discerning person is called to act when God is working in time of spiritual consolation.

We have no indication, however, that Jane, after her deeply consoled prayer and while the "blissful feeling remains with her throughout the day," remembers at all the *thinking* that Ignatius has recommended in rules 10 and 11 for those in spiritual consolation: "let the one who is in consolation *think* how he *will conduct himself in the desolation* which will *come after*, taking new strength for that time" (rule 10), and "let one who is consoled seek to *humble himself* and lower himself as much as he can, *thinking* of *how little he is capable* in the *time of desolation* without such grace or consolation" (rule 11). We note here a point that we have made repeatedly in commenting on Ignatius's counsel to *think* in these ways when in spiritual consolation: such thinking will not arise spontaneously. Jane and all other persons seeking God become capable of such thinking through reflection on just such situations as this and the consequent effort to apply Ignatius's rules increasingly as similar situations arise in daily living.

Thus far, then, Jane's retreat is abundantly blessed, and she is growing spiritually through a grace-filled experience of spiritual consolation. Yet her awareness is totally circumscribed by the experience of the day; she does not consider what has preceded this time of spiritual consolation or what may follow it.

The third day comes:

> Day 3: She arises early next morning quietly hoping for similar experiences of the Lord. She prays over the assigned section of the Canticle of Canticles and experiences a *sweet joy* at the thought of the Lord's love for her. She then decides to prolong her praying periods from an hour to an hour and a half each so as to become more immersed in Christ. She does not inform her director about this plan. She spends seven hours that day in prayer. Her *excitement* grows. That night she cannot fall asleep.

On the morning of her third day Jane experiences "sweet joy at the thought of the Lord's love for her." Clearly, her spiritual consolation of the previous day continues. As the hours of the day pass, "her excitement grows." We may legitimately raise the question: is the "excitement" she feels also *spiritual* consolation? We have no clear sign that it is. On the contrary, we begin to sense that a certain emotional excess and strain have entered her retreat.

On this third day, as Jane increases her prayer to seven hours, her forgetfulness of rule 11 is even more strikingly manifest: "Let one who is consoled seek to *humble himself and lower himself as much as he can, thinking* of how *little* he is capable in the time of *desolation without such grace or consolation.*" Far from humbling herself and thinking of how little she is capable without the grace of such spiritual consolation, Jane, with good will but without adequate reflection, is doing just the opposite. She is stretching her energies, doing more on this day than on the earlier days of the retreat. We sense that she has adopted a rhythm of prayer she is unlikely to sustain. The wisdom of Ignatius's counsel to "seek," "as much as [we] can," to maintain a humble heart when in spiritual consolation is plainly evident here.

Her fourth day shows a change:

> Day 4: Jane gets up with a bad headache, feeling exhausted and under strain. She cannot pray well. *All joy* has *evaporated*. She is *tired* and *sad* and *moody*. Finally in the evening she tells the director about her action of the previous day and its results. The director advises cutting down on prayer time and resting more.

All consolation, spiritual and nonspiritual, has now disappeared. Jane is "tired and sad and moody," obvious signs of desolation. Is it spiritual or nonspiritual desolation? We have no clear indication that this tiredness, sadness, and moodiness have direct and immediate reference to Jane's life of faith, and it seems most likely that Jane is experiencing nonspiritual desolation here. Apparently overcoming some reluctance to do so, she wisely speaks of all this with her retreat director, who proposes a more prudent balance in her daily rhythm of retreat.[10]

The fifth day remains difficult:

> Day 5: She follows the advice, prays less but still has *no enthusiasm* and is filled with *gloom*.

Jane faithfully follows the counsel of her retreat director and corrects the imbalance of the previous days. Nonetheless, her nonspiritual desolation does not pass immediately, and the day is flat and heavy.

We come now to the difficult sixth day already mentioned:

> Day 6: At her morning prayer she becomes very much *disturbed*. She begins to *doubt* the *Lord's presence* to her even in the opening days of the retreat. Probably, she thinks, she should attribute everything to her overactive imagination. *Who is she* to be given a taste of the *sweetness of the Lord*? She begins to grow *discouraged* at the thought that she is *not meant for a deep prayer life*. Her desire for God is just an *illusion*. The rest of the day is one of *disquietude, confusion*, and a sense of *discouragement*.

Jane's nonspiritual desolation has become a springboard for intense spiritual desolation, claiming power over the past and the future. As we read this account we note two things: first, Jane's *spontaneous* reaction of deep discouragement in her time of spiritual desolation and, second, her *forgetfulness* of every one of Ignatius's guidelines (rules 5 through 9, and the second half of rule 11) for resisting in time of spiritual desolation.

Now that Jane is experiencing spiritual desolation, the second half of the balance Ignatius proposes in rule 11 becomes crucial. On this day, when the darkness of spiritual desolation surrounds her, Jane urgently needs to employ Ignatius's directive: "let one who is in desolation *think* that he can *do much* with God's *sufficient grace* to resist *all* his enemies, *taking strength* in his Creator and Lord." Though this kind of thinking will not come spontaneously and though she must think this way *in the face of* the spiritual desolation that seeks to dishearten her, if Jane can remember rule 11 and strive to think in the way described, she will cease to be helplessly oppressed by the spiritual desolation. The desolation will pass in the time God chooses ("let him think that he will *soon* be consoled," rule 8), but Jane will already begin to possess that trusting heart which saves us from feeling despairingly low in spiritual desolation and preserves our spiritual balance in time of such desolation.

The seventh day follows:

Day 7: The director urges her to trust her earlier experiences and to hope in the Lord that he will bring good even from this desolation. She directs her to pray over John 14, especially the opening verses, "Do not let your hearts be troubled." She prays quietly over the passages, rests more, takes walks in the garden.

Jane now acquires a new calmness of heart. There is no clear sign in the description of this day of either spiritual consolation or spiritual desolation. It appears that the spiritual desolation lifts as Jane speaks with her director, follows the director's wise counsel, and adopts a healthy rhythm for the day.

Jane reaches her final day of retreat:

Day 8: On the closing day she returns to chapter 55 of Isaiah: "Come to the water . . . in joy you shall depart." A calm settles on her mind and spirit. She *knows* that *she is loved by God.* She also knows at her deepest level that the experience of the second day was genuine. She has become more aware of her weaknesses, especially her undisciplined imagination and her rapidly fluctuating emotions. She prays for light and strength to manage these and become more balanced emotionally. She ends the retreat in *quiet gratitude.* She looks forward now *in hope* to her ministry—a more wise and serene woman.

Spiritual consolation has returned. The spiritual desolation that God has permitted in Jane's retreat has served as a time of learning for her: she "has become more aware" and is now "more wise" (ninth rule, second cause). She begins to consider the future and "prays for light and strength" to grow in specific areas of her life. We sense that Jane now has a humble heart and is less likely to presume on her human and spiritual energies. If Jane applies rule 11 as she concludes her retreat, now, in her renewed time of spiritual consolation, would be the time to "seek" this stabilizing humility still more, "as much as [she] can." In this way she will further consolidate the spiritual balance Ignatius describes in rule 11; she will continue to grow in spiritual maturity.

What we have seen in the context of a retreat—the alternations of spiritual consolation and spiritual desolation, and the humble and trusting heart that we are called to preserve in the one and the other—applies equally to the spiritual fluctuations of daily life. If Alice seeks to maintain a *humble* heart during her happy and spiritually consoled years in her former parish, and equally strives to maintain a *trusting* heart during her spiritually desolate year in her new parish, the resulting spiritual balance will strengthen her entire journey. If all dedicated people, in the circumstances of life to which God has called them, seek to maintain this balance of a humble heart in spiritual consolation and a trusting heart in spiritual desolation, then they will find themselves progressing safely and perseveringly toward God. As always in these rules, it is toward just such freedom that Ignatius would guide us.

12

⤳

Standing Firm in the Beginnings (Rule 12)

⤳

And yet he felt that now, at this very moment . . . his inner life was, as it were, wavering in the balance, and that the slightest effort would tip the scale to one side or the other. And he made the effort, calling to the God Whose presence he had felt in his soul the day before, and that God instantly responded.

—Leo Tolstoy

A New Stage in the Rules

Thus far in the rules Ignatius has centered on spiritual consolation and spiritual desolation, focusing especially on freeing us from bondage to spiritual desolation. In the final three rules, his language changes, and Ignatius does not refer explicitly to spiritual consolation or spiritual desolation again. He does continue to highlight the enemy's deceptions with the unchanging purpose of freeing us from the spiritual traps contained therein. In rule 12 Ignatius speaks of the enemy's *temptations*; in rule 13 of the enemy's *deceits*; and in rule 14 of the enemy's *attacks*.

Ignatius, in discussing *spiritual desolation*, has already referred to *temptation* in rules 5 ("disquiet from various agitations and temptations") and 7 ("so that he may resist the various agitations and temptations of the enemy"). A distinction may be made between the two in that, whereas spiritual desolation always involves *painful affectivity* (sadness, disquiet, hopelessness, agitation, and similar feelings), the same need not be true of temptation. Temptation of its nature is simply a deceptive suggestion of the enemy. It may come without affectivity ("Why not let prayer go until later?") or, in fact, be accompanied by a sense of attraction.

At the same time, this distinction should not be overstressed. As rules 4 and 7 indicate, the affective "agitation" of spiritual desolation is a fertile

149

seedbed for temptation, generally not far away in times of spiritual desolation. Both spiritual desolation and temptation are the work of the enemy, and both have the same ultimate purpose: to harm us spiritually and to hinder us from "rising from good to better in the service of God our Lord." Although in these final three rules the focus shifts slightly, we remain essentially in the same spiritual arena.

A glance at rules 12, 13, and 14 further reveals an alteration in literary style with respect to the earlier rules. Each of these three rules begins with a metaphor, which is then applied to illustrate *a quality of the enemy's deceptive action* in us. In rule 12, Ignatius employs the somewhat problematic metaphor of a woman fighting with a man; in rule 13, that of a false lover; and in rule 14, that of an astute leader of a group of brigands. These three metaphors illustrate respectively the enemy's *essential weakness* when we respond firmly, the quality of *secrecy* with which the enemy seeks to shroud his deceits, and the enemy's *keen sense of our weakest point* in his attacks.

Having clarified for us how the enemy operates, Ignatius then specifies what our *response* must be to each of these qualities of the enemy's action.[1] Our way of responding, Ignatius tells us, will determine much of the subsequent course of the temptation, deception, or attack: whether these will diminish or increase their hold upon us. As spiritual experience amply demonstrates, each of these three rules is highly beneficial to faithful persons. Alerted to these three specific characteristics of the enemy's deceptions, they will recognize these deceptions more readily and counter them more effectively in daily living.

The Metaphor of Rule Twelve

The metaphor Ignatius adopts in rule 12 requires, for obvious reasons, some discussion. We will present the rule exactly as Ignatius does and then examine the issues involved. He writes:

Twelfth Rule. The twelfth: the enemy acts like a woman in being weak when faced with strength and strong when faced with weakness. For, as it is proper to a woman, when she is fighting with some man, to lose heart and to flee when the man confronts her firmly, and, on the contrary, if the man begins to flee, losing heart, the anger, vengeance and ferocity of the woman grow greatly and know no bounds, in the same way, it is proper to the enemy to weaken and lose heart, fleeing and ceasing his temptations when the person who is exercising himself in spiritual things confronts the temptations of the enemy firmly, doing what is diametrically opposed to them; and, on the contrary, if the person who is exercising himself begins to be afraid and lose heart in suffering the temptations, there is no beast so fierce on the face of the earth as the enemy of human nature in following out his damnable intention with such growing malice.

Different authors deal with this rule in different ways, but none can avoid the difficulty raised by the figure Ignatius uses here. Thomas Green writes simply: "Like a woman. This is a dangerous comparison to use in our feminist age."[2] What can we say about this?

Daniel Gil, in his treatment of this question, aptly notes that Ignatius is not comparing the enemy simply to a woman but to "a *woman, when she is fighting with some man.*" We are dealing, therefore, with an *unnatural situation*: one that does not describe the true nature of either woman or man, created by God not to battle with each other but to share life in love and mutual service.[3]

The same "unnatural" quality is evident also in the metaphors of rules 13 and 14. The man who loves the woman (rule 13) is not a genuine lover, giving of himself out of authentic love for her and a sincere desire for her happiness. He is, rather, a *false* lover,[4] seeking only to seduce the woman for utterly selfish reasons. Nor is the leader (rule 14) an honorable figure, directing his men in a noble cause, but rather a *thief*, seeking to conquer for the sake of "robbing what he desires."

Since Ignatius, through these three metaphors, is describing the *enemy*, whose *only aim is to harm human persons spiritually*, it is not surprising that this "unnatural" quality be found in each of the three figures he sketches. In these final three rules, in fact, Ignatius amplifies the title of the enemy to "the enemy of human nature," emphasizing that the enemy is *against* what is *natural* to the human person. In these three rules, therefore, Ignatius is not discussing the true nature of women, of those who love, or of those who lead. Rather, in seeking to illustrate three anti-human qualities of the enemy's workings, he describes three unhappy instances in which persons have abandoned the fullness of human stature as intended by God: a woman and a man who fight, rather than assist, each other; a man who "uses" love, the noblest human capacity, in a totally selfish way; and a leader who leads, not to build, but only to destroy and plunder.

Clearly, then, any woman and man whose relationship is harmonious and mutually strengthening, any man who sincerely and with self-giving loves the woman with whom he speaks, and any leader who honestly labors for the good of those he serves would not serve Ignatius's purpose here. Ignatius does not have such persons in mind in the metaphors of these three rules. Because they are living according to the fullness of their human nature, they could not serve to portray the qualities of the one whom Ignatius, in this rule, calls "the enemy of human nature."

Still, as Katherine Dyckman, Mary Garvin, and Elizabeth Liebert write with regard to Ignatius's metaphor in rule 12: "A metaphor must work not only for the teller; it must also function for the receiver."[5] Because this metaphor does not, generally speaking, "function for the receiver" today, the commentator is left with the choice of either changing the metaphor, thus conserving the movement between the two parts of the rule—from metaphor to application—as Ignatius wrote it, or omitting any metaphor entirely, focusing simply on the teaching contained in the second part of the rule. As noted, both approaches are used in commenting on this rule.

One current example of a change in metaphor is David Fleming's metaphor of a spoiled child. If "a person is firm" with such spoiled children, they "give up their petulant ways of acting." If, however, a person "shows indulgence or weakness in any way, [such] children are merciless in trying to get what they want, stomping their feet in defiance or wheedling their way into favor."[6] This metaphor may, in fact, "function for the receiver" more broadly than the original metaphor, and Ignatius's point in rule 12 may indeed be expressed with it. What, then, is that point?

The Application of the Metaphor

Ignatius makes that point clear from the outset of the rule: the enemy is "*weak* when *faced with strength* and *strong* when *faced with weakness*." If we apply Fleming's metaphor, then we have the following: if the persons responsible are *firm* in dealing with spoiled children, such spoiled children cease "their petulant ways of acting." If, on the contrary, the persons responsible are *weak* and simply indulge these petulant ways, then these children can become "merciless in trying to get what they want." The key to how this relational situation will unfold lies in the *response* of these persons when the spoiled children *begin* to act in their petulant ways: a *firm* response causes the behavior to *cease,* and a *weak* response causes the behavior to *increase* beyond measure.

Ignatius then applies the metaphor, first, as an illustration of what will follow when dedicated persons respond *firmly* to the enemy's temptations:

> In the same way, it is proper to the enemy to *weaken and lose heart, fleeing* and *ceasing* his temptations when the person who is exercising himself in spiritual things confronts the temptations of the enemy *firmly,* doing what is *diametrically opposed* to them.

When dedicated persons are *firm* in confronting the temptations of the enemy, doing precisely the *opposite* of what the temptation suggests ("Why not let prayer go until later?" "No, I will pray right now, as planned."), then, says Ignatius, the enemy *weakens, loses heart*, and *ceases* to tempt them. A quick and firm response strips the deceptive temptation of all its power.

Second, Ignatius applies the metaphor as an illustration of what will follow when dedicated persons respond *weakly* to the enemy's temptations:

On the contrary, if the person who is exercising himself begins to be *afraid and lose heart* in suffering the temptations, there is no beast so fierce on the face of the earth as the enemy of human nature in following out his damnable intention with *such growing malice.*

When dedicated persons are *weak* in confronting the temptations of the enemy and begin to be afraid and lose heart ("Why not let prayer go until later?" "Yes, maybe I could. . . . It does seem too much right now. . . . Later will do as well . . ."), then, says Ignatius, the enemy becomes *strong* and the temptation *grows*, acquiring fierce energy and effectiveness. A weak and hesitating response gives the temptation increasing power over the one tempted.

The Essential Weakness of the Enemy

We come, in this way, to the heart of rule 12 and to the quality of the enemy's action that Ignatius wishes above all to highlight. As always in these rules, his message sounds a vibrant call to hope: the enemy, he says, is *essentially weak.* When confronted firmly and decisively, the enemy is weak and helpless. If dedicated persons refuse "to be afraid and lose heart" and choose to do "what is diametrically opposed" to the enemy's temptations, then "it is proper to the enemy to *weaken* and *lose heart, fleeing* and *ceasing* his temptations." When faced resolutely, the fundamental weakness of the enemy is revealed. The enemy is, as Gil affirms, essentially a coward. Like a coward, he will only attack when met with weakness; when resisted firmly, he flees.[7]

The enemy is essentially weak: this is a teaching of great value for all faithful persons seeking God. Often they may have exactly the opposite sense of the enemy and his temptations. They may tend to feel weak and helpless and to consider the enemy's temptations strong, even unbearably so. Such persons may feel almost inevitably fated to surrender to these harmful suggestions ("You can't do it! You are not able to stand firmly and resist. You've failed so often in the past, and you will fail again this time. You are too weak . . ."). Precisely here Ignatius speaks a word of invigorating hope based on solid spiritual truth: the *enemy is essentially weak,* and if dedicated persons are willing to strive humbly and with trust in God's ever-sufficient grace to resist firmly, they will see the enemy "*weaken* and *lose heart, fleeing* and *ceasing* his temptations."

Two observations follow. There is, first, what we might call a "snowball effect" to the enemy's temptations. When a snowball is just beginning to form on a mountainside, a person can put out a finger and stop it; but when it has traveled halfway down the mountain slope, gaining mass and speed along the way, it will be immensely more difficult to stop. Indeed, at this point it may simply overwhelm the person. In the same way, Ignatius says, the enemy's temptations, if resisted firmly *when they first begin*, simply cease. They gain no further strength; they do not increase their hold upon the persons so tempted. When, however, these persons respond indecisively, allowing the temptation to linger, then the temptation may grow, "snowballing" and assailing them with growing strength. The longer the enemy's suggestion is allowed to remain, the harder it will be to resist.

This fact leads, second, to a key practical observation: *the crucial moment* in resisting the temptations of the enemy *is when they first begin. Everything else* will depend on how faithful persons respond at this initial point. If they respond firmly when the suggestion first arises, doing, as Ignatius teaches, just the opposite ("Why not let prayer go until later?" "No, I will pray right now, as I had planned."), then the snowball effect will never occur. They will have overcome the temptation when it was still possible to do so by spiritually "putting out a finger." If, on the contrary, they allow the harmful suggestion to remain in their hearts ("Why not let prayer go until later?" "Yes, maybe I could pray later. . . . It does seem too much right now. . . . Later will do as well . . ."), it will gain power and they are likely to succumb to it.[8]

If at such times these persons, instructed by the spiritual wisdom of Ignatius's twelfth rule, recall the *essential weakness* of the enemy, realize that now, when the deceptive suggestion *first presents itself*, is the crucial moment of decision, and strive immediately and firmly to do exactly the *opposite* of what enemy suggests, they are unlikely to be harmed by such temptations. They will be liberated from these deceptions and will progress unerringly toward God.

"He Overcame the Temptation and Remained at Peace"

Some examples will illustrate what we have said thus far in this chapter. In his letter to Teresa Rejadell, Ignatius describes the snowball effect of the enemy's action when not resisted firmly. When the enemy "sets up all possible obstacles to turn us aside from the way on which we have entered," the further progress of his workings depends on our response to his *initial* activity:

> Not only this, but *if he sees that we are weak* and much humbled by these harmful thoughts, he *goes on* to suggest that we are entirely forgotten by God our Lord, and *leads us* to think that we are quite separated from him and that all that we have done and all that we desire to do is entirely worthless. He thus *endeavors to bring us* to a state of general discouragement.[9]

"If we are *weak* and *much humbled*":[10] if dedicated persons do not respond firmly at the start, then, as Ignatius tells us in his twelfth rule, the enemy does not limit himself to his initial action: "he *goes on* . . . and *leads us*. . . . He thus *endeavors to bring us*. . . ." This is the snowball effect of the enemy's action when such persons fail to respond decisively *as that action begins*. The enemy's workings, when not resisted and allowed to snowball in this way, lead ultimately to "a state of general discouragement"; such an interior state, obviously, exposes us to great spiritual harm. Ignatius, therefore, further writes to Teresa:

> We can thus see what causes our fear and weakness: it is a too-prolonged gaze at such times on our miseries. We allow ourselves to be laid low by his misleading suggestions. For this reason it is necessary for us to be aware of our opponent.

"*We allow ourselves to be laid low* by his misleading suggestions." It is precisely from this bondage that Ignatius would free Teresa and all who love the Lord, reminding them that the enemy is *essentially weak* and that, if they will strive firmly to resist "his misleading suggestions" *from the start*, they will be set free from them.

The following account exemplifies this snowball dynamic at work in the course of a day of prayer:[11]

> Steve has completed seven years of seminary training and is on the verge of ordination to the diaconate, as a preparation for priesthood. He has reached, therefore, the moment of definitive decision for the clerical state of life. His preparation for ordination includes an eight-day Ignatian retreat, to be made a few weeks before the ceremony. Steve welcomes the opportunity to pray more deeply as he approaches this key moment in his life and willingly prepares for these days of silence and recollection. Steve is an occasional smoker and, before the retreat, decides to abstain from smoking during the eight days of retreat.
>
> The retreat begins and Steve dedicates himself to the daily rhythm of liturgical prayer with the other seminarians, personal prayer with Scripture, and his individual meeting with the director. He finds the silence helpful and enjoys the setting of natural beauty that surrounds the retreat house. He experiences times of spiritual consolation in prayer and an overall sense of well-being in the retreat.
>
> After supper on the fourth day, Steve finds that he has lost his former sense of peace. He goes for a walk, but a vague interior disquiet persists. Steve decides to smoke a single cigarette and does so. He then goes to his room for his final hour of prayer that evening, unhappy that he has not maintained his resolve to avoid smoking during the retreat. As he begins his prayer, he continues to feel restless and ill at ease.
>
> The prayer is distracted and dry, and Steve, finding it difficult, ends

the prayer period after forty-five minutes. He awakens late the next morning and barely arrives in time for Morning Prayer with the other seminarians. He continues with the times of prayer as planned but finds them empty and burdensome. God seems far away and Steve becomes increasingly frustrated as he strives to pray. A thought comes to him: "You are about to be ordained a deacon, and you wish to become a priest. Look at you! You can't even keep a simple resolution not to smoke for eight days. You can't complete an hour of prayer as planned. You are unable to pray with any fruit at all, after all these years of training. If you can't even do these simple things, how are you ever going to handle the responsibilities of priesthood for the rest of your life?"

In the early afternoon, Steve meets as usual with the retreat director and shares openly with the director all that he has experienced since the day before. The sharing relieves his frustration and doubts, and the director helps Steve to discern the spiritual movements at work in him. Steve recovers his peace, continues his retreat with his habitual good will, and, a few weeks later, is ordained a deacon. His ordination is the beginning of a rewarding year of diaconate and leads, later, to a fruitful priesthood.

Steve is clearly a dedicated person, seeking to love and serve the Lord. On the evening of his fourth day of retreat, however, he experiences what is at least nonspiritual desolation: "he has lost his former sense of peace . . . a vague inner disquiet persists . . . he continues to feel restless and ill at ease. . . ." Steve, apparently, is spiritually unaware at this point, unable to name what he is feeling as desolation and even less able to discern whether it is spiritual or nonspiritual desolation. In his time of desolation, Steve makes two changes to earlier proposals: he sets aside a resolve taken before the retreat began and shortens his hour of prayer (*SpirEx*, 13).

By the following morning the "vague inner disquiet" has plainly become spiritual desolation and has developed into a generalized feeling. Steve feels completely helpless at prayer and experiences a growing frustration. Finally, *on the threshold of ordination*, his *very vocation* is called into doubt: "If you can't even do these simple things, how are you ever going to handle the responsibilities of priesthood for the rest of your life?" We are not far at this point from the "state of general discouragement" that Ignatius describes to Teresa Rejadell. The *snowball effect* of the enemy's action is very clear as the hours of this spiritual sequence unfold. Steve's experience indicates that the snowball effect need not require much time: it may occur within a few minutes, over several hours (as it does for Steve here), or over weeks and months. The key is always the same: to strive to resist the deceptive suggestions of the enemy as close to their beginnings as we can. In the light of the twelfth rule, growth in discernment signifies an increasing ability to discern—to be aware, understand, and take action—at the *very beginnings* of the enemy's workings.

This is a story of success. Steve does not give in to the vocational doubt he experiences but perseveres faithfully in the retreat and receives ordination, "the beginning of a rewarding year of diaconate," which leads "to a fruitful priesthood." His willingness to speak openly with the director about his struggle breaks the grip of the spiritual desolation and of the temptations of the enemy. Nonetheless, we may surmise that had Steve been firm in maintaining his proposals on that evening when the *first* suggestion to change those proposals surfaced, the subsequent snowball effect might never have occurred. For, "it is proper to the enemy to *weaken* and *lose heart, fleeing* and *ceasing his temptations* when the person who is exercising himself in spiritual things *confronts the temptations of the enemy firmly*, doing what is *diametrically opposed* to them." Steve, with the help of his director, is now able "to discern the spiritual movements at work in him" with new clarity. His trial has become a "lesson," and he has taken a significant step toward becoming a spiritually discerning person.

Ignatius, in his twelfth rule, writes of what he himself has experienced. In his *Autobiography* he describes an incident from his early days in Manresa, shortly after his conversion:

> Until this time he had remained always in nearly the same interior state of great and steady happiness. . . . During those days . . . a harsh thought came to trouble him by pointing out the hardships of his life, as if someone were saying within his soul, "How will you be able to endure this life for the seventy years you have yet to live?" Believing that the thought came from the enemy, he answered inwardly with great vehemence, "O miserable being! Can you promise me an hour of life?" So he overcame the temptation and remained at peace.[12]

As soon as the "harsh thought" comes "to trouble him" Ignatius responds "with great vehemence." His resistance to the temptation is immediate, energetic, and decisive; *and the temptation ceases*. There is no snowball effect, no "state of general discouragement"; on the contrary, Ignatius remains "at peace." The essential weakness of the enemy in his temptations is clearly evident here. Ignatius's twelfth rule, like all the earlier rules, is born not of speculation but of experience. If dedicated persons endeavor to respond in this same firm way to the deceptions of the enemy, they, like Ignatius, will find themselves freed from these deceptions and will, also like Ignatius, remain "at peace."

In one of the early *Lives* of Francis of Assisi we read:

> The saint, therefore, made it a point to keep himself in joy of heart and to preserve the unction of the Spirit and the "oil of gladness" [Ps

45:7]. He avoided with the greatest care the miserable illness of dejection, so that if he felt it creeping over his mind *even a little*, he would have recourse *very quickly* to prayer. For he would say: "If the servant of God, as may happen, is disturbed in any way, he should rise immediately to pray and he should remain in the presence of the heavenly Father until he "restores unto him the joy of salvation." [Ps 51:12][13]

Francis, too, seeks to respond quickly and decisively to the first, small beginnings of disquiet: "if he felt it creeping over his mind *even a little*, he would have recourse *very quickly* to prayer." This immediate, prayerful, and resolute response to an enemy who is "weak when faced with strength," renders a snowball effect highly unlikely. In this response, Francis practices precisely what Ignatius teaches in the twelfth rule, a teaching that enables us to shatter much of the enemy's ability to hold us in bondage. Through it, like Francis, we abide "in joy of heart" and preserve within us "the unction of the Spirit and the oil of gladness."

13

⤳

Breaking the Spiritual Silence (Rule 13)

⤳

The Christ in his own heart is weaker than the Christ in the word of his brother; his own heart is uncertain, his brother's is sure.

—Dietrich Bonhoeffer

Communication and Spiritual Freedom

It is not good for us to be alone (Gen 2:18). This biblical affirmation, applicable to our human nature in general, is true of the spiritual life and, in a particular way, of discernment of spirits. We have already noted that, for Ignatius, communication with one knowledgeable in discernment is always a constitutive part of discernment of spirits. Through instruction and assistance in discerning from such a person we grow and are intended to grow in our own ability to discern. Nonetheless, communication of our spiritual experience with a spiritually competent person remains an important part of discernment of spirits; it is not good for us to be alone.

In rule 13 Ignatius explicitly discusses this aspect of discernment. The context, like that of the previous rule, is still the deceits of the enemy and how to overcome them. In this rule Ignatius describes the enemy's desire that *we maintain silence* regarding his troubling deceits; Ignatius will urge us, as we would expect, to do precisely the contrary. As in the preceding rule, there is a metaphor, followed by the application of the metaphor. We will first discuss Ignatius's text and then examine several concrete examples of this teaching.

The text is the following:

Thirteenth Rule. The thirteenth: likewise he conducts himself as a false lover in wishing to remain secret and not be revealed. For a dis-

159

solute man who, speaking with evil intention, makes dishonorable advances to a daughter of a good father or to a wife of a good husband, wishes his words and persuasions to be secret, and the contrary displeases him very much, when the daughter reveals to her father or the wife to her husband his false words and depraved intention, because he easily perceives that he will not be able to succeed with the undertaking begun. In the same way, when the enemy of human nature brings his wiles and persuasions to the just soul, he wishes and desires that they be received and kept in secret; but when one reveals them to one's good confessor or to another spiritual person, who knows his deceits and malicious designs, it weighs on him very much, because he perceives that he will not be able to succeed with the malicious undertaking he has begun, since his manifest deceits have been revealed.

The quality of the enemy Ignatius highlights here is the enemy's desire "to *remain secret* and *not be revealed*." As in the preceding rule, the metaphor depicts an unnatural human situation: a love that is not an authentic but rather a *false love*, seeking only to use the other for selfish purposes. The metaphor is clear. The false lover desires that the intended victim remain silent regarding his seductions since that silence alone permits the further progress of his selfish undertaking. If, however, the intended victim speaks to the proper person about these seductions, the false lover "easily perceives that he will not be able to succeed with the undertaking begun." Once the silence is broken, the false lover is utterly defeated.[1]

Ignatius then applies the metaphor. When "the enemy of human nature" troubles "a just soul" with his "wiles and persuasions" (Jane: you "are not meant for a deep prayer life," and your "desire for God is just an illusion"; Steve: "If you can't even do these simple things, how are you ever going to handle the responsibilities of priesthood for the rest of your life?"), he "wishes and desires" that these "*be received* and *kept* in secret." The enemy desires that the faithful persons so afflicted *receive* (when the troubling "wiles and persuasions" first arise within them) and *keep* (as these "wiles and persuasions" further develop) his workings in their hearts *secret*, carrying them in silence and alone. Provided they maintain this silence, "the malicious undertaking he has begun" can progress (Jane, in discouragement, may eventually give up her prayer life; Steve, filled with doubts, may withdraw from the seminary and ordination).

What the enemy, in proposing "his wiles and persuasions," *does not want* and what "weighs on him very much" is "when one reveals them to one's good confessor or to another spiritual person who knows his deceits and malicious designs." When this occurs, "he perceives that he will not be able to succeed" because "his manifest deceits have been *revealed*" (Jane reveals her trouble to her retreat director, overcomes her discouragement,

and progresses in her prayer; Steve reveals his trouble to his retreat director, overcomes his doubt, and is ordained). This, then, is the spiritual action
Ignatius strongly counsels in rule 13: that when faithful persons are troubled by the deceits of the enemy they must not remain silent and isolated
but should speak of their interior burden with the appropriate spiritual person. If they do so, they will be set free from the enemy's deceits.

A Crucially Important Guideline

Ignatius's rule 13 is *of crucial importance* in the spiritual life. We cannot
overstate the significance of this rule and its remarkable power to liberate
dedicated persons from what may be at times long-standing discouragement and doubt. Experience repeatedly and tellingly demonstrates how
necessary it is that faithful people understand the characteristic of the
enemy that Ignatius describes here and know clearly what their response to
that quality must be. They need to be aware that the enemy will burden
them with his "deceits and malicious designs" and, *at the same time*, urge
them to bear this burden in *silence*. This guideline regarding sharing with
another touches deeply sensitive places in the human heart and must be
grasped well. We will examine, therefore, the *signs* of this characteristic
action of the enemy, the *persons* with whom we should speak, and the specific *content* that we are to share with these persons.

What are the *signs* of such action of the enemy? Faithful people will find
themselves in a time of spiritual confusion, doubt, or discouragement like
Alice, Jane, Steve, Angela, and others we have seen in our reflections. They
may, like Jane and Steve, be considering spiritual changes, born out of their
discouragement and doubt. As this is occurring, they will sense promptings
within such as these:

> You *cannot* speak about this interior trouble. You can speak about
> anything else, but not about this. You *must not* speak about this. If
> you do, the person with whom you speak will never understand you.
> The person will be shocked that you could be so weak or feel such
> things in your heart, will lose the esteem that he or she has for you
> now and will no longer wish to accompany you. The person will crit-
> icize you or laugh at you, and will confirm your fears about your spir-
> itual inadequacy. It will be unbearably painful. . . . It is best to say
> nothing and do what you can yourself to carry this burden.

Such persons may find that they are "too busy" to ask to speak with the
other or do not wish to "take the other's time" for a problem that is "not
all that important." They may find that somehow they never manage to
connect with the other. . . . Certainly, there may be objective reasons that

create difficulty in meeting with a given person at a given time. Yet, when both factors are found simultaneously—spiritual trouble of heart and resistance to speaking with the appropriate spiritual person—then faithful people must ask themselves whether the enemy's action may not be involved. The enemy wishes, says Ignatius, "to *remain secret* and *not be revealed.*"

Who is the *appropriate spiritual person* with whom these spiritually troubled persons should speak? Are there also persons with whom they should *not* speak? These are key questions, and Ignatius answers them carefully in rule 13. His text is succinct but densely packed; the enemy's deceits should be revealed "to *one's good confessor* or to *another spiritual person* who knows his deceits and malicious designs." Ignatius describes, with several modifiers, two such appropriate spiritual persons, one more specific and the other more general.[2]

The first mentioned is a "*good confessor*," known by the spiritually troubled person through personal contact to be such. Ignatius speaks, in fact, of "*one's* good confessor,"[3] thus indicating that the spiritually troubled person has had previous experience of this confessor and in this way knows him to be a "good" confessor. Ignatius's immediately following phrase, "or to *another* spiritual person," indicates that this confessor is likewise a *spiritual* person. As Ignatius clearly states, the word "spiritual" in this context does not signify simply a person of prayer and service: such a person may or may not have the *necessary knowledge and experience* to assist the troubled person wisely. A confessor is spiritual if he is *conversant with the workings of the enemy*: one "who *knows* his *deceits and malicious designs.*"

A compelling image emerges of this first-described person with whom the spiritually troubled person may speak: a *confessor*, a *good* confessor, *known* to the troubled person, chosen previously as confessor because of the confidence the troubled person feels in him, and a *spiritual* confessor, familiar with deceptions of the enemy. Clearly, communication in time of spiritual trouble with a figure of such goodness and such competence will be of great assistance.

If the first description of the appropriate spiritual person with whom to speak is more specific, the second is more general. The first is linked with a sacramental context; the second is inclusive of all spiritual persons knowledgeable of the enemy's workings: "or to *another spiritual person*, who knows his deceits and malicious designs." Here Ignatius mentions only one essential qualification: that this person be familiar with the tactics of the enemy and, therefore, competent to listen to and spiritually assist one troubled by these tactics. This might include suitably trained spiritual directors, retreat directors, spiritually experienced clergy, religious and lay people, a spiritual friend, and similar persons. The key qualification is suitable knowledge of the enemy's deceptive ways of acting. To such persons, the deceptive ways of the enemy will indeed be "manifest," as Ignatius says in concluding the text of rule 13.

We do well also to note the persons *who are absent* from Ignatius's description of the appropriate spiritual persons with whom spiritually troubled persons should speak. All persons who are *not adequately familiar* with the enemy's "deceits and malicious designs" are not appropriate candidates for this role.[4] These may be good, sincere, and faith-filled people. Yet, if they do not possess sufficient knowledge of the enemy's ways, they may, though with good will, either fail to assist or compound the difficulties of these troubled persons. If Jane and Steve in their time of trouble speak of their struggles with a good but spiritually unprepared person rather than with their appropriate spiritual guide, they are unlikely to receive the same assistance, and their trouble may persist. Because both speak with the spiritually competent person at hand, they are set free from their burden.[5]

Finally, what *content* is to be communicated by spiritually troubled persons to the appropriate spiritual person? Ignatius describes this content repeatedly and with varying vocabulary in rule 13. Such troubled persons are to reveal the *"wiles* and *persuasions"* of the enemy, his *"deceits* and *malicious designs,"* his *"malicious undertaking"* and his *"manifest deceits."* Jane is to communicate to her retreat director her discouraging thought that she is not meant for a deep prayer life and that her desire for God is just an illusion; Steve is to communicate to his director his newly surfaced doubt about whether he should be ordained as planned. In short, all faithful persons burdened by the troubling "wiles and persuasions" of the enemy are to communicate these wiles and persuasions to the appropriate spiritual person.[6]

In rule 13, as always throughout these rules, Ignatius is speaking of discernment *of spirits* and of what has direct and immediate reference to our lives of faith and pursuit of God's will. His teaching is very clear: if dedicated persons are *spiritually* burdened by the *enemy's* "wiles and persuasions," they are to speak of these with an appropriate *spiritual* person knowing that, in so doing, they will progress toward freedom from these wiles and persuasions.

This spiritual guide must recognize, therefore, when the interior trouble is *nonspiritual* (psychological) and so beyond the purview of Ignatius's thirteenth rule. Certainly, communication to another person about nonspiritual burdens may be very liberating for the nonspiritually (psychologically) troubled person. Decisions regarding whether a person is emotionally prepared to speak of such psychological burdens may, at times, involve complex affective issues. Such decisions do not pertain to discernment of spirits and are best left to those professionally qualified to make them. Psychological distress and its healing through communication with another are human issues of the greatest importance; they are not, however, the issues which Ignatius is treating in rule 13.

"My Doubts Left Me Completely as Soon as I Finished Speaking"

Some examples of rule 13 in concrete situations will further illustrate Ignatius's teaching. We will consider, first, a moment in the life of Thérèse of Lisieux that exemplifies Ignatius's thirteenth rule with great clarity. This is the unexpected "storm" Thérèse experienced the evening before her final vows as a Carmelite religious.[7] From a very early age Thérèse was utterly certain that God was calling her to Carmelite religious life, and she had pursued this call with unwavering constancy. Both before her entrance and in her first years as a Carmelite, while preparing for her final vows, Thérèse remained totally sure of her Carmelite calling. Then suddenly, the evening before the ceremony, she found herself in vocational turmoil. Her response to this turmoil reveals her keen spiritual awareness, understanding, and capacity for decisive spiritual action.

Thérèse writes:

The *beautiful day* of my wedding [final vows] finally arrived. It was without a single cloud; however, the preceding evening *a storm arose in my soul*, the like of which I'd never seen before.[8]

"A *storm* arose in my *soul*": already we sense the need for spiritual awareness. Spiritual turmoil, of an especially intense nature—"the like of which I'd never seen before"—presents itself on the verge of Thérèse' definitive commitment to religious life.

She continues:

Not a single doubt concerning my vocation had ever entered my mind until then, and it evidently was necessary that I experience this trial. In the evening, while making the Way of the Cross after Matins, my vocation appeared to me as a *dream*, a chimera. I found life in Carmel to be very beautiful, but the devil inspired me with the *assurance* that it wasn't for me and that I was misleading my Superiors by advancing on this way to which I wasn't called. The *darkness* was so great that I could understand one thing only: I didn't have a vocation. Ah! how can I possibly describe the *anguish* in my soul?

This is plainly the language of spiritual desolation: "The *darkness* . . . the *anguish* in my soul." And the desolation is profound: "The darkness *was so great*. . . . Ah! *how can I possibly describe* the anguish in my soul?" Out of Thérèse' intense spiritual desolation a single thought emerges, with *a sense of absolute clarity*: that she *does not have* a vocation to Carmelite religious life. "My vocation," Thérèse says, "appeared to me as a dream, a chimera," and she writes of her *"assurance* that it wasn't for me and that I was misleading my Superiors by advancing on this way *to which I wasn't called."*

Ignatius has instructed us to watch for "the *thoughts* that *come from desolation"* (rule 4) and taught us that "as in consolation the good spirit guides and counsels us more, so *in desolation the bad spirit"* guides and counsels us (rule 5). We sense how Thérèse is urged in this time of spiritual desolation to *change* the former spiritual decision and abandon her lifelong pursuit of Carmelite religious life. Thérèse, a woman of great spiritual perceptivity, is immediately aware of the origin of this "assurance" that she has no Carmelite vocation and specifically names the enemy as its inspiring source.

Now a further quality of this "storm" appears:

> It appeared to me (and this is an absurdity which shows it was a temptation from the devil) that if I were to tell my Novice Mistress about these fears, she would prevent me from pronouncing my Vows. And still I wanted to do God's will and return to the world rather than remain in Carmel and do my own will.

Here Thérèse describes precisely the characteristic of the enemy that Ignatius emphasizes in rule 13. Not only does a "thought" arising out of spiritual desolation awaken in Thérèse the assurance that she has no call to Carmelite life, but she experiences *a resistance to speaking* with her novice mistress—her appropriate spiritual person—about her fears: "It appeared to me . . . that *if I were to tell my Novice Mistress about these fears,* she would prevent me from pronouncing my Vows."

In her time of spiritual desolation, a scenario unfolds in Thérèse' imagination. She sees herself speak with her novice mistress and tell this older religious about her new assurance that she has no Carmelite vocation. Thérèse sees her novice mistress listen attentively and kindly and then agree that Thérèse should not pronounce her vows the following morning. She further sees her novice mistress encourage her "to do God's will and return to the world." With pain, Thérèse sees that the sharing of her vocational fears with her novice mistress will mean the death of all her hopes to be a Carmelite, the one great desire of her life.

As real as this painful scenario appears, Thérèse is keenly aware that "a temptation" of the enemy is at work in it: that there is an "absurdity," an unreal quality to what she is imagining. Her spiritual awareness and understanding *in the midst of spiritual desolation* are remarkable. Thérèse, in her time of desolation, is "myself-reflecting-on-myself-in-desolation" and gains, as a result, full spiritual clarity about the inner movements she is experiencing.

Her clarity inspires her action:

I made the Novice Mistress come out of the choir [place of common prayer for the community] and, filled with confusion, I told her the state of my soul. Fortunately, she saw things much clearer than I did, and she completely reassured me. The act of humility I had just performed put the devil to flight since he had perhaps thought that I would not dare admit my temptation. *My doubts left me completely as soon as I finished speaking.*

"*Filled* with *confusion*": these words reveal how powerfully a person may feel the enemy's urging to maintain secrecy and the courage required to overcome that urging. Clearly, such courage is necessary for Thérèse in this moment, and *she chooses to act* with precisely such courage. In terms of discernment, she moves decisively from spiritual *awareness* and *understanding* to the appropriate *action*. Everything changes when Thérèse does so.

Her novice mistress is at prayer in the choir, most probably together with others of the community. The courage required is, therefore, all the greater in that Thérèse can only approach her novice mistress in a public setting; and, though she is "filled with confusion," she does not hesitate to do so. She asks her novice mistress to leave the place of common prayer. The novice mistress acquiesces, and they move to a private setting and speak.

Thérèse is completely open with her novice mistress; she affirms simply: "I told her the state of my soul." The novice mistress, she says, "saw things much clearer than I did," and "she completely reassured me." For the novice mistress, more than for Thérèse, the "manifest deceits" of the enemy are indeed manifest: "*she saw things much clearer* than I did." And in that greater clarity lies Thérèse' spiritual liberation: "she *completely reassured me.*"

Thérèse's final sentence bears witness forcefully to all that Ignatius affirms in rule 13: "My doubts *left me completely as soon as I finished speaking.*" "*As soon as*": these three little words are spiritually powerful. In fact, "when one reveals" one's spiritual trouble to a person who knows the enemy's "deceits and malicious designs, it weighs on him very much, because he perceives *that he will not be able to succeed* with the malicious undertaking he has begun, since *his manifest deceits have been revealed.*"

A comparison between the *imagined* and *real* scenarios in Thérèse' experience will now be useful. The *imagined* scenario is filled with sorrow and signifies the death of hope: if Thérèse speaks with her novice mistress about her fears she will be compelled to leave the Carmelite community. The *real* scenario, on the contrary, is filled with joy and new hope: Thérèse speaks with her novice mistress, is liberated from fear, and is confirmed in her Carmelite vocation. The *gap* between the two scenarios is the measure of the enemy's mendacity and the falsity of his insinuation that disaster must inevitably follow upon speaking with the appropriate spiritual person. It is this gap and the lie it reveals that troubled persons must recall when urged by the enemy not to break the spiritual silence in their time of darkness.

Thérèse, however, has not yet finished dealing with the enemy:

> My doubts left me completely as soon as I finished speaking; nevertheless, to make my act of humility even more perfect, I still wished to confide my strange temptation to our Mother Prioress, who simply laughed at me.
>
> In the morning of September 8, I felt as though I were flooded with a river of peace, and it was *in this peace* "which surpasses all understanding" [Phil 4:7] that I pronounced my Holy Vows.

We have seen above how Ignatius counsels a retreatant, tempted in time of spiritual desolation to shorten an already planned hour of prayer, to lengthen it slightly instead and thus "accustom himself *not only to resist* the adversary but *even to overthrow* him" (*SpirEx*, 13). Thérèse employs exactly this tactic here. She has already overcome her confusion and spoken openly of her fears with the appropriate spiritual person, her novice mistress. Now she takes further action, seeking not simply to resist the adversary but to overthrow him completely. Thérèse chooses to speak once more of her fears, this time with the superior of the Carmelite community, another spiritually competent woman to whom the deceits of the enemy are manifest. The prioress's refusal to give even the slightest weight to these fears utterly banishes even the most remote possibility of their return. The darkness totally disappears, and the next day, in a time of great spiritual consolation, Thérèse pronounces her perpetual vows as a Carmelite: "I felt as though I were *flooded with a river of peace*, and it was *in this peace* 'which surpasses all understanding' that I pronounced my Holy Vows."

Two additional questions are worthy of our attention here. What might have occurred had Thérèse succumbed to the enemy's urging to secrecy and *not spoken* with her novice mistress that evening? In the light of her almost painfully sincere desire to do God's will, would she have taken her vows the next morning? If she had taken her vows, would she have taken them feeling "flooded with a river of peace"? If she had taken them without speaking, what memory of her vocational decision would she have carried over the years, and how might that memory have affected her in the inevitably difficult moments of later Carmelite life? Her quick and firm choice to speak of her fears to her novice mistress simply excludes all such distressing possibilities.

Moreover, what if Thérèse *had spoken,* but *not to her novice mistress*? What if, unable to face the confusion she felt and afraid "that if I were to tell my Novice Mistress about these fears, she would prevent me from pronouncing my Vows," Thérèse had opted to speak with a fellow novice or another spiritually inexperienced sister? What kind of advice might she have received? Would she have recovered her vocational clarity and peace that evening as, in fact, she did? Would she have felt peace in the ceremony of profession the next morning? How might she have viewed this moment years later? It is apparent that, in this case, such spiritual burdens might indeed have weighed upon her. Thérèse' courage to speak with the *appropriate* spiritual person frees her from them all.

Thérèse, in this experience, lives discernment of spirits to perfection. She is "within" and deeply *aware* of the spiritual movements she feels. Even in her time of anguish and fear, she *understands* with total clarity the deceptive temptations of the enemy. She *acts* immediately and with unerring spiritual instinct, speaking with the appropriate spiritual person. Her perceptive and courageous discernment of spirits shatters the enemy's deceptions, and through this trial she continues to progress in what will prove to be a Carmelite life of great blessing for the entire people of God.

"That Was the End of All My Anxiety, All My Hesitation"

A second example, taken from the writings of Thomas Merton, will illustrate more amply the back-and-forth dynamic that may characterize Ignatius's thirteenth rule in actual practice. The young Merton visited the Trappist monks in Gethsemani, Kentucky. While there, and afterward, a question remained in his mind: Is the Lord calling me to be a Trappist monk in Gethsemani? Merton continued to teach at St. Bonaventure University in upstate New York as he pondered his decision.

The vocational question, with a mingling of attraction and anxiety, increasingly consumed Merton. He knew that he needed to speak with a spiritual guide about this question but hesitated to do so, and the months passed without progress. He wrote:

The fight went on in my mind.

By now, the problem had resolved itself into one practical issue: why don't I consult somebody about the whole question? . . . .

More practical still, here at St. Bonaventure's there was one priest whom I had come to know well during this last year, a wise and good philosopher, Father Philotheus. . . . I knew I could trust him with the most involved spiritual problem. Why did I not ask him?

There was one absurd, crazy thing that held me up: it was a kind of blind impulse, confused, obscure, irrational . . . it amounted to a vague subconscious fear that I would once and for all be told that I definitely had no vocation. It was the fear of an ultimate refusal.[9]

Merton faced a spiritual question of the greatest importance in his life. He knew that he needed to speak with a spiritually competent person in this regard. He identified the appropriate spiritual person in the person of a Franciscan professor whom he knew and respected. Merton, like Thérèse, imagined what would happen if he shared his vocational hopes and doubts. Like Thérèse, he imagined that, if he spoke with Fr. Philotheus, the death of all his vocational hopes would inevitably follow. His fear, he says, was "that I would once and for all be told that I definitely had no vocation." And the imagined scenario effectively restrained him from speaking.

Months passed and he remained in this state of indecision. Then a November evening arrived when the vocational issue could no longer be postponed:

> Finally, on the Thursday of that week, in the evening, I suddenly found myself filled with a vivid conviction:
> "The time has come for me to go and be a Trappist. . . ."
> And yet, in the way, stood hesitation: that old business. But now there could be no delaying. I must finish with that, once and for all, and get an answer. I must talk to somebody who would settle it. It could be done in five minutes. And now was the time. Now.
> Whom should I ask? Father Philotheus was probably in his room downstairs. I went downstairs, and out into the court. Yes, there was a light in Father Philotheus' room. All right. Go in and see what he has to say.
> But instead of that, I bolted out into the darkness and made for the grove. . . .
> In the silence of the grove my feet were loud on the gravel. I walked and prayed. It was very, very dark by the shrine of the Little Flower. "For Heaven's sake, help me!" I said.
> I started back toward the buildings. "All right. Now I am really going to go in there and ask him. Here's the situation, Father. What do you think? Should I go and be a Trappist?"
> There was still a light in Father Philotheus' room. I walked bravely into the hall, but when I got within about six feet of his door it was almost as if someone had stopped me and held me where I was with physical hands. Something jammed in my will. I couldn't walk a step further, even though I wanted to. I made a kind of push at the obstacle . . . and then turned around and ran out of the place once more.
> Again I headed for the grove. . . . My feet were loud on the gravel. I was in the silence of the grove, among wet trees.
> I don't think there was ever a moment in my life when my soul felt so urgent and so special an anguish.

After intense prayer, alone in the darkness of the evening, Merton gained the courage to return to buildings, "going the long way 'round, past the shrine of Our Lady of Lourdes and the far end of the football field," and was ready to try yet again:

> When I came into the courtyard, I saw that the light in Father Philotheus' room was out. . . . My heart sank.
> Yet there was one hope. I went right on through the door and into the corridor, and turned to the Friars' common room. I had never even gone near that door before. I had never dared. But now I went up and knocked on the glass panel and opened the door and looked inside.
> There was nobody there except one Friar alone, Father Philotheus.
> I asked if I could speak with him and we went to his room.
> That was the end of all my anxiety, all my hesitation.
> As soon as I proposed all my hesitations and questions to him, Father Philotheus said that he could see no reason why I shouldn't want to enter a monastery and become a priest.
> It may seem irrational, but at that moment, it was as if scales fell off my own eyes, and looking back on all my worries and questions, I could see clearly how empty and futile they had been. . . . Accident and circumstances had all contributed to exaggerate and distort things in my mind. But now everything was straight again. And already I was full of peace and assurance—the consciousness that everything was right, and that a straight road had opened out, clear and smooth, ahead of me. . . .
> I went upstairs like somebody who had been called back from the dead. Never had I experienced the calm, untroubled peace and certainty that filled my heart.

Merton's text is a clear illustration of Ignatius's thirteenth rule and needs only a little additional comment. Once again, as with Thérèse, the gap between the *imagined* and the *real* scenario is present, the first promising the end of hope, the second confirming hope and giving new life. This *gap* is the clear indication of the deception contained in the enemy's urging to secrecy. The enemy suggests that dedicated people should maintain secrecy because it will serve *their good* to do so; in actual fact it serves only the *enemy's* "deceits and malicious designs." Once Merton does speak, the enemy's deceptions are completely eliminated: "worries and questions" are replaced by "peace and assurance."

It will also be valuable to note the "back-and-forth" dynamic that plays out interiorly in Merton's *heart* ("I will try to speak"—"I am too afraid to speak") and exteriorly in terms of *space* (courtyard—grove—corridor—grove—common room). Merton, in depicting this sequence, describes what dedicated people may, at times, feel when they wish to speak with an appropriate spiritual person. They may, like Merton, be caught between this same desire to speak and a fear of speaking. They may, like Thérèse and Merton, imagine painful results should they, in fact, speak with the appropriate spiritual person. Like Merton, they may allow months or longer to pass without actually speaking. And when, like Merton, they gain the courage to speak, they will attain liberation from their fears and find renewed "peace and assurance" for their spiritual journeys. Should such dedicated people experience this back and forth, this "desire-to-speak/ hesitation-to-speak" dynamic, then is the time to recall Ignatius's thirteenth rule. In the choice to speak, they will find freedom.

"With New Hope in Her Heart"

One final example will place this thirteenth rule in the more ordinary circumstances of daily spiritual living:

Sally is a woman of faith and deeply committed to serving the Lord. She is happy in her life of service, and many are grateful for her faith-filled and loving presence in the parish community and at home. She is familiar with Ignatius's teaching on discernment of spirits. Sally dedicates herself wholeheartedly to her service and, from time to time, exhausts herself. Recently she has once again worked hard at her many commitments and has become somewhat worn. She is try-ing to reduce the activity in her life for a few days in order to recu-perate her energy. As she does so, she experiences a sense of loneliness and a certain interior heaviness. Prayer becomes more difficult and she finds herself beginning to doubt the value of her service to the Lord and whether she can continue to serve as she has.

Several weeks earlier she had called Sr. Joan, a close friend, and they had agreed to have dinner together on this evening. Sally keeps the appointment and, in the course of the meal, tells Joan about the heaviness she has experienced in the past few days. Joan listens and says simply: "It sounds like you are in desolation." As soon as Sally hears these words, she realizes that Joan is right, and that, without having identified it as such, she has been experiencing spiritual deso-lation in the past week. With that new awareness, a large part of her burden lifts. She now has a clear understanding of her spiritual situ-ation and begins to consider how she will respond to it. She leaves the dinner with new hope in her heart.[10]

Here the appropriate spiritual person is a friend who is sufficiently knowledgeable of the enemy's "deceits and malicious designs" to be able to assist a troubled friend. Through her sharing with Joan, the grip of Sally's spiritual desolation is broken. With Joan's help, Sally has made a transition she was not able to make alone; she has progressed from "myself-in-desolation" to "myself-reflecting-on-myself-in-desolation," and in this finds new hope. This incident illustrates only one of the infinitely creative ways in which God may give to spiritually troubled people "another spiritual person" who knows the "deceits and malicious designs" of the enemy. If, in their time of trouble, they seek out and communicate with such spiritual persons, they will find, like Sally, that new hope springs up in their hearts.

14

⤳

Strengthening the Weak Point
(Rule 14)

⤳

Abba Poemen said that Abba Ammonas said: "A person can spend his whole time carrying an axe without succeeding in cutting down the tree; while another, with experience of tree-felling brings the tree down with a few blows. He said that the axe is discernment."

—The Sayings of the Desert Fathers

An Astutely Directed Attack

Ignatius's final rule brings his teaching concerning the enemy's attacks and how to overcome them to yet another level. Earlier, in rule 12, he focused on the *beginnings* of the deceptive action of the enemy and urged firm resistance in those initial moments. Decisive resistance when the deception is just beginning eliminates that deception before it can snowball. The *beginnings* are the time when the enemy's essential weakness is most readily apparent and when he is most easily defeated.

Dedicated people, however, need not await these beginnings to resist the enemy deceptions. People of discernment can prepare their resistance to these deceptions *before the deceptions begin*. They can learn *where* in their spiritual lives the enemy's deceptions are most likely to occur and prepare beforehand. If they do, the enemy may be blocked before he even begins his attack. This is the final refinement of discerning awareness, understanding and resistance to which Ignatius would lead faithful people in these fourteen rules.

Once more Ignatius begins his rule with a metaphor, which he then applies to dedicated people and to how the enemy seeks to deceive them. His text reads:

173

Fourteenth Rule. The fourteenth: likewise he conducts himself as a leader, intent upon conquering and robbing what he desires. For, just as a captain and leader of an army in the field, pitching his camp and exploring the fortifications and defenses of a stronghold, attacks it at the weakest point, in the same way the enemy of human nature, roving about, looks in turn at all our theological, cardinal, and moral virtues; and where he finds us weakest and most in need for our eternal salvation, there he attacks us and attempts to take us.

In rule 12 Ignatius highlights the enemy's *essential weakness* when resisted firmly in the beginnings of his temptations, and, in rule 13, the enemy's desire that his deceptions be kept *secret*. In rule 14, Ignatius centers on the enemy's *astute sense of the weakest point* in our spiritual life and his unerring choice of that weakest point as his place of attack.

In this rule, as in the preceding two rules, Ignatius describes an *unnatural* human situation.[1] This leader[2] is not an honorable figure, wisely directing his adherents in a noble cause. He is, rather, the shrewd head of a group of plunderers and thieves, bent only "upon *conquering* and *robbing* what he desires." We will explore Ignatius's metaphor in some imaginative detail and then examine its application to the experience of dedicated persons.

We may envisage a landscape in Ignatius's Spain: a small stronghold, set upon a high hill overlooking the surrounding plains. The stronghold is defended by stone walls and towers and is accessible through a gate in the walls. A day comes when the inhabitants of the stronghold look into the distance and see an armed group of plunderers approaching. The group of brigands draws near and establishes its camp below, safely out of range of the inhabitants' weapons.

As the inhabitants watch, the leader of this band of thieves, accompanied by his lieutenants, rides up closer to the walls, still safely out of range. Slowly and carefully he circles the entire stronghold, noting the lay of the land, the strength of the walls at each point, the placement of the towers, and the positioning of the central gate. When the circuit is complete, the leader has *astutely identified* the *weakest point* in the defenses of the stronghold. He gathers together his forces and attacks precisely at that weakest point, the place where the inhabitants are least prepared to defend their stronghold. In fact, their "fortifications and defenses" are only as strong as the weakest point in them. Solid and well-maintained walls of stone elsewhere around the stronghold will not save the inhabitants if the gate, a tower, or one section of wall has been neglected and is crumbling.

This, then, is the metaphor: the enemy "conducts himself as a leader, intent upon conquering and robbing what he desires," who, "exploring the fortifications and defenses of a stronghold, attacks it *at the weakest point.*" Ignatius now applies the metaphor to the spiritual issues at hand.

The enemy, affirms Ignatius, attacks a faithful person "in the same way." The "enemy of human nature, roving about, looks in turn at *all our theological, cardinal, and moral virtues.*"[3] The enemy, says Ignatius, examines *every aspect* of our spiritual life and "where he finds us *weakest* and *most in need* for our eternal salvation, *there he attacks us* and attempts to take us." Precisely where each faithful person is weakest (and so where this person would least desire to be attacked), *there* the enemy will attack and endeavor "to take us." As in the metaphor, the enemy reveals an astute sense of each person's weakest spiritual point and infallibly directs his attacks to that point. And again, as in the metaphor, each dedicated person's spiritual "fortifications and defenses" against the enemy's attacks are only as strong as that weakest point.

The example of Sally, cited in the preceding chapter, will serve to illustrate how the fourteenth rule may apply. We will quote once again a part of that example and examine it in the light of the fourteenth rule:

> Sally is a woman of faith and deeply committed to serving the Lord . . . and many are grateful for her faith-filled and loving presence in the parish community and at home. . . . Sally dedicates herself wholeheartedly to her service and, *from time to time, exhausts herself.* Recently she has worked intensely to fulfill her commitments of service and *has become somewhat worn.*

In Ignatius's terms, Sally is clearly a woman who is "rising from good to better in the service of God our Lord." She lives a deep life of faith and service and finds joy in the Lord. Her life is a source of blessing for many others. Sally, in general, is living the "theological, cardinal, and moral virtues" in a rich and fruitful way. The fortifications and defenses of her spiritual life, in general, are vibrant and strong.

There does, however, appear to be one point in which Sally is "weakest and most in need." In this one point the enemy repeatedly and, it seems, with some success, "attacks and attempts to take" her spiritual stronghold. Sally periodically tends to overextend herself in her service, exhausting herself physically and emotionally. Her nonspiritual desolation serves as a ready springboard for spiritual desolation. In this desolation, as we have seen, "prayer becomes more difficult and she finds herself beginning to doubt the value of her service to the Lord and whether she should continue in her efforts to serve."

In this particular case, Sally, with the help of her friend Joan, becomes aware of, resists, and overcomes her spiritual desolation. Yet, unless Sally reflects on and strengthens this weakest point, she will remain susceptible in the future to similar bouts of overwork, exhaustion, and spiritual desolation. How many such debilitating attacks can Sally survive? Even now, in her time of spiritual desolation, she wonders "whether she should continue

in her efforts to serve." The crucial need for all dedicated persons to identify and strengthen any such weakest point in their spiritual fortifications
and defenses is evident.

A Response: Prepare Beforehand

If this is the enemy's tactic—to attack precisely where faithful people are
weakest and least able to defend themselves—and if this tactic has such
potential to harm them spiritually, how must faithful people respond? In
rules 12 and 13 Ignatius described a quality of the enemy (strong when
faced weakly, desiring secrecy) and how faithful persons *should respond* to
this quality (resist strongly, speak to the appropriate spiritual person). In
both rules Ignatius instructed them regarding a characteristic of the enemy
in order to teach them how *to respond effectively*, thus nullifying the
enemy's tactic and freeing them from potential spiritual harm.

Ignatius's purpose remains the same in rule 14, though here he suggests
the response implicitly rather than in the explicit manner he employed in
the previous two rules.[4] If the enemy habitually and most harmfully attacks
each dedicated person in this person's weakest point, then each person, like
the enemy, must *become aware of* this weakest point and *strengthen* it
before the attack begins. Then the enemy, notwithstanding his astute ability to identify the weakest point, will be overthrown *even before he can
begin* his deceptive workings.

We may pursue the metaphor a step further, rendering explicit what is
implicit but clearly understood in this rule. We may consider the same
stronghold upon the hill and imagine a time when the inhabitants are *not*
under attack. These inhabitants know, however, from long experience that
roving bands of thieves do attack their stronghold from time to time. Their
leaders decide to review the fortifications and defenses of their stronghold
in order to prepare for any such future attacks. On a day of peace, they ride
out the gate of the stronghold and circle the entire stronghold, carefully
examining the walls, the towers, and the gate. As they do so, they clearly
identify the weakest point in their defenses. Now they understand why in
the past they have so often been attacked precisely at that point. In their
time of peace, they fortify that point in their defenses, repairing the
stonework, widening it, and raising it.

Some weeks later, a day comes when the inhabitants look into the distance and see an armed band of plunderers approaching. They see the
group establish its camp below and the leader circle their entire stronghold,
noting, as in the previous scenario, the lay of the land, the strength of the
walls at each point, the placement and strength of the towers and the central gate.

But this time, the results are radically different: *the weakest point is no longer weak*. The inhabitants have prepared *before* the leader of the thieves arrived with his followers. Now the leader of the thieves must either simply renounce his attack or face strong defenses should he decide to continue with his attack. This leader's astute sense of the weakest point no longer serves him; his tactic has been anticipated and negated before he and his band even approached the stronghold.

We may now apply the extended metaphor. Faithful persons, like these wise inhabitants, must *examine* all their "theological, cardinal, and moral virtues" that is, the whole of their spiritual fortifications and defenses *before* they are attacked once more by the enemy. They must themselves clearly identify where they are "weakest and most in need."[5] When they have identified this weakest point, they must then apply themselves to *strengthen* this particular aspect of their spiritual lives. If they do so, when the enemy's attack returns, once more focusing specifically on this weak point, they will no longer be exposed to defeat. By wise reflection and spiritual effort they have eliminated a potential Achilles' heel in their spiritual lives and so are far more likely to stand firm in the day of spiritual struggle.[6]

Let us suppose, for example, that Sally, alerted to her spiritual desolation with the help of her friend Joan, decides that she needs to examine her spiritual situation. She decides to review the past years of her life of prayer and service. As she does so, she notes with gratitude the many blessings received from God and the ways she has been an instrument of grace for others. She is gladdened to sense that God is genuinely at the center of her life, that prayer is blessed for her, and that she continues to grow in her ability to serve. Yet, as she examines her experience, she perceives with new clarity *a continuing pattern* of overwork and exhaustion, leading to spiritual desolation. She realizes that, each time this pattern repeats, she expends much time and energy in overcoming the nonspiritual and spiritual desolation it generates within her. Sally has clearly identified her spiritually *weakest point*, the point where she is most susceptible to attack and where she is, in fact, most often attacked.

Sally further determines to strengthen this weak point. She shares her new awareness of this recurring pattern with her spiritual director (rule 13). Simply speaking about this pattern with a spiritually competent listener consolidates her clarity concerning it. Together they explore why Sally may tend to overextend herself in this way and the steps she may take to gain deeper self-knowledge in this regard. They discuss healthy parameters for activity in her life at home and in the parish.

Sally decides to examine this point for a few minutes each day and to write what she discovers in her spiritual journal; through such reflection and journaling she hopes to gain still deeper insight into this pattern in an ongoing way.[7] She also hopes that, assisted by this daily exercise of spiritual awareness, she will more easily perceive even the first beginnings of this pattern and so resist it more effectively *before* it can develop in any substantial way. Sally and her director agree to discuss this particular point each time they meet for the next several months. Sally also plans to discuss these efforts with Joan whom she knows will accompany her willingly as a friend in her striving for a healthier spiritual life.

Obviously, should the enemy attack Sally once more with this same inducement to overextending herself, she will be much less likely to succumb. Like the wise inhabitants of the stronghold, she has reviewed her "fortifications and defenses" *before* the enemy's next attack, and has efficaciously *strengthened* those defenses in prevision of similar attacks in the future. By strengthening that single weakest point, Sally has strengthened the *entirety* of a fruitful spiritual life of love and service. *Everything else* in her rich spiritual life, because it is no longer exposed to harm through that single "Achilles' heel," is increasingly likely to stand firm and grow. By living the wisdom of the fourteenth rule, Sally has transformed her point of greatest vulnerability into the cutting edge of her spiritual growth.

When, like Sally, faithful people identify and strive to fortify their point of specific need, the whole of their spiritual life is greatly blessed as a result. Then, that single point can no longer undermine the rest of their spiritual "fortifications and defenses." It becomes, on the contrary, the source of powerful spiritual growth. The teaching of Ignatius's fourteenth rule has set them free to progress toward the Lord they love.

An Individual Point of Need

In theory, as Daniel Gil indicates, the enemy may attack faithful people at any point of their "theological, cardinal, and moral virtues."[8] In the *Spiritual Exercises,* Ignatius describes the common patterns of the enemy's attacks: awakening a desire to possess that leads to a self-centered existence (*SpirEx,* 142); moving faithful persons "to lack of confidence" in God's help (rule 4); leading them to change their proposals in time of spiritual desolation (rule 5), and so forth. However, in addition to the tactics that apply to *all* persons seeking God, Ignatius assumes that *each* faithful person, like Sally, will have an individual weakest point and will, consequently, be subjected to a *personally directed* attack: "*there* he attacks us and attempts to take us."

What might this weakest point be? For what might dedicated persons look in reviewing all their "theological, cardinal, and moral virtues," seeking to identify this specific point of need? For Sally, this was a tendency to exhaust herself through overwork in her service. We will consider several further examples to expand our understanding of the fourteenth rule as it applies to life.

In earlier chapters we explored Jane's eight-day retreat with the alternations of intense spiritual consolation and deep spiritual desolation she experienced during those days. The following is a description of Jane personally and in her spiritual efforts:

> Sister Jane is in her late thirties. She is an introverted but affectionate personality, having a lively imagination and a wide range of feelings that can be easily moved by idealism and enthusiasm and just as easily downcast by failure and loneliness. She loves Christ and desires to grow in her nearness to God and in service to others. For the past year and a half she has been under spiritual direction and has come to a deepening of her inner life through a daily hour of prayer and monthly days of recollection.[9]

In this description Jane clearly emerges as a rich human being, an "affectionate personality," with "a lively imagination" and "a wide range of feelings." She also appears as a woman of genuine and profound spiritual life. Jane "loves Christ" and "desires to grow in her nearness to God and in service to others." She has taken concrete steps to pursue this growth: during "the past year and a half she has been under spiritual direction," and she makes "a daily hour of prayer" as well as "monthly days of recollection." Clearly, much in her spiritual fortifications and defenses is solid and strong.

Is there a point in which Jane is "weakest and most in need" spiritually? One element in the description given does seem to indicate a particular vulnerability. Jane is endowed with a wide range of feelings that "can be *easily moved by idealism and enthusiasm* and *just as easily downcast by failure and loneliness.*" In fact, in her time of spiritual consolation, Jane somewhat unwisely increases her already abundant time of daily prayer, thereby straining her energies. In her time of spiritual desolation she does appear to be easily downcast and subject to deep discouragement.

In the light of Ignatius's fourteenth rule, Jane would be well advised to examine this human and spiritual point of vulnerability. She might do this personally and with the help of her spiritual director, utilizing, like Sally, any additional means that might increase her self-knowledge and clarify the helpful human and spiritual steps she might take to strengthen her fortifications and defenses in this specific area of her life. If Jane *does* pursue deeper self-knowledge regarding this vulnerability and *does* take active measures to prepare for future struggles regarding it, what then is likely to occur the next time she is moved to strain too hard in time of spiritual consolation or is tempted to feel hopelessly discouraged in time of spiritual desolation? Will she again fall so easily into these traps? And if Jane *does not* take such steps, what is likely to occur the next time she is attacked by the enemy precisely in this area of vulnerability? Is she not positioned to fall again and again into the same traps?

Such is the type of spiritual thinking and action Ignatius counsels in his fourteenth rule. He encourages faithful people to identify any existing weakest point in their spiritual life and to work to strengthen that point. If they *do not*, they will remain susceptible to the enemy's attacks exactly where they are least able to defend themselves. They will, as a result, be continually exposed to harm. If they *do* identify and strengthen their point of greatest need, great spiritual benefits follow; they will be increasingly freed from attack in that specific point, every other aspect of their spiritual journey will be more likely to remain strong, and they will be growing spiritually precisely where they most need to grow. If we imagine Jane's already strong spiritual life now joined to increasing awareness of and decisive action to strengthen her one point of particular vulnerability, we can recognize the richness with which she will progress toward the Lord as her heart so desires.

The following example applies rule 14 to yet another area of spiritual experience:

> Jim has for several years been a member of a religious congregation. He has gotten along well enough and certainly loves the congregation and is enthusiastic about its apostolic work. One serious difficulty, however, showed up along the line; and, despite his goodwill and effort and prayer, this has gotten worse rather than better. He generally feels resentful and distrustful of those in authority, and frequently his spontaneous first response to any directive or even suggestion from his superiors is rebellious. His efforts to be open and obedient put him under constant tension. Worse yet, he finds that even his attitude toward God is often tinged with fear and distrust. He is disturbed and confused by all this, feels guilty and discouraged about ever growing into a truly Christlike man.[10]

Jim is evidently a person sincerely seeking to love and serve the Lord. He has joined a religious community; he "loves the congregation" and "is enthusiastic about its apostolic work." Jim is a man of "goodwill and effort and prayer." There is great goodness in Jim, and, like the others already considered, much in his spiritual fortifications and defenses is strong.

This description reveals, however, that "one serious difficulty" severely hampers Jim's life in community and his relationship with God. He is "resentful and distrustful" toward those in authority and "frequently his spontaneous first response to any directive or even suggestion from his superiors is rebellious." He has tried though without success to be more open and, in fact, "this has gotten worse rather than better." His relationship with God is also affected and "is often tinged with fear and distrust," leaving Jim feeling "guilty and discouraged."[11]

Many questions arise. Clearly there are emotional dynamics at work in Jim's difficulties in religious life and more directly with God. What are these emotional dynamics? How did these dynamics develop? How are these dynamics affecting Jim's relationships with superiors and his prayer?

Nothing in this description indicates that Jim has any clear understanding of these emotional issues and their impact upon his religious and spiritual life. Further, there is no indication that Jim has spoken about his struggles with anyone at all and certainly not with a person psychologically or spiritually competent to assist him in his difficulties (rule 13). Jim is aware of and appears to be laboring valiantly to strengthen his point of need, but in isolation, without visible progress, and without hope.

Jim is a man of sincerity and genuine goodness, with "one serious difficulty" that leaves him vulnerable to emotional tension and spiritual desolation. This difficulty appears to be the point where he is weakest and most in need, the one point from which most of his difficulties stem. If Jim is able to ask for the emotional and spiritual assistance he needs from appropriate persons, he is most likely to find new understanding and new hope in his struggles. Jim is likely to perceive new and healthier ways of facing his present emotional and spiritual struggles; he will become less vulnerable to the disturbance and spiritual desolation he currently feels. Clearly, much in Jim's life depends on how he sets about strengthening his fortifications and defenses in this single point of his life.

A final example concerns a faith-filled woman who, having endured several weeks of spiritual desolation, looks back on that time and writes:

> What I can see now is that the core of the difficulty was *the same old problem*—dressed up a bit differently perhaps but still the same—of doubting God's love for me with all the morass of negativity that brings with it.[12]

"The *same old problem*": the fourteen rule awakens in us a special sensitivity to any language that suggests a long-standing pattern of vulnerability. The words appear to describe this woman's awareness of a consistent pattern of attack centered on "doubting God's love for me," a doubt "that brings with it" a "morass of negativity." The emotional heaviness and the spiritual desolation occasioned by this attack are not difficult to imagine. In his fourteenth rule, Ignatius would encourage this dedicated woman to strengthen *this specific point* of her spiritual fortifications and defenses. If she does so, the enemy's inducement to doubt will gradually lose its power to harm her and much spiritual energy will be liberated in her for loving service.

Know Thyself!

Know thyself. . . . This classic spiritual dictum is critically important in regard to Ignatius's fourteenth rule. Sally, Jane, Jim, and this woman all have different points of individual vulnerability; they, and all faithful people, must strive for a self-knowledge that will permit them to identify any such *personal* point of greatest spiritual need.

Questions such as these may assist in determining that particular point of vulnerability: Is there some situation that frequently discourages me? That frequently strips me of spiritual energy? Are there circumstances in which I often become afraid? Become worn out? In which I feel spiritually helpless? Is there one recurring way in which I find myself spiritually weakened? Does one thing seem to diminish most my energy to love and serve others? Is there something that habitually disheartens me in prayer? That often causes me to doubt God's love for me? Is there *a repeating pattern* of these experiences?

If faithful persons do discover such a pattern, they may well have identified their individual point of vulnerability to the enemy's attack. In gaining this spiritual self-knowledge they are, in effect, using the enemy against himself. In noting the frequency of his attack in a *specific* area of their spiritual life, they learn where they may *most fruitfully focus* their spiritual energies toward growth. If, in addition to the personal reflection proposed here, they also speak with an appropriate spiritual person, they will find great assistance in their effort to identify this point of vulnerability. Again, it is not good for us to be alone. . . .

Having *found* this specific point of vulnerability, they may then begin to *strengthen* that particular point. Any of the classic spiritual resources may be enlisted in this effort: prayer, daily examen of progress regarding this point, journaling, ongoing conversation with a spiritual guide, spiritual reading, and similar means.[13] The fourteenth rule, when practiced in daily living, ensures that faithful people will be constantly growing in their spiritual life. A quality of youthfulness and freshness will accompany them on their spiritual journey, with the happy consciousness of continuing progress.[14]

The Fourteenth Rule and the Preceding Rules

Two concluding observations regarding the fourteenth rule merit our attention. Both concern this rule in relation to the rules that precede it: *the two* with which it forms a subset within the fourteen rules, and the sequence of the rules *as a whole*.

In rule 12, Ignatius teaches that if faithful persons resist when the enemy *first begins* his temptations, the enemy will be completely defeated. He has no strength at all except in the weak resistance of those he tempts. The enemy, Ignatius tells us, is *essentially weak*. Again, in rule 13, if faithful persons speak to the appropriate spiritual person the enemy is utterly routed. *Words alone*, the right words spoken to the right person, are sufficient to undo his "wiles and persuasions." The *essential weakness* of the enemy is again manifest.

The same fundamental weakness of the enemy is evident in the fourteenth rule as well. The metaphor of this rule focuses *not* on the *strength* of the leader and his band of thieves but rather on the *weak point* in the *defenses* of the stronghold.[15] Nothing is said in the metaphor to suggest that the leader and his would-be plunderers possess any particular strength. In fact, once the inhabitants of the stronghold have fortified the weakest point in their defenses, the enemy is helpless and must desist in this attack.

A look, then, at how each of these three rules presents the "enemy of human nature" removes fear and instills hope. Ignatius teaches very simply and very powerfully that, if we are willing to resist him, we will see that the enemy's power never was more than a façade; it will crumble before us. With wonder, like Paul, we will say: "I can do all things in him who strengthens me" (Phil 4:13). As we have said so often in these reflections, Ignatius's entire teaching on discernment of spirits is charged with hope. The final three rules once more convey that uplifting and energizing message.

Finally, consideration of the fourteenth rule in relation to the entire preceding set of rules reveals the itinerary of continually refining discernment they contain.[16] Ignatius begins with persons heading away from God and toward serious sin and describes how the spirits act in such persons (rule 1). He then considers faithful persons, those who are "rising from good to better in the service of God our Lord," and how the spirits reverse their action in these with respect to the persons previously designated (rule 2).

Having sketched the two types of spiritual movements (spiritual consolation and spiritual desolation: rules 3 and 4), Ignatius instructs faithful persons regarding how to resist spiritual desolation *while they are in* spiritual desolation (rules 5 to 9). He then teaches them to prepare for spiritual desolation *before it begins*, storing up, in time of spiritual consolation, the energy they will need for future resistance to spiritual desolation (rule 10). At this point, he invites discerning persons to live with spiritual balance and maturity, neither thoughtlessly "high" in spiritual consolation nor helplessly "low" in spiritual desolation (rule 11).

Ignatius focuses, lastly, on the enemy's temptations and guides faithful persons to resist them *in their very beginnings* (rule 12) and through the courage to speak of his "wiles and persuasions" with the appropriate spiritual person (rule 13). The ultimate refinement of discernment in this set of rules is reached when discerning persons become capable of defeating the enemy's personalized attacks even *before he begins his attack* (rule 14). The spiritual growth described along this itinerary of discernment is immense. We begin with the person *heading away from God* and conclude with the person "rising from good to better in the service of God our Lord," prepared to defeat the enemy *in* and *even before* the *beginnings* of his action.

Ignatius's fourteen rules constitute a program for progressive growth in discernment of spirits. A humble and persevering effort to live according to the wisdom of these rules, assisted by a spiritual guide and with trust in God's always sufficient grace, gradually forms the mature spiritual person, able to discern and overcome the deceptions of the enemy, faithfully fulfilling God's will, and growing in love. This is the goal of all discernment of spirits.

CONCLUSION

∽

Setting Captives Free

∽

The Spirit of the Lord is upon me,
because he has anointed me
to bring glad tidings to the poor.
He has sent me to proclaim liberty to captives . . .
to let the oppressed go free.
                                                    —Luke 4:18

One of the first followers of Ignatius, Blessed Pierre Favre, recounts in his *Memoriale* the spiritual impact of Ignatius upon him when they met as students in Paris. Pierre, a man of profound intelligence, gentleness, and holiness, who won the hearts of many in his apostolate, recalls with gratitude the great blessings God gave him through Ignatius in those university days. He writes:

> May it please the divine clemency to give me the grace of clearly remembering and pondering the benefits which the Lord conferred on me in those days through that man. Firstly, he gave me an understanding of my conscience and of the temptations and scruples I had had for so long without either understanding them or seeing the way by which I would be able to get peace.[1]

Pierre Favre was among the first of the many persons who would find liberation from long-standing spiritual bondage through the assistance of Ignatius of Loyola. Pierre speaks of the temptations and scruples to which for so long he has been subject, "without either understanding them or seeing the way by which I would be able to get peace." This man of faith, in so honestly describing his helpless struggle against spiritual burdens that he neither understood nor knew how to overcome, certainly speaks for other dedicated people who, through the centuries, would share that same sense of struggle and burden.

Pierre speaks also for the countless faithful people who would, as did he, discover in the teaching of Ignatius of Loyola a means of *understanding* at

185

last the stirrings of their hearts, revealing to them that *there is a way out of* spiritual darkness and fear. Like Pierre, they would *see the way* by which they "would be able to get peace." And, also like Pierre, their hearts would expand in praise to the God who set them free through Ignatius's teaching. Ignatius's instruction on discernment and the spiritual liberation to which it leads have been the subject of this book.

In his fourteen rules Ignatius proclaims to all dedicated persons that humble and persevering discernment of spirits—spiritual awareness, understanding, and action—can *set them free* from slavery to spiritual desolation and the deceits of the enemy. The Lord revealed by these rules is the Lord who says to his disciples: "Do not let your hearts be troubled" (John 14:1).

In beginning our reflections on discernment we quoted a text from John Cassian regarding spiritual struggles with the various passions and the teaching of the spiritual elders regarding these struggles. We may consider the same words again, now with deeper understanding, as we conclude our discussion of discernment:

> Although the causes of these passions, once they have been set forth by the teachings of the elders, are immediately recognized by all, nonetheless, before they are revealed, though we are all harmed by them and they are present in everyone, no one knows of them.[2]

What is true of the passions and the corresponding teaching of the elders is also true with respect to discernment of spirits and Ignatius's fourteen rules. Spiritual consolation and spiritual desolation are common experiences for all persons who seek God. All such persons experience, at times, the affective heaviness of spiritual desolation and the accompanying deceits of the enemy. They may feel discouraged in prayer and service; they may be burdened by obstacles, false reasoning, and sadness; they may incline toward changes in time of spiritual desolation; they may consider the enemy strong and themselves weak; they may tend to remain silent when troubled by the enemy. They will experience these and other similar deceptive urgings.

These tactics of the enemy are "present in everyone" and yet "*no one knows of them*," or knows of them with the clarity our tradition makes possible, until they have been set forth by an elder conversant in the wisdom of discernment. In our case, that elder brother is Ignatius. He, in a way uniquely his own in the Christian spiritual tradition, has found clear and practical words to describe the spiritual experience which is, in fact, "present in everyone": ongoing alternations of spiritual consolation and spiritual desolation, with their respective grace and deceptions. Once Ignatius has explained these spiritual movements, they are indeed "recognized by all." The power of these rules in large part consists in this: that Ignatius spiritually *explains us to ourselves.* Having assimilated his rules, many of us, like Pierre Favre, will begin to understand the spiritual stirrings we have vaguely sensed in our hearts but could not comprehend. That new understanding is the gateway to new freedom.

Growth takes time, and growth in discernment is no exception to this universal human law. Progress in the ability to live the spiritually discerned life occurs through continuing prayer, effort, conversation with a spiritual guide, and all the means that Ignatius outlines in his rules.[3] What John Henry Newman writes with regard to prayer is equally true of discernment: "the power of prayer, being a habit, must be acquired, like all other habits, by *practice*."[4] Theresa of Avila's repeated insistence that *perseverance* is the principal prerequisite for a developing life of prayer is also valid of discernment of spirits.[5] *Persevering practice* of spiritual awareness, understanding, and action in daily living: this, with God's grace, is the path that leads to a growing life of discernment.

One day, Jesus returned to his native place in Nazareth. At the Jordan River the Spirit had descended upon him, and the Father had pronounced him "my beloved Son" (Luke 3:22). He had been "led by the Spirit" into the desert, done battle with and overcome the temptations of the enemy (Luke 4:1–13). Then, "in the power of the Spirit" he returned to Galilee and came to Nazareth (Luke 4:14–30). He entered the synagogue on the Sabbath day and, in the presence of the assembly, proclaimed the words of the prophet Isaiah: "The Spirit of the Lord is upon me, / because he has anointed me / to bring glad tidings to the poor. / He has sent me *to proclaim liberty to captives* / and recovery of sight to the blind, / to *let the oppressed go free*" (Luke 4:18; *emphasis added*).

That message of freedom from captivity is still the message of the Savior today. It is the message conveyed by Ignatius, a faithful disciple of the Savior who *proclaims liberty to captives*. It is the message of his fourteen rules for discernment: to *let those oppressed* by spiritual desolation and the deceits of the enemy *go free*. Discernment of spirits is the quest for that freedom, a spiritual adventure that leads surely to the God whose love never ceases to call our hearts.

Notes

∽

Introduction

1. Leo Tolstoy, *Anna Karenina*, trans. Constance Garnett (Garden City, N.Y.: Nelson Doubleday, 1944), 717–21.

2. Ibid, 725.

3. Cf. Sr. Innocentia Richards, trans., *Discernment of Spirits* (Collegeville, Minn.: Liturgical Press, 1970), the English translation of the article "Discernement des Esprits" by Jacques Guillet et al., in the *Dictionnaire de Spiritualité Ascetique et Mystique*, III, cols. 1222–91.

4. Quoted in Joseph de Guibert, *The Jesuits: Their Spiritual Doctrine and Practice. A Historical Study* (St. Louis: Institute of Jesuit Sources, 1986), 45.

5. Pedro Ribadeneyra, writes: "It is unbelievable with what ease our Father recollected himself in the midst of a tide of business, apparently having at his disposal and under his hand, so to speak, the spirit of devotion and torrents of tears" (ibid, 45). Diego Laynez adds that Ignatius "had so much care of his conscience that each day he compared week with week, month with month, day with day, seeking daily to advance" (ibid., 39–40). Luis Gonçalves da Câmara describes Ignatius's sense, in his later years, that "he had gone on continually increasing in devotion, that is, in facility to find God, and now more than ever in all his life. And every time and at any hour that he wished to find God, he found him" (ibid., 41). A full description of Ignatius's life and personality exceeds the scope of this book, focused specifically on one aspect of his spiritual teaching. These details may be found in his many biographies; among them are Cándido de Dalmases, *Ignatius of Loyola, Founder of the Jesuits: His Life and Work* (St. Louis: Institute of Jesuit Sources, 1985); José Ignacio Tellechea Idígoras, *Ignatius of Loyola: The Pilgrim Saint* (Chicago: Loyola University Press, 1994).

6. On the meaning of the word "discernment," see also Thomas Green, S.J., *Weeds among the Wheat. Discernment: Where Prayer & Action Meet* (Notre Dame, Ind.: Ave Maria Press, 1984), 22.

7. Discernment *of spirits* is not the only kind of discernment in spiritual matters. Manuel Ruiz Jurado lists a number of additional types of spiritual discernment: discernment of "the signs of the times," of groups and ecclesial movements, of charismatic phenomena, of the true sense of the church, discernment in community, and discernment of one's vocation. Cf. *El discernimiento espiritual: Teologia. Historia. Practica* (Madrid: BAC, 1994), IX–XI. Jules Toner (*A Commentary on Saint Ignatius' Rules for the Discernment of Spirits: A Guide to the Principles and Practice* [St. Louis: Institute of Jesuit Sources, 1982], 12–15) differentiates between discernment of spirits and discernment of the will of God. In this book I am focusing

only on *discernment of spirits*, that is, on distinguishing among *the stirrings of our hearts* that which is of God and that which is not, and how to respond to these stirrings. The classic eighteenth-century author on discernment of spirits, Giovanni Battista Scaramelli, S.J., writes: "Here by 'spirit' we understand an impulse, a movement or an internal inclination of our soul toward something particular" (*Dottrina di S Giovanni della Croce e Discerniment degli spiriti* [Rome: Pia Società S. Paolo, 1946], 230; my translation).

8. Nos. 313–27, the First Week rules for discernment. Hereafter the book *Spiritual Exercises* is abbreviated *SpirEx*.

9. Green, *Weeds among the Wheat*, 14. Toner (*Commentary*, xvi) writes that "the rules of St. Ignatius of Loyola have for centuries now proved to be the most complete and practically helpful set of directives for discernment of spirits that has yet been formulated."

10. I first learned the richness of this approach from Daniel Gil, S.J., who adopts it in his *Discernimiento según San Ignacio* (Rome: Centrum Ignatianum Spiritualitatis, 1983).

11. *The Jesuits*, 71.

12. Several authors, with differing approaches, have offered commentaries on these rules. I am particularly indebted to three of these: Jules Toner, S.J., Daniel Gil, S.J., and Miguel Angel Fiorito, S.J. Their major works on these rules are the following: Jules Toner, *A Commentary on Saint Ignatius' Rules for the Discernment of Spirits: A Guide to the Principles and Practice* (St. Louis: Institute of Jesuit Sources, 1982); I will also quote from Toner's later work, *Spirit of Light or Darkness? A Casebook for Studying Discernment of Spirits* (St. Louis: Institute of Jesuit Sources, 1995); Daniel Gil, *Discernimiento según San Ignacio* (Rome: Centrum Ignatianum Spiritualitatis, 1983); and Miguel Angel Fiorito, *Discernimiento y Lucha Espiritual* (Buenos Aires: Ediciones Diego de Torres, 1985).

13. Those more suited for the First Week (*SpirEx*, 313–27) and those more suited to the Second Week (*SpirEx*, 328–36) of the *Spiritual Exercises*. "First Week" and "Second Week" here indicate less a specific set of days in the *Spiritual Exercises* than two different tactics of temptation, one by means of spiritual desolation (First Week rules) and one by means of spiritual consolation (Second Week rules). Cf. Gil, *Discernimiento*, 26–27, 51; Fiorito, *Discernimiento y Lucha*, 35–37.

14. Fiorito (*Discernimiento y Lucha*, 7–11) suggests further reasons for a separate treatment of the first set of rules: these rules serve as a general introduction to the other rules for discernment; they deal specifically with desolation; and they draw attention to the spiritual struggle that is part of every life of faith.

15. "Ignatius clearly intends that the retreatants continue, when they return to daily life after the *Spiritual Exercises,* to live according to what they learned in them" (Fiorito, *Discernimiento y Lucha*, 10), speaking about the fourteen rules for discernment we are discussing here. Manuel Ruiz Jurado, S.J., in *El Discernimiento Espiritual: Teologia. Historia. Práctica* (Madrid: Biblioteca de Autores Cristianos, 1994), 125, affirms: "The condensed spiritual experience of the time of the *Exercises* serves as an intensive training for what is to be practiced in life itself" (my translation, as are all subsequent quotations from this book).

16. Jules Toner's *Commentary* is an excellent resource for investigating further complexities of discernment of spirits.

Text of the Rules

1. My translation. My aim, in keeping with the methodology described above in the introduction, has been to reproduce in English, as closely as possible, the Spanish of the rules as found in the autograph version of the *Spiritual Exercises*. This style of translation best facilitates the close examination of Ignatius's own words, which is key to my approach to the rules in this book. The autograph version, from which this translation is made, is that which most faithfully gives us Ignatius's original Spanish text. This version is authoritatively reproduced in José Calveras and Candido de Dalmases, eds., *Sancti Ignatii de Loyola Exercitia Spiritualia* (Rome: Monumenta Historica Societatis Jesu, 1969), 100:374–86. In this translation I have striven to maintain a balance between the closest possible fidelity to Ignatius's own "rough and difficult style" (Toner, *Commentary*, 21) and a sufficiently readable English text. The awkwardness of style the reader will encounter at times in my translation reflects Ignatius's original; the preservation of that awkwardness is necessary if we wish to examine the rules precisely as Ignatius wrote them. In translating, I have consulted earlier translations, especially that of Eldar Mullan, who translated the *Spiritual Exercises* with a similar purpose and whose wording I have employed at various points. Cf. Eldar Mullan, S.J., *The Spiritual Exercises of St. Ignatius of Loyola Translated from the Autograph* (New York: P. J. Kennedy & Sons, 1914), 169–75. I have also occasionally adopted wording from the translations by Louis Puhl, S.J., *The Spiritual Exercises of St. Ignatius Based on Studies in the Language of the Autograph* (Chicago: Loyola University Press, 1951), 141–46, and that of Toner, *Commentary*, 22–27. I have followed this same procedure throughout this book in quoting other passages, beyond the rules themselves, from the *Spiritual Exercises*.

Prologue: What Is Discernment of Spirits?

1. Joseph O'Callaghan, trans., *The Autobiography of St. Ignatius of Loyola with Related Documents* (New York, Hagerstown, San Francisco, London: Harper Torchbooks, 1974), 21–26. Henceforth quoted as *Autobiography of St. Ignatius*.

2. *Autobiography of St. Ignatius*, 23. The page numbers for quotations in the next pages from this *Autobiography* are given at the end of the quotation itself. I have added the italics for the sake of highlighting points central to our discussion and will use the same procedure in subsequent quotations without repeating this note.

3. In *SpirEx*, 32, Ignatius includes our own reflective activity, as well as the influence of both the good and the bad spirit, under the single word "thoughts."

4. Emphasis mine. The verbs I have italicized are, in the Spanish original, "sentir" (become aware); "conocer" (know, recognize); and "recibir" (receive) or "lanzar" (reject).

5. Daniel Gil, *Discernimiento según San Ignacio* (Rome: Centrum Ignatianum Spiritualitatis, 1983), 18–20.

6. *SpirEx*, 8–10, 17.

7. *Confessions*, X.27. My translation.

8. John Cassian, *Institutes* V.2. My translation. These are the "eight principal faults."

9. *Summa Theologica*, I-II, q. 2, a.6, reply obj. 2; q. 31; q. 73.

10. Jules Toner, *A Commentary on Saint Ignatius' Rules for the Discernment of Spirits: A Guide to the Principles and Practice* (St. Louis: Institute of Jesuit Sources, 1982), 41–42. Elsewhere Toner writes: "For most people, what goes on in consciousness is largely, in a phrase from William James, 'a booming, buzzing confusion'" ("Discernment in the *Spiritual Exercises*," *A New Introduction to the Spiritual Exercises of St. Ignatius*, John Dister, ed. [Collegeville, Minn.: Liturgical Press, 1993], 66). Julian Green also writes: "What takes place in our brain in the space of a minute should be recorded, if there were time enough to do it. But indeed, there would not be sufficient paper and also, how could the thread of such innumerable and rapid ideas be followed?" (*Diary*, trans. Anna Green, selected Kurt Wolft [New York: Harcourt, Brace & World, Inc., 1964], 118–19).

11. Blaise Pascal, *Pensées* (Harmondsworth: Penguin Books, 1984), no. 136, p. 67.

12. *The Wall Street Journal*, May 5, 2000, p. W17.

13. *SpirEx*, 17.

14. Gil, *Discernimiento*, 42, my translation, as are all subsequent quotations from Gil's *Discernimiento según San Ignacio*. No English translation of this work exists.

15. We will discuss these factors more in detail in our commentary on Ignatius's third rule.

Chapter 1: When a Person Moves Away from God (Rule 1)

1. R. S. Pine-Coffin, trans., *Saint Augustine Confessions* (Harmondsworth: Penguin Books, 1961), book VIII.12, pp. 177–78.

2. Ibid., II.1. This and the following quotation are my own translation. All other quotations from the *Confessions* in this chapter are taken from the Pine-Coffin translation cited in the preceding note. The page numbers for these quotations are given at the end of the quotation itself.

3. Ibid., II.2.

4. Ibid., VIII.6, pp. 167–68.

5. Ibid., VIII.11, p. 175. Both Fiorito, *Discernimiento y Lucha*, 54–55, 60–61, 105–8, and more briefly Toner, *Spirit of Light or Darkness*, 44–45, use parts of this conversation with Ponticianus and its aftermath to illustrate rules 1 and 2.

6. "de pecado mortal en pecado mortal." In the *Spiritual Exercises* Ignatius uses the term "mortal sin" both to signify *grave sin* in contrast to venial sin (*SpirEx*, 35, 41, 48, 52, 349) and, more broadly, with the sense of *capital sin*, that is, the seven root tendencies toward sin experienced by the Christian (*SpirEx*, 18, 238, 244–45). As a result, a question arises regarding whom precisely Ignatius has in mind in speaking of "persons who are going from mortal sin to mortal sin." Are these persons who are going from one grievous sin to another (first interpretation) or might they also be persons slipping into less serious levels of sinfulness or even simply into tendencies that lead them away from God in any way at all (second interpretation)? Gil, *Discernimiento*, 56, 97–98, and Green, *Diary*, 100–101, adopt the first interpretation; Toner, *Commentary*, 50–51, emphasizes the second; Fiorito, *Discerni-*

miento y Lucha, 40–41, explicitly includes both. I prefer to discuss rule 1 in the light of the first interpretation, which I understand to be the basic sense Ignatius intends here, that is, "mortal sin" understood as grave sin. I choose this approach also for Ignatius's own reasons of clarity. As Toner, *Commentary*, 71, writes: "In Rules I:1–2 [the first two rules], Ignatius, as a good pedagogue, has stated pure cases in order to communicate an initial understanding which is unconfused by complexities." In keeping with the methodology I have adopted in this book, I limit myself in this chapter to explaining what Ignatius essentially says in the text of the rule, aiming, like Ignatius, at an "initial" and "unconfused" understanding. For an excellent discussion of the further complexities, see Toner, *Commentary*, 49–53, 70–78. A presentation of the two interpretations together is found in D. Gil and M. Fiorito, "La primera regla de discernir de S. Ignacio, ¿a qué personas se refiere . . . ?" *Stromata* 33 (1977): 341–60. In this co-authored study, Gil argues for the first interpretation and Fiorito for the second. I will return to this issue in discussing rule 9.

7. Examination of the manuscript of the autograph, the earliest existing Spanish version of the *Spiritual Exercises*, reveals that Ignatius added these first two rules in a second moment, when he had already written the rest of the rules. Cf. José Calveras and Candido de Dalmases, *Sancti Ignatii de Loyola Exercitia Spiritualia*, MHSI, vol. 100, pp. 376; 380; Gil, *Discernimiento*, 142; Fiorito, *Discernimiento y Lucha*, 138–39; Ruiz Jurado, *El discernimiento espiritual*, 224 n. 75.

8. Toner, "Discernment in the Spiritual Exercises," in *A New Introduction to the Spiritual Exercises of St. Ignatius*, ed. J. Dister (Collegeville, Minn.: Liturgical Press, 1993), 64. Cf. also Green, *Weeds among the Wheat*, 103–4, for a fine exposition of this same point, wherein he concludes: "From the point of view of discernment we can take the "evil spirit" or the "devil" to mean whatever forces are working against God, whether they be "natural" or strictly "diabolical" (p. 103).

9. A more literal translation would read: "through the *synderesis* of reason," one of the few places in which Ignatius uses a technical theological term. *Synderesis* refers to the sense of and tendency toward the good, ultimately toward God, which is innate in every human person and that no person, however confirmed in sinfulness, can ever fully ignore. The good spirit, says Ignatius, makes this *synderesis* felt in the one moving away from God. *Synderesis,* writes Servais Pinckers, is the intuitive knowledge or "the primordial perception of the good proper to man" (*The Sources of Christian Ethics* [Washington, D.C.: Catholic University of America Press, 1995], 384).

Chapter 2: When a Person Moves toward God (Rule 2)

1. "remordiendoles las consciencias" (314).
2. Ignatius simply uses the infinitive "morder" (315).
3. William Young, S.J., *Letters of Saint Ignatius of Loyola* (Chicago: Loyola University Press, 1959), 19.
4. Ibid., 22.
5. Ibid., 19.
6. R. S. Pine-Coffin, trans., *Confessions*, VIII.11, pp. 175–76. When Nekhlyu-

dov, the central character in Tolstoy's *Resurrection*, seeks to heed his conscience and change his dissolute life, he hears similar questionings within: "'Haven't you tried before to improve and be better, and nothing came of it?' whispered the voice of the tempter within. 'So what is the use of trying any more? You are not the only one—everyone's the same—life is like that,' whispered the voice" (Leo Tolstoy, *Resurrection*, trans. Rosemary Edmonds [London: Penguin, 1966], 141).

7. Quoted from Jules Toner, *Spirit of Light or Darkness? A Casebook for Studying Discernment of Spirits* (St. Louis: Institute of Jesuit Sources, 1995), 38–39. The universal negatives in this narration are worthy of note: "second-guessing my *entire* retreat . . . a *complete* waste of time." We will return below to this quality of the enemy's action.

8. Cf. Gil, *Discernimiento*, 82.

9. Cf. *SpirEx*, 7 where Ignatius uses this same phrase: the one giving the Exercises is to be gentle with the person in desolation, "giving him courage and strength."

Chapter 3: Spiritual Consolation (Rule 3)

1. Jacques Maritain, ed., *Raïssa's Journal* (Albany, N.Y.: Magi, 1974), 35.

2. Cf. Toner, *Commentary*, 115–16, from whom I take the term "nonspiritual" and who, in his writings on discernment of spirits, makes a clear distinction between these two types of consolation (and desolation).

3. Gil, *Discernimiento*, 116.

4. As Gil, *Discernimiento*, 116, indicates, we can choose to engage in the actions from which nonspiritual consolation normally flows (visiting some place of natural beauty, listening to uplifting music, entering into friendly conversation, etc.), and so experience such nonspiritual consolation. When we cease to engage in such actions, the nonspiritual consolation also ceases. The same is not true of spiritual consolation which no action of our own can "produce" or control, but which can only be received as the free gift of God. Every person who seeks to pray experiences the truth of this.

5. John Clarke, O.C.D., trans., *St. Thérèse of Lisieux: Her Last Conversations* (Washington, D.C.: ICS Publications, 1977), 60. In the original quote Pauline's words are italicized and Thérèse's words set in roman type. I have removed the italics.

6. Among these: *Autograph Directory*, nos. 11, 18, in Martin Palmer, S.J., trans. and ed., *On Giving the Spiritual Exercises: The Early Jesuit Manuscript Directories and the Official Directory of 1599* (St. Louis: Institute of Jesuit Sources, 1996), 8, 9; Letter to Francis Borgia, September 20, 1548, in Young, *Letters of Saint Ignatius of Loyola*, 181.

7. See Gil, *Discernimiento*, 120–31, whose outline of these experiences in "five chapters of consolation" I am following here.

8. *Pensées*, no. 913, p. 309.

9. Augustine writes of finding "more delight in weeping over my sins than I did in committing them." Quoted in Toner, *Commentary*, 102. This conjunction of elevation of the heart toward God and tears for sin is the sign that these tears are indeed tears of spiritual consolation.

10. A companion of Thérèse of Lisieux writes: "One day when I was in her room she said to me in a tone of voice that I cannot reproduce: 'God is not loved enough! And yet he is so good and kind. . . . Oh, I wish I could die!' And she began to sob. Not understanding what it was to love God so vehemently, I looked on in amazement. . ." (Christopher O'Mahoney, O.C.D., ed. and trans., *St. Thérèse of Lisieux by Those Who Knew Her: Testimonies from the Process of Beatification* [Huntington, Ind.: Our Sunday Visitor, 1975], 261).

11. As Raïssa writes: "*Suddenly*, keen sense of his nearness, of his tenderness. . . ." She recognizes clearly the moment this increased awareness of God's presence begins.

12. Halcyon Backhouse, ed., *The Scale of Perfection* (London: Hodder & Stoughton, 1992), 21.

13. Pierre Descouvement, *St. Thérèse of Lisieux and Marie of the Trinity: The Transformative Relationship of St. Thérèse of Lisieux and Her Novice, Sister Marie of the Trinity* (New York: Alba House, 1997), 88. In the next line of her account she explicitly mentions her newly found joy: "After supper I happily proposed to myself to wash the dishes. . . ."

14. "Ignatius was later in life reported by Pedro de Ribadeneira as having . . . said that he believed he could not live 'without consolation, that is, without finding within himself something that neither was nor could be from himself but came purely from God'" (John W. O'Malley, *The First Jesuits* [Cambridge, Mass.: Harvard University Press, 1993], 19–20).

15. *Autobiography of St. Ignatius*, no. 99.

Chapter 4: Spiritual Desolation (Rule 4)

1. Quoted in Toner, *Spirit of Light or Darkness*, 63.

2. Ibid., 66.

3. Ignatius sketches these contrasts explicitly in a single paragraph of his *Autograph Directory*, 12. After exemplifying consolation he writes: "Desolation is the contrary, coming from the evil spirit, and gifts of the same, such as war versus peace, sadness versus spiritual joy, hope in low things versus hope in higher things, base love versus higher love, dryness versus tears, wandering of the mind in low things versus elevation of mind." Cf. Palmer, *On Giving the Spiritual Exercises*, 8.

4. Cf. Gil, *Discernimiento*, 142–46.

5. As Ignatius writes to Teresa Rejadell, the enemy in placing before us the trials we must undergo "fails to remind us of the great comfort and consolation which our Lord is wont to give to such souls who, as new recruits in our Lord's service, surmount all these obstacles and choose to suffer with their Creator and Lord" (Young, *Letters of Saint Ignatius of Loyola*, 19).

6. Ibid., 21–22. The text continues: "The first is an interior consolation which casts out all uneasiness. . . . But when this consolation is absent the other lesson comes to light. Our ancient enemy sets up all possible obstacles . . . and everything in the first lesson is reversed."

7. Barbara Krzywicki-Herburt and Walter Ziemba, trans., *A Freedom Within: The Prison Notes of Stefan Cardinal Wyszynski* (New York: Harcourt Brace Jovanovich, 1983), 8. In the original the scriptural quote is given in Latin.

8. Gil, *Discernimiento*, 151–52.

9. The sixth rule, in inviting us to *examine* our spiritual desolation as one means of resisting it, indicates that discernment of spirits is concerned not only with the thoughts that *come from* spiritual desolation but also with the thoughts that may be the *cause* of spiritual desolation. Having identified these, we are the more enabled to reject them.

Chapter 5: Spiritual Desolation: A Time for Fidelity (Rule 5)

1. Here and throughout, I am following Gil, *Discernimiento*, 19, in adopting the words "instructive" and "normative."

2. We are speaking here of the fourteen rules (*SpirEx*, 313–27) that are the subject of this book. In the second set of rules for discernment (*SpirEx*, 328–36), spiritual consolation and the pitfalls related to it will become the primary focus.

3. The distinction between nonspiritual and spiritual desolation clarifies the difficulties in interpreting rule 5 raised by Katherine Dyckman, Mary Garvin, and Elizabeth Liebert in *The Spiritual Exercises Reclaimed: Uncovering Liberating Possibilities for Women* (New York: Paulist Press, 2001), 260. Further, while Ignatius's rule 5 should not be invoked to prohibit the healthy changes necessary to overcome nonspiritual desolation, nonetheless, if the nonspiritual desolation (the woman's depression because of a harmful relational situation) is *also* serving as a springboard for *spiritual* desolation (she begins to feel far from God's love), then the person should not make the *spiritual* changes suggested by the thoughts that arise from the spiritual desolation (give up prayer, fail to speak with a spiritual director as planned, etc.).

4. Quoted in Toner, *Spirit of Light or Darkness*, 43–44. Toner gives no indication of gender and the account is written in the first person. To avoid an otherwise inevitably impersonal quality in our discussion, I have made a choice of gender.

5. Toner, *Spirit of Light or Darkness*, 77, judges that "the experience does not seem to be one of spiritual desolation." Whether the woman herself considers it to be such or not is unclear from her account. She does understand the restlessness and debate as movements to be rejected actively and, in rejecting them, finds spiritual consolation enter her prayer.

6. Cf. Simon Decloux, *The Spiritual Diary of St. Ignatius Loyola: Text and Commentary* (Rome: Centrum Ignatianum Spiritualitatis, 1990), 83–104.

7. My translation. Since Ignatius's Spanish original is obscure at various points I am translating the rendering of the Spanish text by Santiago Thió de Pol, *La Intimidad del Peregrino: Diario Espiritual de San Ignacio de Loyola* (Bilbao: Mensajero-Sal Terrae, 1990), 169–71. In translating, I have also utilized the English translation in the Decloux text quoted in the preceding note (pp. 50–51).

8. Earlier in this *Diary* Ignatius writes: "I prayed to our Lady, and then to the Son and to the Father, to give me their Spirit" (February 11); "I took the Mother and the Son as my intercessors" (February 13), Decloux, *Spiritual Diary,* 22, 24; cf. *SpirEx*, 63, 147, 232.

9. Young, *Letters of Saint Ignatius of Loyola*, 22.

10. Earlier in the same diary, on February 18, Ignatius writes: "Later, wishing to get up with the thought of postponing my meal, and to take measures, however,

that would not embarrass me until I found what I was looking for, I felt fresh warmth and devotion in tears and dressed with the *thought* of *fasting* for three days" (Decloux, *Spiritual Diary*, 29).

11. Ibid., 51. We might note in passing the high level of spiritual awareness Ignatius has reached at this point in his life as evidenced by his attentiveness to the fluctuations of spiritual consolation and desolation in his heart, as well as to the thoughts which, one after another, pass through his mind.

12. The word "more," since Ignatius does not specify the second term of the comparison (more than what?), is difficult to interpret and is, in fact, diversely interpreted. See Gil, *Discernimiento*, 171–73; Fiorito, *Discernimiento y Lucha*, 151–53. Some of the translations simply omit it (*Versio Prima* in its original form; Louis Puhl, trans., *The Spiritual Exercises of St. Ignatius*, 143; Toner, *Commentary*, who includes it in his translation of the rules on p. 25 but omits it in his discussion of rule 5, pp. 152–54). Gil, *Discernimiento*, 172, suggests three possible interpretations: more than at other times; more than the other spirit; more than our own "spirit."

13. Further discernment is necessary in the spiritual situation considered in the Rules for the Second Week (*SpirEx*, 328–36). In our present set of rules and in the spiritual situation they describe, the norm is clear: in spiritual consolation the good spirit counsels us, and in spiritual desolation the enemy counsels us.

Chapter 6: Spiritual Desolation: A Time for Initiative (Rule 6)

1. I am speaking here, as indicated, of spiritual desolation as Ignatius understands it in these rules: an experience of spiritual heaviness typical of the beginnings of the spiritual journey (*SpirEx*, 9) and also an ordinary part of this journey, over the years, for dedicated people in general. I am not discussing here the "dark nights" described by John of the Cross which pertain to infused, contemplative prayer and which, with Toner, *Commentary*, 271–82, I see as distinct from spiritual desolation. Toner affirms that the dark night is "a spiritual experience in a fuller sense than the desolation which Ignatius describes; and it never depends on the agency of the evil spirit. It comes at a more advanced stage of spiritual growth, and it is not as common an experience as the spiritual desolation described in the Ignatian rules" (271). Cf. Green, *Weeds among the Wheat*, 126 n. 1, who adds a different nuance to this question.

2. Ignatius's elliptic style leaves his phrase "prayer, meditation" open to interpretation as either one or two different (though related) means of resisting desolation. With Toner, *Commentary*, 165–67, and Maureen Conroy, *The Discerning Heart: Discovering a Personal God* (Chicago: Loyola University Press, 1993), 28, I am considering these as two distinct means. Gil, *Discernimiento*, 178, and Fiorito, *Discernimiento y Lucha*, 160, do not make this distinction.

3. Such is Toner's position, *Commentary*, 165: "the first and most essential step in changing ourselves with the hope of conquering desolation is prayer—in this context, prayer of *petition*." Toner's emphasis. As the preceding note indicates, others take different positions regarding such prayer in time of spiritual desolation.

4. It is important to repeat that Ignatius is speaking of *spiritual* desolation here, as described in the fourth rule. He is not addressing situations of nonspiritual des-

olation as, for example, intense psychological stress or the various psychological disorders. Such afflictions exceed the limits of discernment of spirits and require other solutions, including professional help.

5. Toner, *Commentary*, 151. My emphasis.

6. The role of examination as a daily practice in ongoing discernment of spirits is a larger topic than we can discuss in a commentary on Ignatius's rules for discernment such as this, and my intention is to dedicate a separate study to it. On this issue, cf. G. Aschenbrenner, "Consciousness Examen," *Review for Religious* 31 (1972): 14–21.

7. In a similar way, Gill Goulding explores the relationship between "a renewed asceticism" and "creative perseverance," and writes: "A renewed asceticism assists the work of conversion within us and enables creative perseverance to be tempered and sustained. . . . I do not advocate ascetic practices from a misguided, arbitrary and compulsive perfectionism. I suggest them because they are life-giving disciplines, which enable the individual to be transformed in Christ with consequent effects upon all those with whom an individual lives and works" (*Creative Perseverance: Sustaining Life-Giving Ministry in Today's Church* [Ottawa: Novalis, 2003], 130). As André Louf, *The Cistercian Way* (Kalamazoo, Mich.: Cistercian Publications: 1983), 82, writes: "It is right and normal that the body should be part of the spiritual adventure to which man is called. . . . A genuine interior life can grow only through the body. . . . Asceticism is simply our sharing in the paschal mystery of Jesus, the mystery of his death and rising to new life in God."

8. In his *Spiritual Exercises* Ignatius mentions various forms of "exterior" penance, that is, with regard to food, sleep, and other physical penances (*SpirEx*, 82–84), urging that a "suitable" measure be adopted in their exercise according to each person's capability (*SpirEx*, 89).

9. "el intenso mudarse."

Chapter 7: Spiritual Desolation: A Time for Resistance (Rule 7)

1. P. Lachance, trans., *The Book of Angela of Foligno: Complete Works* (New York: Paulist Press, 1993), 171.

2. God does not leave her without assistance. She continues: "After this period I heard God speaking to me with such words as the following: 'My daughter, you are beloved by almighty God and by all the saints in paradise. God has placed his love in you . . .'" (ibid., 171).

3. The enemy *tempts* us (rules 4, 7, 12); God allows us to undergo *trials* (rules 7, 9).

4. "The term *sufficient grace*, as we have said, is not used here in the scholastic sense but rather in a popular way. Though we do not feel its presence with us, this grace is sufficient to complete the action called for by the situation we are experiencing. . . . The one in desolation is to consider that the divine assistance which remains with him is sufficient to live through the desolation without spiritual ruin; that, on the contrary, it will serve toward his eternal salvation" (Gil, *Discernimiento*, 189).

5. This transition is well illustrated in one of Gerard Manley Hopkins's final sonnets, written in a time of deep spiritual desolation: "Not, I'll not, carrion comfort,

Despair, not feast on thee; / Not untwist—slack though they may be—these last strands of man / In me ór, most weary, cry *I can no more*. I can; / Can something, hope, wish day come, not choose not to be" (W. H. Gardner, ed., *Gerard Manley Hopkins: Poems and Prose* [Harmondsworth, Middlesex: Penguin Books, 1981], 60; italics in the original).

6. Young, *Letters of Saint Ignatius*, 19.

7. Ibid., 22.

8. *The Book of Her Life*, chapter 30, paragraph 8, in *The Collected Works of St. Theresa of Avila*, vol. 1, trans. Kieran Kavanaugh and Otilio Rodriguez (Washington, D.C.: ICS Publications, 1987), 256; quoted in Fiorito, *Discernimiento y Lucha*, 95.

9. Fiorito, *Discernimiento y Lucha*, 97.

Chapter 8: Spiritual Desolation: A Time for Patience (Rule 8)

1. Elisabeth Leseur, *My Spirit Rejoices: The Diary of a Christian Soul in an Age of Unbelief* (Manchester, N.H.: Sophia Institute Press, 1996), 68.

2. Ibid., 77. Juliette was Elizabeth's sister; she died of tuberculosis at the age of thirty-two, two years after the writing of this letter.

3. "trabaje de estar en paciencia."

4. "Patience," from the Latin *patior*: to suffer, to bear, to endure.

5. Fyodor Dostoevsky, *Crime and Punishment*, trans. Sidney Monas (New York: Signet Classics, 1968), 413. Emily Dickinson also captures perfectly this quality of pain: "Pain has an element of blank / It cannot recollect / When it began, or if there were / A day when it was not. / It has no future but itself . . ." (R. Linscott, ed., *Selected Poems & Letters of Emily Dickinson* (New York: Doubleday, 1959), 89.

6. E. Colledge and J. Walsh, *Julian of Norwich: Showings* (New York: Paulist Press, 1978), 204. The subsequent quotations are all taken from pp. 204–5 of this volume.

Chapter 9: Why Does God Allow Spiritual Desolation? (Rule 9)

1. Toner, *Commentary*, 183.

2. Ibid., 183; emphasis added.

3. Gil, *Discernimiento*, 199

4. Toner, *Commentary*, 191, suggests two other such motives. One is "the desire to be one with Jesus in his redemptive poverty, suffering and humiliation"; the other is that "by enduring desolation in a Christian way we learn to understand and sympathize with others in desolation." Fiorito, *Discernimiento y Lucha*, 186, offers yet another motive linked to Ignatius's counsel to return to and pray further with experiences of both spiritual consolation and spiritual desolation in prayer (*SpirEx*, 62, 118). Cf. Brian O'Leary, "Review and Repetition," *The Way Supplement* 27 (1976): 58.

5. Gil, *Discernimiento*, 199, gives these three causes as conversion, realism, and humility.

6. See Toner, *Commentary*, 49–53, where the author speaks of "spiritually

regressing Christians" and "spiritually maturing Christians," incorporating both the spiritual regression of which we spoke in commenting on rule 1 (serious regression involving a complete turning away from God through grave sin) and that which we are describing here in rule 9 (lesser but real regression in some aspect of the spiritual life in those whose life remains fundamentally oriented toward God). See above, chapter 1.

7. My translation, in partial dependence on Decloux, *The Spiritual Diary*, 173. Once again I am integrating into this translation the rendering of the Spanish in S. Thió de Pol, trans., *Ignatius of Loyola, La Intimidad del Peregrino: Diario espiritual de San Ignacio de Loyola* (Bilbao: Mensajero—Sal Terrae, 1990), 193.

8. C. S. Lewis concludes his account of how God worked in his life with a similar insight: "The hardness of God is kinder than the softness of men, and his compulsion is our liberation" (*Surprised by Joy: The Shape of My Early Life* [New York: Harcourt, Brace & Company, 1955], 229).

9. Gil, *Discernimiento*, 202.

10. This comparison recalls Ignatius's description of different responses to the call of Christ the King to share in his task of conquering "all the enemies" (*SpirEx*, 95) of his redemptive work. Cf. *SpirEx*, 91–98.

11. Quoted in Toner, *Spirit of Light or Darkness*, 39.

12. This will be the teaching of Ignatius's thirteenth rule: that we speak of the enemy's agitations and temptations with a competent spiritual person, familiar with the deceptions of the enemy. See below, chap. 13.

13. Quoted in Maureen Conroy, *The Discerning Heart: Discovering a Personal God* (Chicago: Loyola University Press, 1993), 87. The author gives the quotation without offering further details regarding the writer.

14. See Toner, *Commentary*, 187–90.

15. Ibid., 188.

16. Thomas of Celano, *Second Life*, no. 118, in *St. Francis of Assisi, Writings and Early Biographies: English Omnibus of the Sources for the Life of St. Francis*, ed. Marion Habig (Chicago: Franciscan Herald Press, 1973), 460.

17. Fiorito, *Discernimiento y Lucha*, 191.

18. Ibid., 195.

19. In *SpirEx*, 77, Ignatius calls for a similar examination of times of prayer. If the examination reveals that some aspect of the prayer has not gone well, the person is to seek the cause of this and plan the changes to be made once the cause has been identified.

20. In seeking the cause we will often find it advantageous, if not indispensable, to speak with a competent spiritual person. See chap. 13 below.

21. Toner, *Commentary*, 150.

Chapter 10: Spiritual Consolation: A Time to Prepare (Rule 10)

1. In this book we are considering Ignatius's first set of fourteen rules (*SpirEx*, 313–27). In the eight rules of the second set (*SpirEx*, 328–36) his focus shifts to spiritual *consolation* and the issues of discernment relative to it. See *SpirEx*, 8–10.

2. Gil, *Discernimiento*, 210–12, presents rules 10 and 11 (which also, in its first part, speaks of spiritual consolation) as Ignatius's counsel to one in spiritual con-

solation not to be deluded into expecting that the consolation will remain forever (rule 10) nor to become vainly self-satisfied when in consolation (rule 11). With Toner, *Commentary*, 192–96, I am presenting rule 10 as Ignatius's teaching regarding the importance of preparing, when in spiritual consolation, for future spiritual desolation. I understand rule 11 to be Ignatius's portrait of the spiritual balance to which he would guide us as we experience the alternating times of spiritual consolation and spiritual desolation (see chapter 11 below).

3. Quoted in Joseph L. Dirvin, C.M., *Mrs. Seton: Foundress of the American Sisters of Charity* (New York: Farrar, Straus & Giroux, 1975), 25.

4. In rule 11 Ignatius will speak yet again of "thinking," both in time of spiritual consolation and in time of spiritual desolation.

5. Here the question of *examen* arises. For an exposition of Ignatian examen as an exercise in daily spiritual awareness, see George Aschenbrenner, "Consciousness Examen," *Review for Religious*, 31 (1972): 14–21.

6. Toner, *Commentary*, 194. The subsequent quotations are all from this page.

7. Tony Hendra graphically describes precisely this "complete loss of composure" in his own spiritual experience when doubt and desolation unexpectedly intervene after a year of clarity and spiritual consolation: "Suddenly . . . I was falling, in an elevator with its cables severed, accelerating down into the blackness of the shaft . . . plunging into a chasm with no bottom" (*Father Joe: The Man Who Saved My Soul* [New York: Random House, 2004], 88).

8. Toner, *Commentary*, 194 (emphasis mine).

9. See above, chapter 9, n. 7.

10. Toner, *Commentary*, 195

11. The first five of these points are found in Toner, *Commentary*, 195–96. I am expanding somewhat his treatment of these five and I have added the final two.

12. Gil, *Discernimiento*, 15–16, counsels memorizing their basic content: "In addition to receiving instruction or explanations from the one giving the Spiritual Exercises, it is highly desirable in general that the retreatant not only keep the text of the rules close at hand but that he also learn their essential content by heart. Once he has memorized them, the rules will be more present to the retreatant, and he will apply them more often in accordance with the different situations he encounters."

13. We will return to this point in discussing Ignatius's fourteenth rule (chap. 14).

Chapter 11: Spiritual Consolation and Spiritual Desolation: Finding Our Balance (Rule 11)

1. E. Colledge and J. Walsh, *Julian of Norwich: Showings* (New York: Paulist Press, 1978), 205.

2. "Peter said to him, 'Even though they all fall away, I will not. . . .' But he said vehemently, 'If I must die with you, I will not deny you.'" See Toner, *Commentary*, 197, and Gil, *Discernimiento*, 215, who both quote this text regarding Peter in Matthew 14. My treatment of Peter's experience follows that of Toner. Ignatius makes a similar point also in *SpirEx*, 14.

3. In rule 10 we think of *future* spiritual desolation in order to prepare for it. In rule 11 we think of *past* spiritual desolation in order to gain, from the memory of it, a fruitful humility during present spiritual consolation. Cf. Gil, *Discernimiento*, 217.

4. Gil, basing his observation on Ignatius's presentation of the Incarnation in the *Spiritual Exercises*, suggests *gratitude* as another. Mary, in the Incarnation, responds to God's gift through "*humbling* herself and *giving thanks* to the Divine Majesty" (*SpirEx*, 108). Such gratitude opens the hearts of those consoled to look beyond themselves, to see spiritual consolation in relation to God, and to realize its nature as a gift of God (Gil, *Discernimiento*, 218).

5. Colledge and Walsh, *Julian of Norwich: Showings*, 205.

6. Letter of June 18, 1536, in *San Ignacio de Loyola: Obras Completas,* ed. Ignacio Iparraguire and Candido de Dalmases (Madrid: Biblioteca de Autores Cristianos, 1982), 662 (my translation).

7. "Abba Poemen said: 'Vigilance, self-knowledge and discernment; these are the guides of the soul'" (Benedicta Ward, trans., *The Sayings of the Desert Fathers* [Kalamazoo, Mich.: Cistercian Publications, 1975], 35).

8. As we observed earlier, Ignatius describes *how* to exercise such daily spiritual awareness in his teaching on daily examen, which is, for Ignatius, a key exercise in the whole of the spiritual life.

9. Toner, *Spirit of Light or Darkness*, 65. The subsequent quotations are all taken from this source (65–66).

10. In this Jane practices Ignatius's thirteenth rule—she speaks with a competent spiritual person.

Chapter 12: Standing Firm in the Beginnings (Rule 12)

1. In rules 12 and 13 Ignatius describes this response explicitly; in rule 14 only implicitly.

2. Green, *Weeds among the Wheat*, 119. Green continues: "But Ignatius clearly does not mean *every* woman here. Nor, I think, *only* women." Toner, *Commentary*, 26, takes a similar approach in adding a modifier into Ignatius's test: "The enemy resembles a *shrewish* woman" (emphasis mine) and comments: "The text, I think, as well as Ignatius's respect for and friendship with women, calls for such a qualification" (26 n. 7). Conroy, *The Discerning Heart*, 26, simply omits the metaphor; and Fiorito, *Discernimiento y Lucha*, 211, writes that "it might be better to exclude the comparison; however, St. Ignatius utilized it in his rule and, trusting in his text, we will do well to keep it in mind."

3. Gil, *Discernimiento*, 230; see also pp. 231–32.

4. "vano enamorado."

5. Katherine Dyckman, Mary Garvin, and Elizabeth Liebert, *The Spiritual Exercises Reclaimed: Uncovering Liberating Possibilities for Women* (New York: Paulist Press, 2001), 259.

6. David Fleming, *Draw Me into Your Friendship: A Literal Translation and a Contemporary Reading of the Spiritual Exercises* (St. Louis: Institute of Jesuit Sources, 1996), 257. This metaphor too must be understood well. In employing it, we will assume that the persons responsible for the children are upright and capa-

ble, sincerely seeking the good of the children. See also St. Athanasius's *Life of St. Anthony*, chapter 6, wherein the enemy is said to be as "weak as a child" (Philip Schaff and Henry Wace, eds., *Nicene and Post-Nicene Fathers,* Second Series, Volume 4, *Athanasius: Select Works and Letters* (Peabody, Mass.: Hendrikson 1994), 197.

7. Gil, *Discernimiento*, 231.

8. This is the difference between the response of Eve (Gen 3:1–6) and of Jesus (Matt 4:1–11) to the suggestions of the tempter. The first responds indecisively, dialogues with the serpent, and, as the process of temptation unfolds, finds that the temptation gains in power, eventually surrendering to it. The second decisively rejects the tempter's suggestions in the very moment they are first proposed.

9. Young, *Letters of St. Ignatius*, 22.

10. "y mucho humillados." Obviously "humbled" here does not have the rich meaning we have seen in earlier rules but rather describes an unfounded and harmful sense of spiritual helplessness.

11. The incident is recounted with the permission of the person involved. The person's name has been changed to preserve anonymity.

12. *Autobiography*, 33–34.

13. Thomas of Celano, *Second Life*, 125, in *St. Francis of Assisi: Writings and Early Biographies. English Omnibus of the Sources for the Life of St. Francis,* ed. Marion Habig (Chicago: Franciscan Herald Press: 1973) 465–66. The biblical quotations are italicized in this version. Among "the instruments of good works" in his classic *Rule*, St. Benedict places the following: "To dash one's evil thoughts against Christ *immediately*, and to reveal them to one's spiritual advisor" (emphasis mine) (Anthony Meisel and M. L. del Mastro, trans. and eds., *The Rule of St. Benedict* (New York: Image, Doubleday, 1975), 53. In this "instrument" Benedict combines the counsel of Ignatius's twelfth and thirteenth rules.

Chapter 13: Breaking the Spiritual Silence (Rule 13)

1. See Katherine Dyckman, Mary Garvin, and Elizabeth Liebert, *The Spiritual Exercises Reclaimed: Uncovering Liberating Possibilities for Women* (New York: Paulist Press, 2001), 259, for a reflection on this metaphor from the perspective of women today. The authors affirm that "the subliminal negative effects compromise the usefulness of this metaphor."

2. I am following Fiorito, *Discernimiento y Lucha*, 232–33, in analyzing Ignatius's description of the appropriate spiritual person with whom to speak.

3. "*su* buen confessor."

4. Cf. Gil, *Discernimiento*, 246.

5. Regarding the search for such spiritually competent persons, Fiorito writes: "We believe, nonetheless that . . . at times it is not possible, at least not immediately, to find the ideal person. In such cases we must continue trying until we find this person . . . since the act itself of manifesting our temptations weakens their grip and renders them more intelligible to the one who so manifests them. . . . We should never cease to search for such a person and to ask the Lord that he grant us to find a good confessor or a spiritual person who 'knows the deceits and malicious designs (of the bad spirit),' remembering the promise of the Lord: 'Ask and it will be given

to you; seek and you will find. . . . For everyone who asks, receives; and the one who seeks, finds' (Matt 7:7)" (*Discernimiento y Lucha*, 234–35).

6. Cf. *SpirEx*, 17.

7. Fiorito, *Discernimiento y Lucha*, 143–44 and 239–40, uses this incident as an illustration of both Ignatius's fourth and thirteenth rules.

8. John Clarke, trans., *Story of a Soul: The Autobiography of Saint Thérèse of Lisieux* (Washington, D.C.: ICS Publications, 1996), 166. "Beautiful day" in this quote and "dream" in the next are italicized in the original. The following quotations of Thérèse's narrative are all from this source.

9. Thomas Merton, *The Seven Storey Mountain* (London: Sheldon Press, 1975), 333. The following quotations are taken from this volume, 333, 363–66. Merton also writes of these events in his journal: P. Hart, ed., *Run to the Mountain: The Story of a Vocation* (San Francisco: HarperCollins, 1995), esp. 457–59.

10. This incident is used with the permission of the person I have called Sally. A few details have been changed to preserve anonymity.

Chapter 14: Strengthening the Weak Point (Rule 14)

1. Gil, *Discernimiento*, 252–53.

2. "caudillo," a word Ignatius uses with negative connotations in the *Spiritual Exercises*, as in the meditation of the Two Standards, *SpirEx*, 138–40. Cf. Gil, *Discernimiento*, 252.

3. *Theological* virtues: faith, hope, charity; *cardinal* virtues: prudence, justice, fortitude, temperance; *moral* virtues: religion, devotion, obedience, chastity, gentleness, humility, etc. Gil, *Discernimiento*, 255.

4. Gil, *Discernimiento*, 223–24, writes of what he calls the "progressively incomplete redaction" of rules 12, 13, and 14. In these three rules Ignatius discusses three tactics of the enemy. In rule 12 Ignatius describes explicitly *the two possible responses* (firm—weak) in both the metaphor and the application. In rule 13, in both metaphor and application, he describes explicitly *only the first* response (the troubled person chooses to speak). The second possible response (the troubled person chooses not to speak) and its consequences (the enemy's deceptions will persist and cause harm) remain implicit, though clearly understood. In rule 14, in both metaphor and application, Ignatius describes only the tactic of the enemy (attacking the weakest point), *without describing either possible response explicitly*: neither the *first* (prepare beforehand) nor the *second* (failure to prepare beforehand), and the consequences of the one and the other (the enemy's attack is defeated; the enemy defeats the person). All this remains implicit, though clearly intended, as the parallelism of rule 14 with the preceding two rules plainly indicates. Gil comments: "St. Ignatius describes explicitly the points he wishes to highlight. The rest can remain implicit" (224).

5. The dynamic here is something like that of rule 10. There, in the context of spiritual consolation and spiritual desolation, Ignatius counseled preparing *in time of spiritual consolation* for the eventual return of spiritual desolation. Here, in the more specific context of a faithful person's weakest point, Ignatius again counsels preparing *before* the time of need.

6. When discerning persons become capable of such refined awareness and

preparation, they are on the threshold of the spiritual situation described in the Second Week Rules for Discernment (*SpirEx*, 328–36). In that new spiritual situation the enemy employs different tactics and must be resisted accordingly. Cf. *SpirEx*, 9–10.

7. This is the Ignatian particular examen (*SpirEx*, 24–31).

8. Gil, *Discernimiento*, 257. The quotations from the *Spiritual Exercises* and the rest of this paragraph closely follow Gil's exposition on p. 257.

9. Toner, *Spirit of Light or Darkness*, 65.

10. Ibid., 48–49.

11. Ibid., 80, comments: "It looks very much as though Jim has an emotional problem, an authority hang-up, and needs psychological therapy. He blames himself for his emotional response to authority figures as if it were a moral failure for which he is responsible and could overcome just by goodwill. As a consequence (and prompted by the 'father of lies') he falls into spiritual desolation."

12. Used with the permission of the writer.

13. The daily examen mentioned here is the Ignatian particular examen (*SpirEx*, 24–31). Regarding the particular examen, Aschenbrenner writes: "When we become sensitive and serious enough about loving God, we begin to realize some changes must be made. . . . But the Lord does not want all of them to be handled at once. Usually there is one area of our hearts where He is especially calling for conversion which is always the beginning of new life. He is interiorly nudging us in one area and reminding us that if we are really serious about Him this one aspect of ourselves must be changed" ("Consciousness Examen," *Review for Religious* 31 [1972]: 19).

14. "Through the practice of one virtue all the virtues grow" (John of the Cross, *The Ascent of Mount Carmel*, book I, chapter 12, 5, in *The Collected Work of St. John of the Cross*, trans. Kieran Kavanaugh and Otilio Rodriguez [Washington, D.C.: Institute of Carmelite Studies, 1973], 100).

15. Fiorito, *Discernimiento y Lucha*, 249, who adds: "As we can see, St. Ignatius loses no opportunity to show us the innate weakness of the enemy 'of human nature' (*SpirEx*, 7 and passim)."

16. Cf. Gil, *Discernimiento*, 53–54, 277–78. Gil makes this point throughout his commentary on these rules.

Conclusion

1. Edmond Murphy and Martin Palmer, trans., *The Spiritual Writings of Pierre Favre* (Saint Louis: Institute of Jesuit Sources, 1996), 65.

2. *Institutes*, V.2 (my translation).

3. As Fiorito, *Discernimiento y Lucha*, 258–59, writes, discernment of spirits may be obtained in one of two forms: either as a "gift or charism of the Spirit," or "by application of the rules for discernment." He continues: "St. Ignatius explains, in his spiritual teaching found in the *Spiritual Exercises*, the second form, through discernment of 'the different movements—or spirits—which are caused in the soul, the good, to receive them, and the bad to reject them . . .' (*SpirEx*, 313); nonetheless he gives repeated and clear proofs of possessing—if one reads his *Autobiography* and his many letters—the 'connatural' grace or charism of discernment. Above

all, however, St. Ignatius was given the grace to write—for those who wish to be spiritually discerning through 'discernment of spirits'—his rules for discernment, which we have examined in this book." The first path to discernment (as gift or charism of the Spirit) may be simply given by God; the second, common path to discernment (through learning and applying the rules for discernment), occurs gradually and through repeated practice. This second path has been the focus of our reflections in this book as well.

4. *Plain and Parochial Sermons*, vol. 1 (Christian Classics; Westminster, Md., 1966), 264.

5. *Life*, VIII.4, 5, 9; XIX.4.

Select Bibliography

Angela of Foligno. *Complete Works*. Translated by Paul Lachance. New York: Paulist Press, 1993.

Conroy, Maureen. *The Discerning Heart: Discovering a Personal God*. Chicago: Loyola University Press, 1993.

De Guibert, Joseph, S.J. *The Jesuits: Their Spiritual Doctrine and Practice. A Historical Study*. St. Louis, Mo.: Institute of Jesuit Sources, 1986.

Dirvin, Joseph, C.M. *Mrs. Seton: Foundress of the American Sisters of Charity*. New York: Farrar, Straus & Giroux, 1975.

Dyckman, Katherine, Mary Garvin, and Elizabeth Liebert. *The Spiritual Exercises Reclaimed: Uncovering Liberating Possibilities for Women*. New York: Paulist Press, 2001.

Fiorito, Miguel Angel, S.J. *Discernimiento y Lucha Espíritual: Comentario de las Reglas de Discernir de la Primera Semana del Libro de los Ejercicios Espirituales de San Ignacio de Loyola*. Buenos Aires: Ediciónes Diego de Torres, 1985.

Francis of Assisi. *St. Francis of Assisi: Writings and Early Biographies. English Omnibus of the Sources for the Life of St. Francis*. Edited by Marion Habig. Chicago: Franciscan Herald Press, 1973.

Gil, Daniel, S.J. *Discernimiento según San Ignacio: Exposición y Comentario Practico de las Dos Series de Reglas de Discernimiento de Espíritus Contenidas en el Libro de los Ejercicios Espirituales de San Ignacio de Loyola (EE 313—336)*. Rome: Centrum Ignatianum Spiritualitatis, 1983.

Green, Thomas, S.J. *Weeds among the Wheat. Discernment: Where Prayer & Action Meet*. Notre Dame, Ind.: Ave Maria Press, 1984.

Ignatius of Loyola. *La Intimidad del Peregrino: Diario espiritual de San Ignacio de Loyola*. Translated by Santiago Thió de Pol, S.J. Bilbao: Mensajero—Sal Terrae, 1990.

_____. *Letters of St. Ignatius of Loyola*. Translated by William Young, S.J. Chicago: Loyola University Press, 1959.

_____. *Sancti Ignatii de Loyola Exercitia Spiritualia: Textuum Antiquissimorum Nova Editio Lexicon Textus Hispani*. Edited by José Calveras, S.J., and Candido de Dalmases, S.J. Rome: Institutum Historicum Societatis Jesu, 1969.

_____. *San Ignacio de Loyola: Obras Completas*. Edited by Ignacio Iparraguirre, S.J. and Candido de Dalmases, S.J. Madrid: Biblioteca de Autores Cristianos, 1982.

_____. *The Autobiography of St. Ignatius Loyola with Related Documents*. Translated by Joseph O'Callaghan. New York: Harper & Row, 1974.

_____. *The Spiritual Diary of St. Ignatius Loyola: Text and Commentary*. Edited by Simon Decloux, S.J. Rome: Centrum Ignatianum Spiritualitatis, 1990.

_____. *The Spiritual Exercises of St. Ignatius of Loyola: Translated from the Autograph*. Translated by Elder Mullan, S.J. New York: P. J. Kennedy & Sons, 1914.

_____. *The Spiritual Exercises of St. Ignatius: Based on Studies in the Language of the Autograph*. Translated by Louis Puhl, S.J. Chicago: Loyola University Press, 1951.

Julian of Norwich. *Showings*. Translated by Edmund Colledge and James Walsh. New York: Paulist Press, 1978.

Leseur, Elisabeth. *My Spirit Rejoices: The Diary of a Christian Soul in an Age of Unbelief*. Manchester, N.H.: Sophia Institute Press, 1996.

Merton, Thomas. *The Seven Storey Mountain*. London: Sheldon Press, 1975.

Palmer, Martin, S.J., trans. *On Giving the Spiritual Exercises: The Early Jesuit Manuscript Directories and the Official Directory of 1599*. St. Louis, Mo.: Institute of Jesuit Sources, 1996.

Pascal, Blaise. *Pensées*. Translated by A. J. Krailsheimer. Reading, Pa.: Penguin Books, 1966.

Ruiz Jurado, Manuel, S.J. *El Discernimiento Espiritual: Teologia. Historia. Práctica*. Madrid: Biblioteca de Autores Cristianos, 1994.

Teresa of Avila. *The Collected Works of St. Teresa of Avila, Volume One: The Book of Her Life, Spiritual Testimonies, Soliloquies*. Translated by Kieran Kavanaugh and Otilio Rodriguez. Washington, D.C.: ICS Publications, 1976.

Thérèse of Lisieux. *Story of a Soul: The Autobiography of St.Thérèse of Lisieux*. Edited by John Clarke, O.C.D. Washington, D.C.: ICS Publications, 1996.

Toner, Jules, S.J. *A Commentary on Saint Ignatius' Rules for the Discernment of Spirits: A Guide to the Principles and Practice*. St. Louis, Mo.: Institute of Jesuit Sources, 1982.

_____. "Discernment in the Spiritual Exercises." In *A New Introduction to the Spiritual Exercises of St. Ignatius*. Edited by John Dister, S.J. Collegeville, Minn.: Liturgical Press, 1993.

_____. *Spirit of Light or Darkness: A Casebook for Studying Discernment of Spirits*. St. Louis, Mo.: Institute of Jesuit Sources, 1995.

Index of Names

～

OF RELATED INTEREST

THE JESUS MEDITATIONS

By Michael Kennedy

A Guide for Contemplation
With accompanying CD read by Martin Sheen.

Have you ever longed to walk beside Jesus on the dusty roads of Palestine? Have you ever wondered what it would feel like to be in the crowd when Jesus was healing and preaching? These powerful meditations will help you imagine being right there with Jesus. Entering into the world of these meditations will change forever your relationship with Jesus, with yourself, and with the world around you.

978-08245-1929-2

crossroad

OF RELATED INTEREST

THE CALL TO DISCERNMENT IN TROUBLED TIMES

*New Perspectives on the Transformative Wisdom
of Ignatius of Loyola*

By Dean Brackley

A major book to help the discerning modern mind understand the Christian experience today. Fr. Brackley uses the
timeless insights of Ignatius to explain a genuine spiritual
methodology: true ways of decision making for living better,
more fulfilled lives. These exercises help you know yourself,
your talents, your yearnings, and your relationship to the rest
of the world.

978-0-8245-2268-1

crossroad

OF RELATED INTEREST

DIRECTIONS FOR COMMUNICATION
Discoveries with Ignatius Loyola

By Willi Lambert

Willi Lambert's study of the life and writings of St. Ignatius indicates that the integration of management and spirituality was not a casual matter for Ignatius, but rather an "experienced reality" that was grounded in his approach to life. The book yields a fruitful and fascinating model of communication for people of all walks of life, and offers both practical and deeply spiritual insights into the art of communicating with oneself, with others, and with God.

978-0-8245-1853-0

Support your local bookstore or order directly from the publisher at
www.CrossroadPublishing.com

To request a catalog or inquire about quantity orders, please e-mail
sales@CrossroadPublishing.com

crossroad

About the Author

Fr. Timothy Gallagher, O.M.V., has dedicated years of his life to an extensive ministry of retreat work, spiritual direction, and teaching in the Ignatian spiritual tradition. He received his doctorate from the Gregorian University in 1983. A member of the Oblates of the Virgin Mary, he has published two books on their founder, the Venerable Pio Bruno Lanteri. He served for twelve years in formation work in this religious community and has taught at Our Lady of Grace Seminary Residence (Boston) and at St. John's Seminary (Brighton, MA); he was also provincial for two terms for the USA province of the Oblates. He currently lives at St. Clement's Shrine, Boston, MA, and is completing a new book for Crossroad on the prayer of examen.